LAWRENCE OF LUCKNOW

LAWRENCE
OF LUCKNOW

A story of love

JOHN LAWRENCE

Edited by Audrey Woodiwiss

Hodder & Stoughton
LONDON SYDNEY AUCKLAND TORONTO

British Library Cataloguing in Publication Data

Lawrence, John
   Lawrence of Lucknow.
   1. India. Social life, 1785-1858 – Biographies
   I. Title
   954.031092

   ISBN 0-340-23918-2

Published by Hodder and Stoughton,
a division of Hodder and Stoughton Ltd,
Mill Road, Dunton Green, Sevenoaks, Kent TN13 2YA
Editorial Office: 47 Bedford Square, London WC1B 3DP

Maps drawn by Alec Spark

Photoset by E.P.L. BookSet, Norwood, London

Printed in Great Britain by Butler and Tanner Ltd, Frome and London

This book is dedicated to the beloved memory
of Letitia Catherine Lawrence 1809–65,
wife of the Reverend Henry Horace Hayes. She was
an invalid but by what she was she made it possible
for her brothers to become what they were.

CONTENTS

LIST OF ILLUSTRATIONS

All illustrations are from the author's private collection unless otherwise credited

Between pages 76 and 77

Henry Lawrence and the Reverend James Knox
Letitia and Honoria Lawrence
Ranjit Singh, Dost Mahommed Khan[1] and Akbar Khan[1]
Kabul during the First Afghan War[1], Afghan soldiers in winter dress[1] and a
   sowar of the cavalry[1]
General Sir George Pollock[1], George Lawrence[1] and Lord Ellenborough[1]
The Residency in Nepal. Honoria Lawrence and her sons Alick and Henry
Henry Lawrence in his bath tub, and the Lawrences' cottage in Koulia
Maharajah Dhulip Singh[2] and Maharajah Gulab Singh[3]

Between pages 172 and 173

Henry Lawrence[4], John Lawrence[1] and Lord Hardinge[1]
A battle during the First Sikh War[1]
Herbert Edwardes[1], Henry Lawrence dictating to the Rajah Dina Nath and
   Henry Lawrence in England *c.* 1847
Lahore 1849[4] and the Sikh sirdars *c.* 1850[1]
George Lawrence, Herbert Edwardes, Henry Lawrence, and the Marquis
   of Dalhousie[1]
The Durbar at Udaipur, 1855[4]
Mount Abu, 1854, and silhouettes of Henry, Honoria and Harry
Henry Lawrence in Lucknow, 1857. Lucknow after the siege

The author and publishers would like to thank the following for allowing them to
reproduce copyright material:

1. The National Army Museum, London
2. The Royal Collection, Windsor Castle, Berkshire
3. F. S. Aijazuddin
4. The India Office Library, London

ACKNOWLEDGMENTS

First of all I am grateful to my wife, Audrey, for her help and encouragement throughout a difficult time. Without her, this book would not have been written. She not only typed the book while she was learning to use a word processor, but she has edited it with great skill and thoroughness.

I am also grateful to Fr Laurence Sundaram S.J. for reading the book in draft and making various suggestions, nearly all of which I have adopted. The Indo–British Historical Society put me in touch with Fr Sundaram and I am grateful for this and also for their encouragement and to Mr Theon Wilkinson, the secretary of the British Association for Cemeteries in Southern Asia (BACSA) for help in identifying some Anglo–Indian words. The staff of the India Office Library have all been kindness itself since the beginning of this work over twenty-five years ago: I am particularly grateful to Dr Richard Bingle and Mrs Kate Kattenhorn. I am also grateful to Mr Ian Robertson, the Director of the National Army Museum, for his co-operation and for making it possible to launch this book at the National Army Museum.

I am grateful to my publishers, Hodder and Stoughton, for their patience and for the help of Ion Trewin and Mrs Christine Medcalf, who has done more than her duty and to Simone Mauger who saw this book through its last stages. Also to my neighbour Dr William Dobson-Smyth for taking the picture of the author which appears on the dust cover and to the British Academy who gave timely help in the form of a grant.

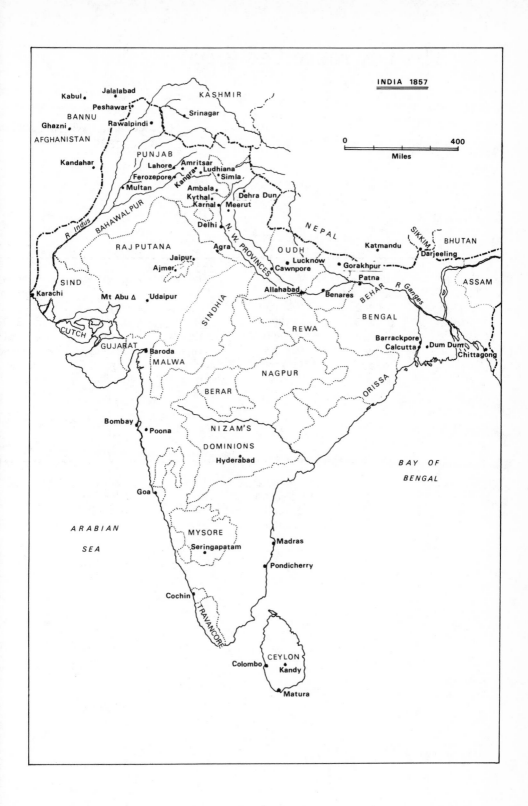

INDIA 1857

0 _____ 400
Miles

Kabul · Jalalabad
Peshawar ·
BANNU
Ghazni ·   Rawalpindi ·
AFGHANISTAN
Kandahar ·

KASHMIR
Srinagar ·

PUNJAB
Lahore · Amritsar · Ludhiana
Ferozepore · Kangra · Simla ·
Multan ·   Ambala ·
Kythal · Dehra Dun
Karnal · Meerut ·
Delhi ·   N.W. PROVINCES

R. Indus
BAHAWALPUR

RAJPUTANA
Jaipur ·
Ajmer ·   Agra ·
Cawnpore ·

NEPAL
Katmandu · SIKKIM BHUTAN
Darjeeling ·
OUDH
Lucknow · Gorakhpur ·
Patna ·   ASSAM
Allahabad · Benares · BEHAR R. Ganges

SIND
Karachi ·
Mt Abu △ Udaipur ·

SINDHIA

BENGAL
REWA
Barrackpore ·
Calcutta · Dum Dum ·
Chittagong

CUTCH
GUJARAT Baroda ·
MALWA

BERAR
NAGPUR
ORISSA

Bombay · Poona ·
NIZAM'S
DOMINIONS
Hyderabad ·

Goa ·

ARABIAN
SEA

BAY OF
BENGAL

MYSORE
Seringapatam ·

Madras ·
Pondicherry ·

Cochin ·
TRAVANCORE

CEYLON
Colombo · Kandy ·

Matura ·

The Lawrence Pedigree

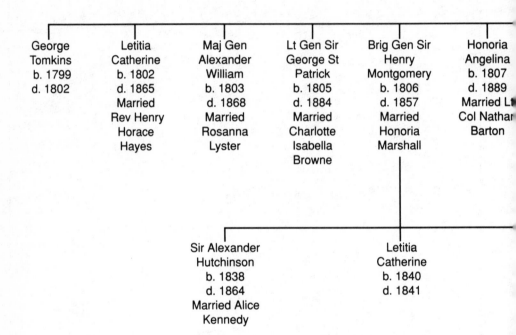

Lt Col Alexander William Lawrenc
b. 1762 d. 1835

George
Tomkins
b. 1799
d. 1802

Letitia
Catherine
b. 1802
d. 1865
Married
Rev Henry
Horace
Hayes

Maj Gen
Alexander
William
b. 1803
d. 1868
Married
Rosanna
Lyster

Lt Gen Sir
George St
Patrick
b. 1805
d. 1884
Married
Charlotte
Isabella
Browne

Brig Gen Sir
Henry
Montgomery
b. 1806
d. 1857
Married
Honoria
Marshall

Honoria
Angelina
b. 1807
d. 1889
Married Lt
Col Nathar
Barton

Sir Alexander
Hutchinson
b. 1838
d. 1864
Married Alice
Kennedy

Letitia
Catherine
b. 1840
d. 1841

Letitia Catherine Knox
b. 1774 d. 1846

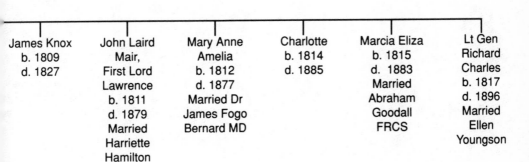

James Knox
b. 1809
d. 1827

John Laird
Mair,
First Lord
Lawrence
b. 1811
d. 1879
Married
Harriette
Hamilton

Mary Anne
Amelia
b. 1812
d. 1877
Married Dr
James Fogo
Bernard MD

Charlotte
b. 1814
d. 1885

Marcia Eliza
b. 1815
d. 1883
Married
Abraham
Goodall
FRCS

Lt Gen
Richard
Charles
b. 1817
d. 1896
Married
Ellen
Youngson

Sir Henry
Waldemar
succeeded by
ecial remainder)
b. 1845
d. 1908
Married Emily
L'Estrange

Honoria
Letitia
b. 1850
d. 1923
Married
Henry
George Hart

Sir Alexander
Waldemar
b. 1874
d. 1939
Married Anne
Elizabeth Le
Poer Wynne

Sir John
Waldemar
b. 1907

Preface

The first biographer of Henry Lawrence was his friend, Herbert Edwardes. A close associate of Henry in his most creative years, he was given all the unsorted papers that Henry and Honoria Lawrence had accumulated over many years; he also collected all the extant material about Henry. This manuscript material now constitutes 116 items in the India Office Library, some of which amount to only a few pages but many are stout volumes. Henry's writing was notoriously illegible and the labour of reducing all this material to order was enormous. According to Herbert Edwardes' widow the task killed her husband. Before he died he had completed the first volume, and left copious material for the second. The work was completed by Herman Merivale, who could hardly do more than stitch together the material left by Edwardes. It is impossible to say what Edwardes would have added or omitted or how his judgment would have matured had he lived to complete the biography. Consequently the second volume of the work is incomplete. It is this volume which covers the years of Henry Lawrence's power in the Punjab, Rajputana and Oudh. There was from the outset a need for a new biography.

The papers collected by Herbert Edwardes came to my grandfather and were passed down to my father. Although they had been roughly sorted and tied up in bundles with red tape, and were not easy to use, my father and grandfather were ready to lend them to any responsible person. Towards the end of the last century they were lent to General Macleod Innes. Unfortunately some of them were lost in a fire while they were with Macleod Innes, who had known Henry in his youth. However, he wrote a good short biography. Between the wars J. L. Morison borrowed the papers to write *Lawrence of Lucknow*, and we hoped that this would supplement and complete the work of Herbert Edwardes. It would be too much to say that this hope was realised but my respect for Morison's judgment has grown steadily. Some of the book is well written but there are too many dull passages. Maud Diver, a relative of the Lawrences, borrowed the papers for her life of Honoria Lawrence, which said a good deal incidentally about Henry, but the main subject was his wife.

xvii

My father always felt a filial obligation to complete the work left unfinished by Herbert Edwardes. In the early years of the century he started a new biography, but he was too close to his grandfather to write a satisfactory book. The attempt was abandoned but he hoped that one of his children would succeed in what he had failed to do. It was always in the back of my mind that this task might fall to me in the last resort.

I inherited the Henry Lawrence papers on the first day of the Second World War; there was no question of writing a book for the following six years. After the war I placed the papers on permanent loan at the India Office Library and then established a charitable trust to ensure that they were kept together in this country. In their new home they have been organised and bound into volumes. Researchers have dipped into them but no comprehensive study has been made.

Eventually it became probable that no new biography of Henry Lawrence would be written in this generation unless I wrote it myself. I realised that I lacked much of the knowledge and experience that a writer on Anglo–Indian history ought to have, but eventually I set my hand to the task, hoping in spite of all to write a useful and readable book. I had after all already written a successful *History of Russia*, now in its sixth edition, there was some family tradition which would be lost if I did not record it, and I believe that the genetic kinship gives me some advantage. Subsequent generations of the Lawrences can claim no more than modest talent, while their ancestors were remarkable, but in reading the record of their doings I sometimes find myself exclaiming with a smile: 'How like our family!'

For many years I paid the expenses of two ladies who were retired missionaries of the CMS and who went to the India Office Library a day a week to make notes on the Henry Lawrence papers. First Mrs Cecily Holland, the widow of the great missionary Canon Willie Holland, undertook this work. On her sudden death, my brother George took over the work for a short time and, when he gave up, he was succeeded by Miss Mildred Gibbs, the historian of the Anglican Church in India. Both of these ladies had lived for many years in India, and had learned to love its people and way of life. I owe them an inestimable debt. The notes they left me amount to about a quarter of a million words. Without their work I could hardly have been able to go ahead.

Soon after Miss Gibbs' retirement from active work Audrey Woodiwiss joined me and the first fruits of our joint labours was *The Journals of Honoria Lawrence* published by Hodder and Stoughton in 1980, which was well reviewed both here and in the Indian subcontinent. At first I intended to make the present book a joint biography of Henry and Honoria Lawrence. Never were husband and wife more closely associated in all that they did, but the plan for a joint biography did not work. There is ample unused material for a fresh biography of Honoria Lawrence but that must be a separate undertaking.

A historian and biographer ought, I believe, to have in his mind at least the outline of a philosophy of history. For myself I do not believe that human history is 'just one thing after another', nor do I believe that history is cyclical. There is a pattern and a purpose. There was a beginning and there will be an end. Such views are out of fashion but there is no reason to think that in such matters the present age is wiser than other ages. And it has been well said that he who is married to the fashions of his age is sure to be widowed in the next. We cannot indeed hope to descry the pattern of history with any approach to precision but in a few years historians may be prepared to try again. In any case it makes a difference if a statesman or a historian acts or writes on the supposition that the events of history have their part in a larger purpose, larger than we can hope to understand.

Take a map of the Eurasian land mass. Observe those two subcontinents, the European and the Indian, and consider what great and diverse gifts these two have given to the world. Their meeting is one of the great formative events in world history. This meeting began five hundred years ago with Vasco da Gama, but in one sense it is still near its beginning. Europe and India still have much to give each other. The British contact began with the foundation of the East India Company nearly four hundred years ago. This developed into the two hundred years of the British Raj. The Raj is gone but many of the links forged by it continue. At one time the Raj was absurdly idealised, now it is absurdly denigrated. It may be hoped that the time is approaching when British rule in the Indian subcontinent can be regarded objectively, like the Norman conquest or the Roman Empire. The British Raj should be seen as one episode, albeit an episode of crucial importance, in the meeting of Europe and India. Anglo-Indian history is very interesting in itself, but more than that, both its defects and its achievements have consequences which will influence the development of humanity far into the future.

For more than ten years I have spent many of my working hours thinking and reading about India during the time of the Lawrences but I could not divest myself of an interest in many other subjects. To read all that I should like to read about India would have taken at least another ten years. Therefore I have had to leave many avenues unexplored and many documents unread. With more time and energy much could be added, but I have become increasingly aware of how much is filtered out in the ordinary process of writing history.

My first concern has been to read as much as I can of what Henry and Honoria wrote, either in manuscript or in print. Among other things I have been right through the volumes of *The Calcutta Review* in order to identify as many as I can of their contributions. The result is set out in the appendix. Some of Henry's contributions are listed in Edwardes and Merivale. Others are mentioned in the Henry Lawrence papers. Others again can be identified by characteristic phrases and thoughts which occur elsewhere in the writings of the Lawrences. Henry's work was extensively subbed by both Honoria and Sir John Kaye, and sometimes Henry supplied rough notes for others to put into shape.

As well as reading what the Lawrences wrote I have tried to read as much as I can of what they read. And some of their books are on my shelf. I have read as much as I can of the writings and biographies of their contemporaries. I have not neglected current writing on India by both Indians and Europeans. I have visited as many as I can of the places that figure in their lives. Something has to be left out and I am conscious that I have said nothing about Henry Lawrence's lifelong interest in foreign missions.

PART ONE

BEGINNINGS

1806–22

CHAPTER 1

A Soldier's Home

At the hottest hour of the day in the hottest time of the year, at 1.30 p.m. on 4th May 1799, a group of British soldiers rushed through the river Kaveri under fire from rockets and muskets and scaled a breach in the walls of Seringapatam. The defenders were not ready for such an untimely attack, and six minutes later the British flag flew on the walls. There was more hard fighting that afternoon but the result was hardly in doubt. Tippoo Sultan, the Tiger of Mysore, lay dead and the state of Mysore lay at the feet of the British. They did not annex it but restored it to the previous Hindu dynasty. On that day Britain had become the arbiter of South India and within five years she had become paramount in India.

The only officer to survive the forlorn hope which took the breach was a young Irishman, Lieutenant Alexander Lawrence. A ball hit him in his left arm just as his detachment reached the top of the glacis, where the storming party had paused at the critical moment. Lieutenant Lawrence, although wounded, ran along the line of his men 'hurrahing them to move on', but they stayed where they were. Therefore he ran through the files calling out, 'Now is the time for the breach!' At that the men came on. The Lieutenant received a second ball 'in his right hand which carried off one finger and shattered another into several pieces', but he seized his sword in his left hand and 'did not give it up till he saw the few remaining men gain the breach'. Then he fainted from loss of blood. After the battle one of the men of his regiment noticed that an officer, whom he took to be dead, was wearing the facings of his own regiment's grenadier company. On turning the body over he recognised Lieutenant Lawrence and found that he was alive. He raised him with a violent effort – Lawrence was six foot two and stout in proportion – and staggered off with his burden to the camp, swearing as he toiled along that 'he would not do so much for any other man of them'.[1] The facings that he wore on that day were before me when I wrote this book but have now been stolen.

Alexander Lawrence recovered and had a large family. Five of his sons grew up and went to India. Four were soldiers and became Generals. John, the only civilian, became Governor-General. They imprinted much of their own character on the government of the Punjab and the North-West Frontier. Henry, the subject of this biography, was the fourth son. The Lawrences were a united and loving family, among whom home influences were unusually strong and lasting. Their father Alexander was probably born in 1766 at Coleraine in County Derry. It is not certain who his father was but the Lawrences were well established in Ulster. They were respectable but not of 'the quality'.

Alexander, orphaned at the age of ten, was left in the care of his two sisters who sent him to school for two or three years 'and then took him away without apparently knowing what to do next'. Alexander 'took the matter into his own hands' and joined the navy as a volunteer on 24th July 1781, for a bounty of £5. He was fourteen but he said he was eighteen. For nearly two years he served in the cutter *Nimble*, which his brother William also joined as Acting Surgeon on the same day. At 8 p.m. on 3rd March 1783 Alexander was discharged from the navy in Margate Roads. Evidently he had decided to join the army, for the very next day he embarked at the Mother Bank off Cowes as a volunteer in the 36th or Herefordshire Regiment on the East India Company's ship *Stormont*.[2]

The Herefordshire Regiment had served in Ulster and it appears that Alexander must have had acquaintances or relatives on board the *Stormont*. Four months later they landed at Madras and Alexander Lawrence began twenty-five years' service in India and Ceylon.

The army and navy had a custom of taking on as unpaid volunteers young men of good family who had no means to buy their commissions. They were treated as officers and when a vacancy occurred among the regular Ensigns they were promoted in the field subject to the approval of the War Office. Alexander Lawrence twice won his commission in the field and both times it was disallowed, the first time because the Commander in Chief's recommendation was in the wrong form and the second time because he did not have the right friends. He had to purchase his commission but advanced by degrees without further purchase to the rank of Lieutenant Colonel, no small achievement in those days for a man with neither money nor influence.

The portraits of him in later life indicate a man who had taken hard knocks. The lower part of his face shows determination, but his bright eyes are not those of a hard man. A deep gash across his left cheek was not caused in war. Herbert Edwardes tells the story:

Going home one moonlight night from mess in India, with the major of his corps, a dispute arose between them. The major in a fit of passion drew his sword, and cut his companion down before he could stand on his defence. It was a fierce bad deed repented as soon as done; and in an agony of remorse and sorrow the assailant helped home his desperately wounded friend. There was no concealing such a thing; and the Colonel of the regiment was determined to sift it to the bottom, and bring the major to a court martial. So soon as the wounded man could leave his bed, the whole of the officers were assembled, and the colonel solemnly called on Captain Lawrence to say if it were true that Major – had struck him a foul blow. He replied, 'Colonel, what ever took place, was between Major – and myself; nobody else saw it. He's sorry for it. And not another word will I tell about it.' Nor could threats or persuasion move him.

His wife's nephew, James Knox, said he was 'the nearest thing that I ever knew to the descriptions of the chivalry of the olden time'.

The first seventeen years of his service were nearly all hard fighting in South India where he distinguished himself by gallantry, close obedience to orders, and 'the spirit to overcome all difficulties and hardships' but his exceptionally strong constitution was weakened by fevers got from lying on the wet ground at night in Lord Cornwallis' campaign against Tippoo in 1791-2.

In 1795 Alexander Lawrence was at the taking of Cochin in South India from the Dutch, an incident of the Napoleonic Wars in which the defenders made only a token resistance. After service in Ceylon and South India he was back at Cochin on 1st January 1798, where the Commandant was Captain George Knox, one of the Knoxes of Prehen near Derry. Captain Knox, a son of the Reverend Dr George Knox, rector of Lifford in Co. Donegal, was accompanied by his sister, Catherine Letitia, and on 5th May 1798, a year less one day before the final assault on Seringapatam, she married Alexander Lawrence in the old church in Cochin, the oldest western church in further Asia, where Vasco da Gama was buried. It was then in the hands of the Dutch Reformed Church and the aged Dominie, the Rev. P. Corneliss, married both Protestant and Catholic Europeans, recording them in a shaky hand that is hardly legible.

Both Alexander and Catherine Lawrence had strong characters. 'I should say that on the whole we derived most of our metal from our father,' said John Lawrence, the future Viceroy. He adds that his mother 'had great administrative qualities. She kept the family together and brought us all up on very slender means. She kept the purse and managed all domestic matters.' The gifts of administration which she exercised in the household were inherited by her sons and one of her daughters, and employed in a wider field, sometimes with more than a touch of genius. The 'gunpowder' in Henry came from his father.

The Knoxes came from a more cultivated circle than the

Lawrences. I have a row of the volumes of *Rollin's Ancient* (and other) *History* won by Dr George Knox as prizes in 1748 at Trinity College, Dublin. The miniatures of him show a clear-eyed, thoughtful face. Colonel Lawrence, although thoughtful, only needed a few books such as Rollin, Josephus and the works of Hannah More. He said it was enough that the family filled three post-chaises whenever they moved, without carrying a library about the country. So all surplus books were disposed of. But the Colonel 'was staunch to the old comrade volumes which had marched about the world with him, and when his daughter had read Rollin's Ancient History aloud from beginning to end, and closed the last volume with an exultant bang as if to say, "We've done with it!" he at once put down the mutiny by saying, "Now, if you please, you'll begin it again at the beginning".'

Mrs Lawrence was described by James Knox as 'the counterpart of her husband in mind'. She bore her husband twelve children over eighteen years. Eleven of them grew up. When childbearing was over but while the youngest children were still in the nursery, she had to give increasing time to nursing a sick husband. And he was not disposed to accept outside help. Two of his children were once staying with kind and wealthy friends 'who . . . wrote to Colonel Lawrence proposing to adopt them. The old soldier threw himself into a post-chaise at once, and brought away the children'. He replied to another similar offer by saying, 'God gave me the children and meant me to keep them, not to give them away to other people'.

Most of Henry's brothers and sisters come into his story. The first child, George Tompkins, was born 14th March 1799 and died on 6th January 1802, the day on which the next child, Letitia Catherine (1802-65) was born. There will be much to say about Letitia but her birth, coinciding as it did with her brother's death, nearly cost her mother's life. The remaining children were Alexander (1803-68), George St Patrick (1805-84), Henry Montgomery (28th June 1806-57), Honoria Angelina (1807-89), James Knox (1809-27), John Laird Mair (1811-79), Mary Anne Amelia (1812-77), Charlotte (1814-85), Marcia (1815-83) and Richard (1817-96). The boys were all remarkable, as was Letitia, and Charlotte was much loved, but, fairly or unfairly, the other girls did not leave a happy memory of themselves, not at least in my branch of the family.

Enough is known of Alexander Lawrence's courage and resource to show where his sons got their soldierly qualities of courage, determination and quick thought in an emergency. Besides the heart of a soldier he had the physique to go with it. 'He was a capital rider, a good sportsman and an excellent runner.' Herbert Edwardes thought that if he had lived in Queen Victoria's reign he would have been rewarded with the D.S.O. and the V.C. His service in the field was over by 1800 when his regiment was moved to Ceylon, where peace reigned, and he had to settle down to the quiet task of commanding a detachment at Matara, which is celebrated for its diamonds. It was there that Henry Lawrence was born. Once a lady at Galle in Ceylon asked Mrs Lawrence whether she had brought any diamonds. 'Yes,' said she, called her nurse, pointed to Henry, and said, 'There's my Matara diamond.'

In 1808 the Lawrences sailed for England, Alexander's first sight of home since 1794 when he had been back on sick leave. After furlough he had appointments at Richmond, Yorkshire, where John Laird Mair was born, at Hull and in Guernsey. In 1815 he was ordered to Ostend where he heard the guns of Waterloo. The Duke of Wellington had been a Colonel at the taking of Seringapatam. Colonel Lawrence reminded him of this and asked to be allowed to come to the front with a picked body of men from the garrison at Ostend. Characteristically the Duke answered that he remembered Colonel Lawrence well, and as too good a soldier to wish for any post other than the one that was given to him.

On 6th January 1816 on the way back to Ireland with his regiment in a fierce gale Colonel Lawrence was taken desperately ill. An abscess in his liver burst, and it was not thought that he could survive the night, but his hardy constitution still held out and with great difficulty the ship managed to dock at Dartmouth to put him on shore. 'The surgeon had prepared everything for carrying the sick man to the ship's side' but fifty years later 'it was still remembered how he refused to be carried, gathered his cloak around him, bade his wife "Catherine, stand aside!" and grasping his favourite stick *Sweetlips* in his hand marched firmly to the boat.' For a month he lay between life and death in an inn at Dartmouth, but he surprised the doctors by recovering.

He had, in his own words 'served his King and Country with indefatigable zeal for thirty-five years and with many a hard struggle had reached that rank which might have been of service to his sons'. He could 'safely say that he never made a guinea by the service', and now there was nothing for it but to sell his commission and take his pension. He sold the commission for £3,500 and retired, living at Cheltenham for three years, and for the remainder of his life at Clifton, Bristol.

He had counted on a pension of £300 p.a. but was only allowed £100 p.a. for his wounds, which he said, 'would do little more than pay his doctors'. To quote his own words: He had 'nothing to produce but wounds and loss of health. His left arm is considerably wasted away by a ball being in it since the siege of Seringapatam, it often giving him excessive pain; his right hand dreadfully mangled; his health so bad as to be always in the doctor's hands.' The story of his long fight for a pension commensurate with his services and with the disabilities incurred therefrom is well documented and it shows why he became embittered against the War Office. He did all he could to dissuade his sons from entering the King's service and to deflect their ambition to the service of the East India Company, which was more generous to its servants.

His wife's first cousin and dear friend Honoria Knox had married a director of the East India Company, Mr John Huddleston. He had been in the Company's service in the Madras Presidency, where he rose to be a member of Council. On coming home he became an MP as well as one of the Company's directors. In these two capacities he continued to work for improvements in the condition of India. In particular he worked for the abolition of *suttee* in British India, and his labours in that cause have been compared with those of his friend Wilberforce for the abolition of slavery. Mr Huddleston was fond of his Lawrence cousins and watched over their interests. First he asked the Company to grant from its own funds a small increase to Colonel Lawrence's pension. They gave him a present of a hundred guineas and a pension of £80 p.a. for life which they raised to £130 p.a. in 1820 to 'mark their sense of his merits'. In telling him the news Mr Huddleston wrote: 'There was not a dissenting voice in either the Committee or the Court . . . there were only cheers and echoes. And I wish the matter (the amount) had been equal to the manner.' The War Office in December 1821 allowed him a further £90 p.a. but refused any further increase on the pretext that his grant from the East India Company should be deducted from any pension that might otherwise be paid by the War Office. So the generosity of the Company helped the Crown to wriggle out of its responsibilities.

By this time Mr Huddleston was able to get the boys cadetships in the Company's service. The old warrior was to live to see his sons launched in their careers. His labours had given them a start, but he was not to know in this life how successful they were to be.

Looking back on his life, John Lawrence said, 'My father was a very remarkable man. He had left home at fourteen years of age, and had to struggle with the world from the beginning to the end. But he possessed great natural powers; ever foremost in the field, and somewhat restless in times of peace. I have heard old military men, when I was a boy, say that he was one of the hardiest and best soldiers they ever met, and that he only wanted the opportunity to do great things.' John adds, 'I fancy he was rather headstrong and wayward.' He was 'much liked by his equals and his inferiors' but was 'not disposed to submit readily to imbecility and incompetence in high places. When I was going out to India, my poor old mother made me a speech somewhat to the following effect: "I know you don't like advice, so I will not give you much. But . . . don't be too ready to speak your mind. It was the rock on which your father shipwrecked his prospects."'

Alexander Lawrence had very little money, but he was quixotic in his generosity, always helping old ladies or sharing what he had with an old comrade who was in want. If he had no ready money to help others, he sold capital, until the small patrimonies which he and his wife had inherited were gone. (This was before the Married Woman's Property Acts.) To the end he did not seem to understand the consequences of his generous improvidence, and in his last illness he ordered the bond of a brother officer to be destroyed, lest his executors should demand payment. But his elder children soon began to see what was happening. When Alexander and George went to India at the age of sixteen, each of them began to send money home of their own accord. Their father did not like this and their mother had much ado to get him to accept it. 'It was good for the boys,' she said, 'that they should begin life with denying themselves and helping others.'

Alexander Lawrence had a loving heart, but it was hidden behind a granite exterior and his home might easily have become unbearably grim for his children, particularly in his later years when his bad health took up much of his wife's time. She had followed her wayward and unpractical husband from youth to age with uncomplaining love through their wanderings from place to place. Her shrewd common sense never deserted her and with the scantiest means she somehow held her large family together and, wherever they were, gave them a house that they could look on as home. But she had no time for sentimentality. Emily Metcalfe described her as like 'a Roman mother of warrior sons'. Her 'domestic management seems to have been hard and unyielding. There were no luxuries; hardly even were there any of the comforts of life. It could not have been otherwise.'

Nurse Margaret 'was a prodigious favourite'. She was the daughter of a schoolmaster and brought with her copies of Cicero's *Letters* and Hervey's *Meditations among the Tombs*, which were eagerly read by Letitia and Henry. In the nursery Nurse Margaret would sometimes break the strict rules of the household by giving the children jam. Henry alone would refuse it, because 'Mamma said we were to have bread and milk'. From the grown-up point of view he must have been an extraordinarily good child, not to say a prig. Throughout his youth he was serious to the verge of excess, and in later life he had his critics; but none called him a prig. As he developed, it became clear that he was too humble to take himself as a standard and too enquiring to become set in his ways.

Catherine Lawrence had a favourite sister, Angel Knox, who was well named. At intervals she spent a total of seven years in the Lawrence household. One of the earliest lessons Henry Lawrence taught his eldest son, another Alexander, was the story of Aunt Angel. She was very small and feeble, 'not beautiful, not rich and not clever . . . God does not require us to be clever, nor is it necessary for our happiness that we should be so'. Angel Knox had only just enough to live on, but according to Henry she 'gave away more money during her life than any person I know'.

When she was a girl she had an aunt who lived in a large house in a lonely part of Ireland. She was very fond of Angel, and so was everybody else. So, when she had visitors, she used to send for Angel, who was often at her aunt's for weeks and months together. This aunt had sons, the eldest of them a sailor who returned home from time to time, and it is a reasonable guess that his ship returned periodically to the naval base on Lough Swilly and that the aunt's house was somewhere in Donegal. When he came home he and Angel often met; and they grew to love each other. After one of these visits he wrote to his mother, told her how his love for Cousin Angel had grown upon him, how he wanted to make her his wife and hoped that his mother would approve. His mother asked Angel if she knew anything of this. She knew it well though neither had ever spoken of it.

The mother was kind but stiff. She 'did not approve of cousins marrying', etc., 'and hoped they would get over it'. When the young Commander came home again, Angel was there too. They had not got over it.

One day the mother spoke to Angel, and hoped it had all passed away. Angel said they both felt as certain of each other's love as ever but that it would be better for her to go home, if the marriage had not her aunt's consent. Divining what had happened, the son suddenly left his mother's house. And the servant who brought his horse back, delivered a letter to Angel in the presence of her aunt. Angel read it and put it in her pocket. Her aunt asked if it was from her son. Angel said it was but did not offer to show it, nor did her aunt ask to see it.

Angel escaped to her room, could not appear for dinner and went to bed. During the night her aunt came into her room and thinking that Angel was asleep, went to the pocket of her dress, took out the letter and read it, put it back and went away. Angel felt that she could not speak. It was easier to lie still and endure. But early next morning she wrote a note to her aunt, and asked if she might have the carriage to go home for the last time, adding, 'You know what he says, but it requires *both to be agreed*. And I will never marry into a family where I am not desired.' She returned home and told no one. The cousins never met again. He never came home, and died at sea. Angel's father never knew. But years after, when her sister Catherine Lawrence came home from Ceylon, she told Angel that she had seen her cousin with his ship. Angel burst into tears and then told the story.

When Aunt Angel was living with the Lawrences, her room was the happy resort of all the children. There seemed to have been no trace of bitterness or frustration in her heart.

Latterly, as their father's failing health absorbed more of their mother's care, the Lawrence children came more and more under the influence of Aunt Angel. Their mother told them it was a blessing to have her living with them, and that some day they would understand it. Herbert Edwardes adds that 'on none of them does she seem to have made the abiding impression that she did on Henry'. He guesses that it was '*her* gentle finger' which first struck in his heart the note of practical compassion for all who are miserable, whatever the reason.

Lest this paragon seems too good to be true, it should be added that some of the brothers found that she gave them more religious teaching than they wanted. All the family were in their several ways Christian, but John was exceedingly reticent about his beliefs, and Bosworth Smith, his biographer, attributes this to a reaction against Aunt Angel's teaching.

An even greater influence in Henry's life was his sister Letitia, four years his senior. The records of her undramatic life are sparse but her impact on the lives of her brothers was great.

Bosworth Smith says that 'she had the courage and force of command of the most famous of her brothers' but combined this with a womanly character. This picture, which is confirmed by family tradition, is filled in by a friend, whom Bosworth Smith called 'Mrs B.' 'John Lawrence's eldest sister (says Mrs B.) was an extraordinary woman. Strong of mind and of will, quick in apprehension yet sound and sober in judgment . . . At the house of Mr Huddleston, among other distinguished men, she had often met Wilberforce and the Thorntons, and had quietly drunk in their wit and conversation from the sofa to which, as an invalid she was long confined. Perhaps her brother Henry, who more nearly resembled her in character and disposition, was most amenable to her influence but John, too . . . cherished . . . a boundless reverence for all she said and thought.' John was undemonstrative but when he heard of her death, 'in the bitterness of his soul the remark was wrung from him that he would never have gone to India as Viceroy had he thought that he would never see her again'.[3] 'In their intercourse with her, their [her brothers'] rougher and more tempestuous side seems altogether to have disappeared. They told her every difficulty, shared with her every joy and sorrow, and corresponded with her in the most unrestrained and intimate intercourse, until her death', when John Lawrence destroyed her letters as being too personal to be entrusted to a biographer. She became the adviser and guide to the whole family, including her sisters-in-law. 'Her will was law, not so much because it was a resolute will as because she never sought her own',[4] whether in tender correspondence or in family conclaves gathered round her sofa.

This mutual confidence was, of course, the work of time. 'As often happens in large families, where all have to help each other, the eldest sister was not only playfellow, counsellor and friend, but a kind of small mother' to all the younger children. And she was closest to Henry. She as the eldest explored books and shared them with him. The formal education of the Lawrences was skimpy and unimaginative, and just before Henry went to India, he and his sister were up in her room immersed in the Life of George Washington, whose character made a lasting impression on Henry, when Letitia, looking up between the chapters, said it was a pity they had not been better taught. Henry replied gently, 'Well, that's past. We can now teach ourselves.'

In 1812, when the family went to Guernsey, Letitia was ten; she was left at school at Southampton in the family of the Rev. Dr Mant, a member of a well-known clerical family. He was most kind to her, but the separation was a most terrible grief to both her and her brothers. At Henry's suggestion 'the boys saved up all the Spanish pieces and crooked sixpences that were given them in Guernsey and sent them in a bag to Letitia'. But she was so unhappy that Dr Mant advised sending her home. Whatever was done to comfort her, every morning her pillow was wet with tears. This was the height of the Napoleonic Wars. Communications between Guernsey and the mainland were often intercepted by privateers, but Letitia wrote to her brothers and parents; so sea captains, 'rough, kindly men', were sent to take a look at her and report. At last the Colonel himself was able to slip across. Letitia thought that this was just another sea captain and came into the room timidly, to see her father looking out of the window with his back to her. He had not heard her come in but felt her arms round his neck, turned round and burst into tears. She, too, cried dreadfully. To soothe her, he took her and the daughters of two brother officers to the play *Speed the Plough*. 'He then promised to come again next day, but did not. From London he right valiantly wrote to say he could not trust himself with another sight of her, as he could not take her away altogether; but sent her, as consolation, a £5 note. Letitia tore it into fragments; declared she had been deceived, and was walked off to bed by Miss Mant in great disgrace.'

When the time came for Henry to go to India, 'the prospect of the approaching separation was bitterly felt by these two, and many were the plans which Letitia made for keeping her brother at home. Confiding her griefs to old Mr Huddleston, one day she declared she "would rather set up shop with Henry than let him go to India". "You foolish thing," he said, "Henry will distinguish himself. All your brothers will do well, I think; but Henry has such steadiness and resolution that you'll see him come back a General. He will be Sir Henry Lawrence before he dies."'

CHAPTER 2

School Days

In 1815 at the age of nine Henry Lawrence was sent to school at Foyle College, Derry, where he remained for four years without ever coming home from Ireland. This was the first of many hard separations, but this time there were mitigations. His elder brothers, Alexander and George, went with him, the headmaster, the Rev. Dr James Knox, was his uncle and during four of the six years Aunt Angel Knox lived at the school. George was a little boy but a good boxer and in his first term he won an epic fight with the school bully. After that he became the protector of all new boys.

Dr Knox, who lived to be over ninety, was highly regarded by his pupils. His great-nephew Robert Young of Culdaff describes him in the act of giving a patriarchal blessing on his setting out for America, and eventually for India. He 'bent over me as I knelt before him dressed in the style of nigh a century previous i.e. double breasted coat with standing collar, knee breeches and stockings, with buckles on his shoes. Add to this his snowy wig, hanging down in curls on his shoulders, as he leaned on his gold mounted stick' and laid his hands on his great-nephew's head. This was the uncle-headmaster to whom the three Lawrence boys were entrusted, and such was the blessing he gave to Henry Lawrence's two little boys thirty years later. Dr Knox was 'a very good man, but it does not seem to have been a very good school'.[1]

The boys spent their dreary holidays at school. Another unfortunate, T. Brooke, who spent a vacation at Foyle College, says 'we got up something like a play'. But they did not know what a play was. So 'how the amusement was suggested, I am at a loss to conceive'. However 'burnt cork and an abundance of paint' made up for everything. Henry threw himself into the work with enthusiasm and 'became the hero of the piece'. This part of Ireland was family territory and the sense of kinship is strong among the Irish, whether they are Catholic or Protestant. Another aunt had married one of the Youngs of Culdaff, a country house near Malin Head, the northernmost point of Ireland, lying at the tip of the Inishowen peninsula which stretches up between Lough Foyle and Lough Swilly. Sometimes during the holiday the boys were asked to stay at Culdaff with their cousin James Young who was also at Foyle College. It was a picturesque rambling old house with endless nooks and corners that made it attractive to children. Through the demesne ran shady avenues in different directions and at some distance in front of the house there was a beautiful, well-stocked and spacious garden.

The most direct route from Derry to Culdaff led through Moville, the home of the Montgomerys, and this was a natural stopping place. A few years later Robert Montgomery, the grandfather of Field Marshal Montgomery, was a contemporary of John Lawrence at Foyle College. Robert Montgomery went to India and in 1850 became with Henry and John Lawrence the third member of the triumvirate that ruled the Punjab. An alternative route from Culdaff to Derry, led down the shores to Lough Swilly through Cardonagh, to the little village of Fahan. At Cardonagh another cousin, the Rev. George Marshall, Henry's future father-in-law, was rector and at Fahan, Honoria, Henry's future wife, was being brought up by her uncle, Admiral Heath. However, Henry and Honoria did not know each other as children.

Foyle College left good memories, if not entirely so. In after years Henry wrote to George Broadfoot, his friend and predecessor on the Sikh frontier, 'education consisted in kicks. I was never *taught* anything.' However when he left Foyle College, he could read Caesar and Virgil. And John Lawrence blamed himself for not using his opportunity of acquiring a better education. Henry may have expected too much. He became himself an inspired teacher in Edwardes' phrase, who 'went through life in a teachable and teaching spirit', first making good his own lack and then passing on to others all that he could.

At Foyle College he seems to have been given to reverie, 'caring little for the sport of the other boys'. By contrast when John Lawrence arrived at Foyle College, he thoroughly enjoyed the rough games, and single combats of champions of the school's two factions, and the defence of a clay castle which the boys had constructed in a field and which was regularly manned and relieved at six-hour intervals by day and by night. The boys had 'a custom always in the afternoon' to break windows. Henry did not join in. Therefore they enticed him to throw stones at a mark on the wall. He missed, as expected, and broke a pane of glass. Without a word he went to the headmaster, knocked on the door and said, 'I have come to say, sir, that I have broken a window.'

In 1818 Mr Huddleston, as a director of the East India Company, nominated Alexander for a cadetship at the Company's Military Academy at Addiscombe near Croydon, and the Colonel and his wife travelled to Ireland to fetch Alexander away. This was the first time that the three elder brothers were separated. From Addiscombe Alexander went to India, where he became a dashing cavalry officer in the Madras Army. After making a shotgun marriage with the daughter of a sergeant, and commanding his regiment, he rose to be a Major General. Madras being a long way from the Punjab, Alexander saw little of his brothers after their school days, and he played no part in the stirring events of their public life. He appears, however, from time to time in their papers, and was active in contributing to the fund organised by the brothers to procure for their mother a comfortable life in her old age.

George and Henry stayed on for one more year at Foyle College, and were knit together for life in brotherly affection. In July 1819 they, too, left Derry and travelled by themselves to their parents' home at Clifton, 'which in those days was regarded as a great feat'. George went to Addiscombe, while Henry with his brother John went to the school of a Mr Gough on College Green, Bristol. Of this school John said years afterwards, 'I was flogged every day of my life except one, and then I was flogged twice.'

John had been a baby when Henry left for Foyle College. Now he was a boy of eight and it was during this year, before Henry followed George to Addiscombe, that the brothers began to know each other. They loved each other but in the end they could not work together.

When John was about five he had a bad attack of ophthalmia and had to be kept in a darkened room for a whole year. He would lie on a sofa holding the hand of Letitia or Nurse Margaret while they read to him. In later life he would often say that by its feel he would be able to recognise the hand of either of them anywhen and anywhere.

He used to describe how three years later as 'a little urchin of eight' he trudged twice a day to school and back with unequal steps beside Henry, 'a bony powerful lad of thirteen', across Brandon Hill, which divided Clifton from Bristol. In the evenings, exhausted by the long day, he used to lie flat on the hearth rug doing his prep. Henry was gentle but not meek. John tells a story how the headmaster got on a table and made a great speech to the boys denouncing 'a poor Irish usher named Flaherty . . . as a viper that he had been harbouring in his bosom'. To make it worse one of the boys had taken Flaherty's part. This boy had deeply wounded him; he was an assassin. John did not understand what it was all about, but as he trotted home beside Henry he looked up and asked who the assassin was. Henry answered very quietly, 'I am the assassin.'

The school bully was a boy named Thomas. Henry and John shared a room, and one day John saw his brother getting up very early. 'Where are you going?' 'To Brandon Hill to fight Thomas.' 'Who is to be your second?' 'You, if you like.' So off they went, but Thomas never came to the rendezvous, they 'returned with flying colours and Thomas had to eat humble pie'.

In 1823, when John was twelve (and Henry was a cadet in India), he left Mr Gough's grim academy to spend two years at Foyle College, followed by two more years at Wraxall Hall in Wiltshire where the boys played less violent games than at Foyle. There was little fighting and little cricket. Marbles, prisoner's base and kite flying were the chief recreations. John Lawrence, unlike Henry, took his full share in school-boy escapades at all his schools. He was a tall overgrown lad, rough but kindly, hot tempered but good natured. Often taciturn when he was with a friend, his sallies could be rough but they were forgiven. His 'exuberance of innocent glee' was irresistible. 'A venerable Scotch lady, unaccustomed to such ebullitions', yet fascinated by them, summed him up as 'a diamond but a rough one'.

While the elder boys were at Foyle College, John was much in the company of his father, and listened to many tales of Indian battles and hairbreadth escapes. His blood was stirred and he set his heart on being a soldier, but to his disgust Mr Huddleston nominated him to be a 'writer' in the Indian Civil Service, where the pay and prospects were much better than in the Indian Army. Under the then system of patronage three cadetships could be exchanged for one writership. John, however, was determined that unless he could be a soldier he would not go to India at all. His father said, 'Look at me, after all that I have gone through. If you wish to end your career in this way be a soldier. If you want to be independent, be a civilian.' But neither his father, nor Henry, nor all his friends could move him. So they turned to the 'family oracle'. A friend who was there said that 'the scene in Letitia's room can never be forgotten by those who were present'. John was seated at the foot of the invalid's couch and put his case 'with all the vehemence of his ardent boy's nature', saying, 'a soldier I was born and a soldier I will be'. But Letitia urged him without hesitation to accept the gift that was offered. And in the end he 'reluctantly but bravely yielded' to Letitia's calm advice and good judgment.

John went to the East India Company's College at Haileybury for four years. Army cadets sailed for India when they were sixteen but future civil servants stayed at home until they were eighteen. The staff of Haileybury, both British and Oriental, were distinguished, the Rev. T. R. Malthus was professor of political economy and of history. His house was the resort of philosophers and statesmen from all parts of Europe. Sometimes the lectures were over the heads of the pupils. Indeed parts of the course would have been more use as a refresher course on first furlough, if only there had been regular furloughs.

Henry was back from India for his health, when John went to Haileybury. He accompanied him to school 'with parental care' and walked him up and down the library 'explaining some rather recondite matters' which might be useful in the examinations. But John was not listening. So an anxious parent asked Henry to transfer his attentions to his own son. Which Henry did.

At Haileybury John Lawrence was 'neither industrious nor very idle'. He liked mooning about the quadrangle and the reading room, roaming over the wild neighbouring heath or organising an Irish revel of bonfires for St Patrick's day or the Battle of the Boyne. But in a desultory way he read a great deal, mainly history and biography, and he remembered all that he read. He kept Plutarch by him all his life and would in moments of difficulty read the life of one of Plutarch's heroes until he came on some passage that fitted his own situation. He won a number of prizes and medals but did not impress his teachers as a man likely to excel. Each term he brought his prizes home and gave them to Letitia. 'They are her books. I should not have had them but for her. I work with her in my mind.'

All the stories recorded of Henry's school days are to his credit, as is the way of Victorian biographers. From a boy he was kind to all who were down, whatever the reason for their misfortune. There was a poor old man who sat on Brandon Hill selling pincushions. Henry gave him a penny or a sixpence when he could, and brought him to the notice of Aunt Angel. Bit by bit the old man became a pensioner of the Lawrences. In this house there were no luxuries, but there was always something to give away. When he was driven home by fever a few years later, one of Henry's enquiries was for 'the old man of Brandon Hill' who lived to welcome him. Letitia, in telling the story to Herbert Edwardes, added, 'He *never* lost sight of anyone in whom he had ever taken the slightest interest.'

Mr Huddleston gave a cadetship for Henry but the Colonel gave it away to someone who had befriended him. However, another Director of the East India Company gave him another cadetship and in August 1820 Henry followed his brother George to Addiscombe. George was a solicitous elder brother and as soon as he could he wrote to his mother that 'dear Henry has passed his examination . . . with great credit to himself, and is now pretty well settled, I mean as well as can be expected, considering there are one hundred and fourteen cadets in the seminary and that he has only been here two days.'

Life at Addiscombe was basic, but healthy. Each of the boys slept in a tiny partitioned room known as his 'kennel'. They paraded for every aspect of their life. The classes were lengthy and they went to chapel twice a day. But they were well fed and they enjoyed their life. Henry did well in his studies but was not outstanding. In his last term he 'acquired a knowledge of military surveying and no one more thoroughly enjoyed the excursions over the country in carrying on his surveys'. Surveying was to be the foundation of his career. His contemporaries remembered him as 'a very rough Irish lad, hard bodied, iron constitutioned'. 'Imagine a rather tall, rawboned youth of sixteen, with high cheekbones, small grey eyes, sunken cheeks, prominent brows' and reddish brown hair inclined to wave. 'Imagine this frame full of life and energy, buoyant with spirits and overflowing with goodness, yet quick of temper . . . and you have before you Pat Lawrence.' At Addiscombe Henry was always called 'Pat', and his fiery temper was 'off in an instant' at any reflection on Ireland; but it was easy to make him laugh. His love of his family was even more marked than his attachment to the land of his fathers and, 'thoughtless as boys are,' he was known to all as a devoted son and brother. It was remarked that he was always ready to side with the losing party or the weak. And 'when anything mean or shabby roused his ire, the curl of his lip and the look of scorn he could put on was most bitter and intense'.

James Abbott, who was one of his distinguished lieutenants, in after life recalls that 'his frame was not very robust, but the energy we have so often admired in him in after years, and which seemed to wax in vigour in proportion to the decline of his bodily strength, was something observable'.

He could quarrel and he could make it up. One little boy, Robert G. Macgregor, was distinguished by a large blue swallow-tailed coat with gilt buttons which he was wearing one day when the boys were on their 'Sunday March' to Croydon church. The boy tells the story:

> Lawrence came up laughing and asked me . . . 'Who made your coat? You have not taken your grandfather's by mistake?' I was angered and gave it him back in kind. There was a struggle and an aggressive shove. We then parted, Lawrence saying that we would have it out after church. But as soon as he could after our return march after church, Lawrence voluntarily came up and, holding out his hand, said with a laugh 'I was wrong and rude and in fault. Let us be friends!' We were so then and ever after.

Soon after this Robert G. Macgregor saved 'Pat' Lawrence's life. Henry was learning to swim in the Croydon Canal when he got out of his depth 'into one of the holes which abound there'. The other boys tried to help him but none of them could swim, so they only got a ducking for their pains. They stood on the edge of the danger with their hands stretched out but unable to help, when his new friend heard a hubbub and a rush of boys come to call him. 'I went to Addiscombe from a school on the Thames under a capital scholar and first rate flogger, who used to cane us into as well as out of the water'.

So he could swim well, and in a few strokes got Henry ashore, 'though quite exhausted and breathless'.

It was the same friend who introduced Henry to the poems of Sir Walter Scott. He learned long passages by heart and 'spouted' them at every opportunity. His favourite incident was the encounter between Fitz James and Roderick Dhu and, when he was outnumbered in some boyish encounter, he would suit the action to the words and thunder out

> His back against a rock he bore,
> And firmly placed his foot before;
> 'Come one, come all! This rock shall fly
> From its firm base as soon as I'.

This same Robert Macgregor tells us that 'rank in India depends on the place held by the cadet in the last month's report before leaving the College . . . I was told that Lawrence was above me. When I told him this he said, with one of his pleasing smiles, "I am sorry you are disappointed, and would just as soon you had been first".'

But Henry was seen walking with a chosen friend more often than taking part in sports. If the young Henry Lawrence stood aloof from the recreations of his contemporaries at school, and as a young officer, part of the reason was lack of money, much as he loved 'manly sports' without being very good at them. Subscriptions were required to join in all games at Addiscombe and he was determined not to ask his father for more pocket money than the college minimum which was given him. Only once in some dire emergency he asked one of his sisters for help by return of post. She sent him a £5 note and in her agitation forgot to seal it; but it arrived safely all the same.

In the holidays he once went to a ball with Alexander, George and Letitia, to whom he said portentously on the way home, 'What a wretched unprofitable evening! Not a Christian to speak to. All the women decked out with flowers on their heads, and their bodies half naked.' He disliked display much and frivolity excessively. In India, knowing what the Indians thought of the European custom of men and women dancing together higgledy piggledy, he had an extra reason for not liking balls. But he mellowed and came to look with pleasure on all the innocent enjoyments of youth. When he was at Mount Abu in Rajputana, his 'return to the station was the signal for dinner parties, picnics' etc, 'not that he ever cared for such things but . . . since they had to be endured' he helped to make them go off well. And when he dropped in on the parties of the young, 'he was the soul of the party'.

At Addiscombe his best subject was mathematics. He was thought to be backward for his age and a slow learner, but made up for it by unflinching application. His need to understand the reason for everything that he was expected to learn sometimes made him slow. One of his contemporaries wrote: 'He was thrown at each step into a reverie, and could not advance until he thoroughly understood the ground he occupied . . . I have often seen him lay down the single stick to carry out one of these investigations suggested by some unusual sentiment of his antagonist, and then return to the game with additional zest . . . His character was original in the extreme. Nothing in it was borrowed.'

Alexander and George had gone into the cavalry, which required no examination but, backward as he was considered Henry was determined to get into the artillery. 'Lest it be supposed that no Lawrence could pass for the artillery.' He worked hard and passed out of Addiscombe at the top of his class. To the end of his life he remained first and foremost an artillery officer.

Many years later John Lawrence said to Herbert Edwardes:

I remember my brother Henry one night in Lord Hardinge's camp turning to me and saying, 'Do you think we were clever as lads? *I don't think we were*', but it was not altogether that we were dull . . . We were both bad in languages and always continued so; and we were not good in anything which required a technical memory; but we were good in anything which required thought or judgment. We were good, for instance in history. And so far from Henry being *dull*, I can remember that I myself always considered him a fellow of power and mark; and I observed that others thought so.

Yet none of his teachers thought that he was likely to distinguish himself.

He left Addiscombe on 10th May 1822 and had a pleasant interlude at home at Clifton until he sailed for India in September at the age of sixteen. He spent this time devouring books with Letitia, except for some days touring on the Wye with Mr Huddleston, Letitia and a Miss Slack. Morison observes that 'the friendship between Henry and Letitia grew stronger with their developing characters'. And the sermons of the great Baptist divine, Robert Hale, in Bristol, added to the depth of his religion.

At this time he and Letitia built a little castle in Spain for themselves. She would come to India with him and they would both set up a school in the hills; but their father's health was failing and their mother could not be left in poverty to nurse him as well as bringing up their younger brothers and sisters. It was Letitia's lot to stay at home and help her mother, while Henry went to India and joined his brothers in scraping together every rupee they could for their parents.

His exile had a purpose, but his outfit would be a sore strain on the family's finances. In all the years Aunt Angel had been with the family, Colonel Lawrence never allowed her to contribute to the common purse. But as each nephew left home, she got permission to fit him out. So Aunt Angel bought Henry's outfit. And then he was gone.

PART TWO

INDIA

1823–26

CHAPTER 3

India in 1823

Henry Lawrence arrived in India in February 1823, joining the head-quarters of the Bengal Artillery at Dum Dum a few miles from Calcutta. The British had already been in India for three quarters of a century as rulers of a great province, and for much longer as traders. The East India Company, of which Henry was a servant, was an extraordinary institution. Since 1600 they had been traders but in the breakdown of the Mogul Empire at the beginning of the eighteenth century they had been forced to employ an army for safety. Then one thing led to another until, contrary to the expressed will of the Directors of the East India Company, they were forced to expand from their tiny bases in India, sometimes willingly but more often unwillingly, until they found themselves in possession of an empire. In Sir John Seely's words it was almost true that the British 'conquered the world in a fit of absence of mind'. The Crown in this unusual situation instituted by degrees a control of the Company. But when Henry went to India it was still 'John Company' or the 'Company *behadur*', who decided where each man should go. The British had been the paramount power in the subcontinent for more than seventy years, but it was only a few years before Henry's arrival that the conclusion of the Pindari wars had finally established that Pax Britannica which was to last for over a hundred years. Much had happened since Clive won the battle of Plassey in 1757. In 1823 the British Raj was taking shape but it was still malleable, and the great Anglo–Indians of the first two generations Sir Thomas Munro, Sir John Malcolm and Mountstuart Elphinstone, had already seen its end in its beginning. Sir Charles Metcalfe had written: 'We are to appearances more powerful in India than we ever were. Nevertheless our downfall may be short work. When it commences, it will probably be rapid.'

There are many strands in the long relation between Britain and India. Two eminent British writers, Rudyard Kipling and E. M. Forster, have painted very different pictures of British rule. Both did see what they thought they saw but there is much that neither of them perceived. Affection and frustration are closely interwoven and it is a mistake to allow the frustration to obscure the warm feelings without which the story is incomprehensible. The fiercest resentments on both sides were often those of a rejected lover. In the ups and downs of their relations Britain and India have been aptly compared to a couple who have long been married.

Indian civilisation is very old, but the British met India at a time of unparalleled disarray. In India, at the best of times, private virtues are better developed than public spirit and the Great Anarchy which followed on the break-up of the Mogul Empire in the eighteenth century had brought public morality to a depth seldom equalled anywhere. The Mogul emperors represented legitimate authority and for nearly two hundred years they had had the means to enforce it. But after the death of Aurengzeb in 1707 there was no legitimate ruler with the ability to make his rule effective. There followed a time of troubles when force and treachery increasingly took the place of lawful authority. As the struggle proceeded many men of strong character and great ability came forward as contestants for a share of the Mogul inheritance, but every decade their standards of conduct were eroded, until men who began their careers as realists were in danger of becoming satanists. The history of the native courts gives examples of treachery, cruelty and corruption. It is not surprising that Europeans were shocked by what they found in India, but later Henry Lawrence was to remind his friends that those guilty of horrifying conduct in public life had been trained in a very bad school. It was for the British to show them higher standards.

The Moguls were a dynasty of Turki-speaking Moslem conquerors from Central Asia who for two hundred years gave India a greater degree of unity than she had ever had before. Their rule had great virtues. They built some of the most beautiful architecture in the world, and the memory of Akbar's civil service survived into the Raj but like almost all Asian monarchs, the continuance of their rule was precarious and its quality unpredictable. Akbar (1542–1605) was a great ruler but too much depended on one man. The ruler's will was supreme and no framework of institutions or enforceable customs curbed the caprice, bad judgment or cruelty of despots. A good man would rule well, sometimes very well, but on his death everything went back into the melting pot. Revolt was the only effective remedy and there was no guarantee that it would provide better government. Moreover where polygamy prevails, it is almost impossible to secure an orderly succession when a ruler dies. The sons of different wives are rivals. Civil wars are the rule after the death of a sovereign; and the leading contenders among his children are always tempted to anticipate their father's death by revolt, and then to protect their own safety by killing their brothers. The Ottoman Turks in their great days went so far as to make it a rule that when a new Sultan succeeded to the throne all his brothers should be killed.

In the case of the Moguls, too, there were revolts in every reign and disputed successions on every death. Yet in the event one great ruler, Akbar, was succeeded by three more than competent rulers, Shah Jehan, Jehangir and Aurangzeb, who all held the empire together for nearly two centuries and enlarged its boundaries. But by the death of Aurangzeb the Mogul Empire was already overextended and had developed internal weaknesses. The Moguls were Moslems, but Akbar had taken his Hindu subjects into full partnership. By the death of Aurangzeb, however, a Moslem minority was ruling by force over a Hindu majority, and some Hindus, notably the Mahrattas, were resisting successfully.

The history of India in the eighteenth century is a sad story of invasion and destruction, famine, pestilence and growing corruption. Treachery had been a persistent element in Oriental politics but in India there had also been heroic faithfulness. Now however, in public life 'bad currency drove out good'.

The British had been in India as traders since 1600. They had fought the 'Portugals' and the Dutch for the right to trade with India, but to the Moguls they came as traders and suppliants, preferring peace but ready to defend themselves. Later, as disorder grew, foreigners in India had to raise regular armies for their own defence. It then became apparent that discipline in war and national solidarity in civil life made it possible for small numbers of Europeans to overcome large Indian armies. Indians were potentially as good soldiers as Europeans, but though firearms had now taken the place of chariots, their tactics and organisation had hardly changed since their defeat at the hands of Alexander the Great.

The French were also in India as traders, and in this age of Anglo-French rivalry the two soon came into conflict. Thanks to Clive and Stringer Lawrence (no relative) the British won. The British sought no empire but in the course of defending themselves they gained one and did not at first know what to do with it. At a later stage some of their servants deliberately enlarged their dominions, often on grounds that were defensible but sometimes without scruple. The East India Company before the invention of telegraph and steamships had an imperfect control over its servants, but the Company as such never wanted to extend its political commitments.

The collapse of the Mogul Empire began at the centre, because Delhi was where struggles for the succession were concentrated and Delhi was the magnet that drew invaders. By the end of the century villages near Delhi were sometimes completely isolated for long periods, being cut off from their neighbours by jungle, tigers and bandits.

The unhappy successors of Babur and Akbar reigned over shrinking domains and were not always able to assert their power outside the capital, but for some time Mogul life continued with little change in outlying provinces such as Bengal. Indeed, one fragment of the Mogul Empire, the domains of the Nizam of Hyderabad, maintained the continuity of its administration till after the end of the British Raj. But the rulers of these provinces had become virtually independent.

The British by now had toeholds in India centred on the three presidencies of Calcutta, Bombay and Madras. All three were seaboard cities founded for trade. They became the centres from which the subcontinent was ruled. Calcutta was the seat of the Governor-General, but the other two presidencies each had their own traditions and for a very long time their own armies. Clive's victories made Britain the arbiter of the rich province of Bengal, which included most of Bangladesh as well as the present West Bengal and Bihar. The British began to rule as the appointed representatives of the distant and impotent Emperors in Delhi, and at first there was no intention of changing the Mogul system of government, but this plan did not work.

The earliest years of British rule were shameful. British clerks and merchants in confederation with their Indian assistants were as grasping and as oppressive as their Indian predecessors, and they exacted in addition trading privileges that ruined those classes which nourished commerce and industry. The soil of Bengal was rich and in those days India was under-populated, as a consequence of war, pestilence and famine. Land was to be had almost for the taking, until under British rule settled government eventually increased the population to the point where there was a shortage of land. For the last hundred years land hunger has been a cardinal problem, but not before. Eighteenth-century Bengal could survive much misgovernment, but after the battle of Plassey in 1757 the double yoke of British oppression, added to that which was already there, ruined Bengal and brought the Company to the verge of bankruptcy.

Bad as this was, it did not last long, and Clive's second term of office as Governor of Bengal from 1765 to 1767 brought an improvement. The appointment of Warren Hastings as Governor in 1772 marked an epoch. He suppressed corruption and gave Bengal an honest and efficient government, which was the foundation of everything that followed for the best part of two hundred years. Indeed his work still has daily consequences, for the independent governments of India, Pakistan and Bangladesh have inherited much from the traditions of British rule. Hastings' achievement is seen to be the greater when it is remembered that he had no power to overrule the Council appointed to work with him, and that a strong faction in his Council, led by Philip Francis, not only went to all lengths to thwart him, but caused him to be impeached on his return to England. Posthumously he has been almost entirely vindicated, but in his lifetime and for long after he was subjected to an obloquy that has few parallels in history.

Warren Hastings had his share of human weakness, but he was a good and perceptive man, well capable of exerting strength when needed but naturally inclined to be gentle. Before Clive's victories he had lived as a young man among Indians, as no other Governor-General did. John Lawrence alone among later Governor-Generals as a young man also lived for a time almost entirely among Indians, but even in his youth he was a representative of the supreme power. Hastings, on the other hand, had been a young foreigner who had to be always on his good behaviour. He loved and appreciated the Indians, and wanted to employ them as much as possible in the administration, but was continually frustrated by place hunters who pushed their friends and relatives into the most lucrative and influential positions. In consequence the Indian Civil Service became what he never intended it to be, a preserve of the British upper and upper-middle class. As an old man, Hastings wrote to his namesake, the Marquis of Hastings, who had been appointed Governor-General in 1812:

Among the natives of India there are men of as strong intellect, as sound integrity, and as honorable feelings as any of this kingdom. I regret that they are not sufficiently employed, nor respected so much as they deserve to be.

The Hindus are gentle, benevolent, more susceptible of gratitude for kindness shewn them than prompt for vengeance for wrongs sustained, abhorrent of bloodshed, faithful and affectionate in service and submissive to legal authority. They are superstitious; but they do not think ill of us for not behaving as they do . . . Even from their theology arguments, which no other can afford, may be drawn to support the most refined mysteries of our own . . . The least therefore that can be expected from the most enlightened of all nations . . . is to protect their persons from wrong, and to leave their religious creed to the Being who has so long endured it, and who will in His own time reform it.

As well as the virtues of the Indians, Warren Hastings saw the faults of his own people. He moderated greed, and his successors carried his work further. Arrogance was more subtle, but in the instructions which he had drawn up humility is given a special mention as one of the 'national principles which should ever characterise the name of an Englishman'. And in his farewell message to the Company's servants he specially commends 'gentleness and moderation . . . towards the native inhabitants'. These were the ideals of Warren Hastings and they were never entirely forgotten.

In the half century since his reforms great changes took place. The turning point was the Governor-Generalship of Lord Cornwallis who, with a reputation untarnished by the surrender of Yorktown, succeeded Warren Hastings. Where Warren Hastings wanted to rule India through Indians, Cornwallis, looking around him at the debris left by Indian anarchy, concluded that only British people could be entrusted to rule justly and without corruption. Under him the Indian Civil Service became what it remained, British, just, incorruptible and conscientious, often humdrum but sometimes with more than a touch of genius. Henceforth Indians did not come to Government House. Henry Lawrence summed Cornwallis' policy up in an aphorism: 'Lord Cornwallis hit upon the expedient of securing official honesty among Europeans by high official pay; he expected to obtain the same virtues from the natives by an opposite process.'[1] The fault of the ICS was not any great oppression but an unwillingness to share their responsibility with Indians, at least, until it was almost too late. They were often overbearing and sometimes harsh, but some of them were sensitive as well as honest, and the British Raj was comprehensive enough to nourish many critics of its own weak points. If there was injustice there were those within the system who raised their voices in protest. For every Napier there was an Outram.

In 1784 Pitt's India Act had converted the East India Company from a trading company into an autonomous body that was responsible to Parliament for the good government of British India. Corruption had been almost completely eliminated, though the standards were not yet as strict as they were later, but in British India after Cornwallis the Indians were almost entirely excluded from positions of responsibility in governing their own country. And the British had drawn away from easy social intercourse with Indians. There had been a short time when the British had been powerful but not all powerful in India and met the Moslem aristocracy on equal terms. The two groups of rulers liked each other; the Moslems sometimes thought the British uncouth, but they were prepared to teach them better manners. They appreciated their manly characters and were prepared to work with them. But once the British became supreme they despised their subjects and human relations between the two groups deteriorated sharply.

Caste had always made relations with Hindus more difficult, but earlier generations of Anglo–Indians had kept Indian mistresses from whom they learnt much about the country. Now, however, this was becoming unacceptable. The change is often blamed on the rise of

Evangelical religion and this must presumably have been an element, but the charge is exaggerated. Anglo–Indian society as a whole was never very ardent in its religion, though there was always a vital leaven of Christian faith in a creative minority, and among the rest a diffused Christianity which is hard to evaluate but could be powerful in moments of tension. Evangelicals, however, were always a minority even among those who took their religion seriously. And those who were not religious, or whose religion was not Evangelical, were not more tolerant of liaisons with Indian women. It seems that there were at least two other factors in this change of *mores*. British women now came to India in greater numbers and they did not want rivals for the affection of their men. And India was once more quietly imposing on her conquerors her own unique ways of emphasising social divisions, without anyone being particularly aware of what was happening. The foreign rulers were being drawn into the Hindu caste system. The British had in effect constituted themselves a new caste whose *dharmat* was to govern, with the Eurasians as a sub-caste to assist them in subordinate positions.

The institution of caste is very ancient, being thought to date back to the Aryan invasions of India in the second millennium BC though it has greatly evolved since then and is still evolving. The Sanskrit word for caste means colour, and the origins of caste are racial. The Aryan invaders disliked mixed marriages as much as the Hebrew prophets or white South Africans. So the light-skinned priests and warriors kept themselves apart from the darker aborigines who followed humbler occupations. And those who did particularly disgusting work were considered untouchable. A system that was once relatively simple gradually became complicated. Almost every occupation became hereditary and was the prerogative of a particular sub-caste, or indeed one of the sub-groups of the untouchables, who ranked too low to have – at least in theory – any caste at all. In general it was not permissible to eat food prepared by someone of a lower caste. One consequence of this was that the social meal hardly existed among Hindus. In practice one could only eat with those of one's own group. One of the indirect consequences of the British Raj was to modify, though by no means do away with, the influence of caste, and to promote a degree of social mixing which had not existed for many centuries if not millennia.

After the end of the eighteenth century the British in India did little to overcome the social barriers between them and the Indians. But it should be recognised that there are difficulties in the way of social friendship with people who are polluted by your presence at table. Regretting her ignorance of the true feelings of Indians, Honoria Lawrence wrote: 'No stone or iron ever formed such a division between people as caste does . . . Separation of food goes further to keep people apart than difference of colour or language. 'Tis like a screen of glass that always keeps you at a certain distance and prevents contact, though at first you may not see anything to prevent approach.' This particular difficulty did not apply to the very important Moslem minority, but in their case *purdah* was a barrier that prevented male Europeans from meeting half the population.

That British arrogance that Warren Hastings feared is not to be excused, but the achievement of the Anglo–Indians was remarkable and it was not surprising that they became rather too full of themselves. Tiny numbers of British had conquered the subcontinent and had given it a rule that was just, tolerably efficient and in the last resort light handed. Supreme power was held by such small numbers of people that gross oppression would have been impossible. The Indian Civil Service never at any time exceeded fifteen hundred men, and the numbers of Europeans in the army and other services were not very large. The British could only rule by consent. They could hardly expect to be popular with subjects from whom they differed in so many ways, but their rule could not have lasted long, nor could it have been so generally peaceable, if it had not been accepted, and on the whole willingly accepted, in the period with which we are dealing. However, it was precarious and fragile. The wiser heads saw that this was so, but most Anglo–Indians took it for granted that the *sepoys*, the native soldiers, on whom the whole structure depended, would remain loyal to their masters and that British rule would continue indefinitely. They did not see that the loyalty of Indian subjects had to be earned continually afresh. Bishop Heber wrote in his famous diary that 'We are not guilty of injustices or wilful oppression but we shut out the natives from our society, and a bullying and insolent manner is continually assumed in speaking to them.' Bad manners can leave a deeper wound than injustices.

Anglo–Indian society was generally humdrum and sometimes trivial, yet in the first half of the nineteenth century it could be said that 'no monarchy in Europe has produced within a given time so many men of the first talent in civil and military life as India within the same period.'[2] The Anglo–Indian community was in some ways like a Greek city state. It was close knit, it was competitive; and a shared experience, with a common purpose in which they believed, challenged many to scale the heights. Moreover, the actors in the drama knew that the plot was not of their devising. Men had not yet forgotten Providence, and the best of them were spurred on by the thought that they were serving a purpose which was higher than they could comprehend.

The expansion of the British dominions increased the area of settled government but one of its first results was to push the freebooters into that shrinking area which remained independent under Indian rulers. Organised armies of marauders on horseback, known as Pindaris, operated from the native states which were unable to control them. They would descend suddenly where they were least expected, rob, murder and torture, and be gone before any army could come near them. They did not respect any boundaries and their incursions into British territory proved their undoing. After their suppression travel and property became safe throughout India. A European lady could travel by herself anywhere in India with the minimum guard, which was more for the sake of appearances, as safely as if she had taken the stage coach from London to Bath. Europeans were treated with a respect amounting to awe. However the chief beneficiaries of the new security were the Indians themselves, and trade and agriculture began to revive.

The boundaries of the British dominions were, however, not yet settled. On the west the Sutlej was the frontier and to the east lay Burma, at that time an isolated country whose rulers imagined that their capital Ava was the centre of the universe. In 1824 their acts of aggression on the border with Bengal led to a war, and the mutiny at Barrackpore a few miles from Calcutta gave advance warning of the storm that was to break over northern India a generation later.

CHAPTER 4

A Lieutenant of Artillery

When Henry Lawrence's parents saw him off at Deal, whence he sailed in September in 1822, it was a long farewell as there was no question of furlough for cadets for at least ten years and an officer serving in the Company's army could only expect one home leave in the course of his service. The only exception to these rules was sick leave. But Henry's brothers Alex and George were already in Calcutta waiting for him. And it was an added comfort to his mother and to Henry himself that one of his fellow passengers was another Addiscombe boy, an artillery cadet called John Edwards, 'a warm hearted affectionate lad'. On the journey out Henry and John Edwards became firm friends and when they arrived in Calcutta, the two sixteen-year-olds set up house together at Dum Dum, where they were stationed. John Edwards was deeply religious and Henry's biographer, Herbert Edwardes, implies that he turned Henry to a deeper concern for the meaning of life. But after a few months John became ill and was sent for his health on a sea voyage to Penang and China. After that the two friends only met twice, but the warmth of their feeling for each other was never quenched. When Edwards was dying in 1831, he sent Henry his blessing and left him a mourning ring inscribed on the inside 'Love one another, being his mother's last injunction to us on leaving England'.

At this time Henry Lawrence gives the impression of a too serious schoolboy. On the evidence of his contemporaries, he paid more attention than most to 'drill and regimental matters, and took to professional reading'. 'He did not join the regimental hunt, nor frequent the billiard room or regimental theatre'.[1] This was a necessary consequence of the extreme frugality that his brothers and he practised in order to save up for the old age of their parents. His spare time was largely spent on 'hard and regular reading', mostly history. But his love of poetry remained. Colonel Sam Fenning, a brother officer in the Bengal Artillery, who knew him at this time, wrote: 'the last work he had in hand, I well remember, was the Universal History in twenty or twenty-one volumes, which he read through.* You might come into his room and see him closely bending over his book with both hands on his temples mentally devouring its contents.' He had a retentive memory and 'his mind thus became stored with facts and principles held' for use when needed.

Few letters survive from this time but on 16th October 1824, when he had been in India nearly two years and was eighteen, he wrote to his little sister, Mary Anne, 'but I am getting a very old fellow . . . I am so tall and so black, just like a native soldier.'

His favourite relaxation was chess, at which he played for hours. He always tried to match himself against a better player and when defeated often lost his temper. 'For the fun of it,' said one of his antagonists, 'when we saw checkmate on the board we began to draw back our chairs as if preparing for retreat. Lawrence would perceive this, but say nothing, till the winning party made the move and rushed to the door, saying "Checkmate!" when Lawrence half in anger, half in jest, would often send the board after him.' But when he won a chance game from a superior, he hastened to say, 'You play better than I do.' And from studying the moves of others 'he shaped out for himself ere long a skilful style of play, much beyond the promise of his commencement . . . Much of what he acquired in after life was by the same patient practice; an emulous observance of what was right or careful avoidance of what was wrong in the ways and means by which others worked.'

After John Edwards left, Henry wrote to Letitia: 'On his departure I took up my quarters with a lad of the name of Ackers, who has been a couple of years out. He had been dreadfully ill and is obliged to go home and, I am afraid, not to come back.' Mortality was so high, particularly among new arrivals, that one may wonder how there were any British left in India. But two months later Henry wrote to Letitia about one, Lewin, who had been a friend of both George and Henry Lawrence at Addiscombe, when Henry had considered him 'a worldly minded lad'. On the voyage he had been on the same ship as the Rev. George Craufurd, one of the more notable chaplains of the East India Company. Craufurd had been appointed assistant chaplain to the Old Church in Calcutta, where the renowned Thomas Thomason was chaplain. During the voyage Lewin had 'opened his heart to Mr Craufurd' and a change had taken place in him. Henry wrote to Letitia that now 'his whole care seems to be what good he can do. And of course he is designated a Methodist, but I wish we had a few more such *Methodists*.'

On arriving in India Mr Craufurd, though attached to the Old Church, 'was soon charged also with the care of the neighbouring artillery station at Dum Dum, the importance of which with its

*No doubt the Rollin won by his maternal grandfather at Trinity College, Dublin in 1748. See Chapter 1.

European soldiery and numbers of young officers claimed half the week at least'. There was in Dum Dum a large untenanted house called Fairy Hall which, James Abbott tells us, 'almost deserved its title, so prettily was it shaded with wood and enlivened with water'. Craufurd took Fairy Hall and made it 'a little heart of Christian life in the midst of the cantonment'. Lewin went to live there and 'the other constant inmates were lieutenants Sam Fenning, Cookson and D'Arcy Todd'. These earnest young men were fine human beings but they wore their religion on their sleeves and were mocked for it. The more reserved Henry Lawrence came to join them and, though they thought much of him, they could not make him out.

Thirty-six years later one of them, probably Sam Fenning, said: 'I cannot say what led Lawrence to join us. I doubt whether religion had reached his heart at this time. He did not speak upon the subject nor disclose his feelings, that I am aware of, to anyone.' Another brother officer, who was among Mr Craufurd's flock though not an inmate of Fairy Hall, says that though Henry Lawrence shrank 'from all outward demonstrations; he mingled as freely as ever with his old associates, locking up the sacred fire in his heart, but exhibiting its effects in self conquest, increased affection for his fellow creatures, and more earnest application to his professional duties and studies'.

Lewin's touching but humourless diary tells us a little more:

Wednesday, February 11th, 1824. We returned thanks to God for his infinite mercy in hearing our prayers for our dear brother Lawrence. He did not go to the theatre this evening.

Saturday, October 2nd. Lawrence is impatient of friendly rebuke and counsel. Coolness in argument is unknown to him. Quite at a loss how to act towards him.

Sabbath, March 26th 1826 (at Arracan) Lawrence does not seem to comprehend the doctrine of original sin.

He never did comprehend it, in the sense that Lewin meant; but he had an abiding feeling for the weakness of human nature and man's need for God's help. His temper remained 'a scourge to him' all his life, and it is easy to see him losing his temper in arguments with these good but gushing Evangelicals. His commitment to the truth in Jesus was complete, but in religion he was one of those blessed souls who feel little need to express their faith in verbal propositions.

Mr Craufurd's attention was first drawn to Henry Lawrence by what that group called Lawrence's 'plain face'. 'He professed less than either he felt or practised' and he kept aloof. 'Once he said almost sharply to Mr Craufurd, you take a great interest in me; as much as if you were my brother. What's the meaning of it? and to the last he never quite opened his heart. He used to ask Mr Craufurd questions as to the Bible, like one who really meant them. "What I want to be assured of" he said one day, "is that this Book is God's. Because, when I know that, I have nothing left but to obey it." After coming to Fairy Hall he joined in all the Bible readings at which Mr Craufurd expounded and prayed, but he would never pray aloud himself.' Craufurd remembered him making his Communion at the Old Church in Calcutta but he used not to do so at Dum Dum. Presumably he felt that an intensely private act was more private in Calcutta than among his Fairy Hall friends at Dum Dum. His approach to faith was like his method of learning to play chess, or to do anything else. He had to teach himself and to test the foundations first but, after that, he moved forward with sureness. Herbert Edwardes writes that among the memories of Letitia 'nothing is more distinct than this, that he attributed his first deep impressions of religion to Mr Craufurd'. But Craufurd did not know this until Herbert Edwardes told him so, thirty-seven years afterwards, when he was living in retirement in England, having succeeded to the family baronetcy.

The months at Fairy Hall were interrupted by the war with Burma. 'For thirty years the Bull-Frog Kings of Ava had been inflating themselves for the conquest.' The eastern boundary of Bengal was a most satisfactory frontier for the British dominions, but the Burmese kings, having conquered the whole of the valley of the Irrawaddy, hoped to expand to the west into Bengal. The British, being satisfied, were studiously conciliatory, but the court of Ava met every embassy 'with studied insult or contempt. Conciliation only swelled their pride.' In September 1823 the Burmese seized British territory. The intruders were expelled but the King of Burma ordered the invasion of Bengal, and then arose in his Grand Council Chamber and 'with vows and vehement gestures declared that from that moment Bengal was severed from the British dominions'. On 17th March 1824 the Governor-General, Lord Amherst, declared war on Burma, and Henry Lawrence was ordered to join one of the four corps into which the British Indian forces were divided. This corps under General Morrison was to move along the coast of East Bengal and attack the Burmese province of Arracan. As soon as he heard that Henry Lawrence was going to the war, Mr Craufurd offered him a Scott's Bible. This great commentary in three volumes had changed many lives, being instrumental among other things in Cardinal Newman's first conversion. Craufurd said, 'Now Lawrence will you please take this with you and read it, if I give it to you?' Lawrence looked at it and said, 'It's a big book.' All three volumes are on my shelf and weigh two stone (28 lbs); they must have weighed more in the damp climate of Bengal. Craufurd replied, 'You can take a volume with you at any rate.' 'Very well,' said Lawrence, 'I will take one volume with me, and I promise that I'll read it.' And there are signs that they were read.

The first stage of the journey to the front was by sea and Mr Craufurd came to see him off, sleeping on deck beside the young officer. Little was said at parting but they exchanged looks that were full of meaning.

The record of the next two years consists mainly of fragmentary diaries and letters home. As an artillery officer Henry Lawrence's first task was to load his guns on board the ships assigned to them. When this was done 'the commanders declared that they could not possibly take the tumbrils and ammunition on board'. This was absurd but the naval authorities were determined that their ships should sail light. So Henry rushed back to Calcutta, got the Quartermaster-General interested, and brought him in his own buggy to the Commodore, who ordered everything to be shipped. They arrived safely a fortnight later on 18th June at Chittagong, in what is now Bangladesh. They waited six months 'preparing to move a force of 10,000 men' as Henry wrote long afterwards, 'most of our cattle having been procured from the banks of the Nerbudda in central India at least 1,000 miles from Chittagong'. When they did start, they were in a hurry. Their march was along the shore, or as near as they could get to it, in order to keep in touch with their supply ships. On the first day they had hard work getting their guns across the Chittagong river in the heat of the day and then were ordered to march on at once that night. Henry describes the scene:

When the bugle sounded to strike the tents, we were just going to our mess. So we hastily crammed something down our throats and returned to our tents to get our troops off the ground. The whole encampment was now one continued blaze; for the servants, as soon as the order was given to march, set fire to all the straw to warm themselves, as well as to serve for a light while packing up. Stray bullocks frightened by the flames and noise, rushing up and 'down the camp, soldiers and camp followers rushing here and there about their several duties and our own servants yelling to each other. [They started about 8 p.m.] and what with the darkness of the night, the badness of the road, the bullock drivers falling asleep, and many of them being *unable to see at night*, we were obliged to stop almost every hundred yards, either to get the guns out of a ditch or to bring up fresh bullocks. We did not reach the encamping until past three o'clock in the morning, having been seven hours in accomplishing little more than nine miles.

They had to make another march that morning. They left tents unpitched and every man was allowed to spend the time as he liked, sitting or lying on the road for about two hours, when they started again. The going was easier by daylight and they reached their next camping ground by ten o'clock. Henry says he was 'quite sick with fatigue' but fortunately their tents were already pitched. 'So I soon got under cover and into bed, went without my breakfast, and was quite well and hearty by dinner time.'

The march continued. Soon they were out of the cultivated country in jungles and hills. It was hard going but they seem to have enjoyed themselves. To overcome obstacles gave them a sense of achievement and Henry enjoyed the tropical scenery, some sport and a little sight seeing. One day they had to get themselves, their guns, their ammunition and their baggage etc. across a river with the help of 'two small matted rafts'. Henry had everything taken to pieces and got it across without wetting any of the ammunition.

My men worked like horses and I showed them the example. We managed to get everything over by half past two and to our no small satisfaction found our tents pitched a short way on the other side. My men had been up to their middles in water during the hottest part of the day and not a man was ill after it. Nor did I hear a grumble, though they were terrible growlers in cantonments, where they have nothing to do.

On 28th January 1825 he wrote to his parents:

The Brigadier [Grant] came to my tent at four o'clock; said he had called before and found me *asleep* (I was *very* tired). He told me he had heard there was a deep ravine on the next day's march and he wished to know exactly how far it was and if we could pass before daylight. I offered to go and reconnoitre it. Path horribly bad. Mugh★ guides told me there were a great many tigers. The descent to the ravine almost impassable. On returning I met the Brigadier, made my report, and told him we could soon make it tolerably passable. He then said I should march with a company of Mughs and one of Sepoys one hour before the other troops to give me time to get over it. He said he knew papa and that he was a fine old soldier and had seen a deal of hard service. It made me feel, as I often do, proud of my father. He said he would have asked me to dinner but that he had *nothing to eat*, but asked me to go and take a glass of wine with him. I went and sat about an hour with him. He sent me *four eggs – quite a treat*.

★The Mughs, who are kindred to the Burmese, were the inhabitants of this province.

On 20th February Henry wrote to his parents that a few days earlier he was suddenly sent across the river Tek Naaf, the previous boundary of Burma, for 'the embarkation of the remaining guns and ammunition. I could not make out the meaning of this order, as there were already three officers there, one of them a captain.' But as soon as he arrived they were sent back to headquarters and Henry was told to take over. It turned out that 'the General was much annoyed at the dilatory manner in which Captain R. of our corps sent the ammunition over the Tek Naaf. The Brigadier said "Ah! if Mr Lawrence was there he would soon get it over"'. And over it came, though *'with some trouble'*. In telling this to his parents, Henry added, 'Don't think that I wish to convince you that I have done anything out of the common way, but merely to show you that I have satisfied my superior officers. And pray, don't think so ill of our regiment as to imagine that my services are more efficient than any captain's, except R's.'

By the beginning of April 1825 the long march was over, and the army stood outside Arracan, the Burmese provincial capital. Henry describes the final battle with zest. First he and the others had to get their guns quietly in position during the night. 'I think I felt more anxious, I will not say afraid, while we were placing the guns in battery, than when the heaviest fire was on us. There was a certain *stillness* – a momentary expectation of something unpleasant – which prevented me feeling at ease.'

The morning began with an exchange of fire. 'My 12-pounder, which had been laid ready to open fire when our troops advanced, burst a shrapnel close to them. Then we ceased firing, and our troops advanced in beautiful style. Oh,

> '"Twere worth ten years of peaceful life
> One glance at their array".'

The Burmese were defending strong positions, but the British Indian troops

> drove the enemy before them from one hill to the other, and we turned our guns on them as they fled, . . . and by 8 a.m. April 1st 1825 the whole place was in our possession.
>
> I went and took a look at the hill opposite, which was very strong indeed, both by nature and art. It was so steep that it was with great difficulty I could reach the top. So what must it have been for our poor fellows who had a heavy direct and flanking fire to withstand, as well as the difficulty of the ascent. In the Pass were the bodies of about a dozen of our poor Sepoys, who had fallen. They were perhaps the most gallant souls in their regiment. I heard that on the

29th (the date of the previous unsuccessful attack), a Sepoy was the first man up the hill, and that just as he gained the top he was seen to roll all the way down, most likely never to rise again. From the mortar battery those who were killed on the 29th could be plainly seen, and our men perceived one Sepoy still moving.

Three British soldiers, a Sergeant and two gunners, volunteered to rescue him and did so at great risk to themselves. He was a fine looking fellow but seemed dreadfully wounded and some of the wounds had been inflicted by 'the Burmahs' as he lay helpless after they had stripped him, but 'he seemed in good spirits and called for water, which our men gave him with a little biscuit, which he readily took in spite of caste'. After this battle the Burmese resistance in the province of Arracan melted away. In November Henry Lawrence was promoted to the rank of First Lieutenant.

The army's next task was to find a passage through the mountains and join forces with the corps that was already in the Irrawaddy valley. But in May the rains set in, bringing a very virulent form of malaria, and 'in a month General Morrison no longer had an army'. Upwards of one third of the army, European and native, died. Arracan was called Death's Bazaar, and for weeks together Henry and his Colonel were the only officers of artillery out of eighteen or twenty, who sat down together at table. Then Henry went down, too, was sent on three months' sick leave to Calcutta, returned to Arracan and remained till he succumbed to a second and more serious attack after the declaration of peace on 24th February 1826.

On being sent back to Calcutta, Henry went straight to George Craufurd, who nursed him as if he was his son. 'With shaven head and gaunt look', Henry Lawrence had become 'the very ghost of the athletic lad who marched from Fairy Hall two years before.' He never got rid of the Arracan fever, a virulent form of malaria, and everything that he did afterwards was done in the teeth of crippling bouts of illness that shrivelled him up. The doctors ordered him home to England and, for the benefit of the long sea voyage, he was advised to proceed by the China route. On 2nd August 1826 he embarked on the *Macqueen*, one of 'the right royal merchant ships' of the East India Company that 'kept the Chinese waters against friend and foe' under the terms of the Company's monopoly. Waking in the morning, before they sailed, he found George Craufurd watching beside his bed. 'Talk of the affection of women,' he told Letitia, 'nothing could exceed the tenderness of that good man.'

He visited Penang and Singapore, Macao and finally Canton, where he bought some souvenirs among which are some of the very few personal possessions that passed to his descendants. Here he met his life-long friend, E. A. Reade, who indicates that already his mind was turning to surveying. He reached Liverpool in the spring of 1827 at the same moment that Letitia and their cousin, Angel Heath, arrived from Ireland. Letitia recognised him on his ship in the distance and said, 'That's Henry'. They met on shore and he insisted on 'dragging his sister and her friend all over Liverpool hunting for his chum Ackers who had left India sick three years ago'. They found him at last 'quite hearty in his father's house'. Then they went to Clifton and his unsentimental mother wrote in her diary: 'returned from Arracan after the Burmese war, my best beloved Henry Montgomery, not twenty-one years old but reduced by sickness and suffering to more than double that age'.

PART THREE

HONORIA

1827–37

CHAPTER 5

Honoria Lawrence

While Henry Lawrence was on his way home, stricken in health, his sister Letitia had also been very ill. To convalesce she went to stay several months with her cousins, the Heaths, at Fahan on the shores of Lough Swilly. Angel, the daughter of Admiral Heath by his first wife, was an old friend of Letitia's and Admiral Heath brought up his niece, Honoria Marshall, one of the many children of the Reverend George Marshall, the rector of Cardonagh, a few miles further up the shore of Lough Swilly. In 1827 Honoria was nineteen, small and active with fair hair and blue eyes. Angel was much older and unmarried, a sort of maiden aunt to Honoria. Letitia was twenty-five. The state of her health made it doubtful whether she could marry and have children, but she was happy in her unpossessive love for her family and her friends. So before Henry and Honoria met they had heard much about each other from Letitia. Ten years later, when she was on the way out to India to marry Henry, Honoria wrote to Letitia about this time: 'You were a crushed flower, just putting forth a little. I was anticipating an untried life, confiding in a strength I did not possess, yet laying up for myself a store, of which I then little knew the value, in your unchanging love, and the reflections of its beams in Henry's mind.' So Henry's heart was open to Honoria before he met her.

When the unexpected news of Henry's return reached Clifton, Colonel Lawrence sent for Letitia at once, fearing that if she was not at home, Henry would soon be off to Ireland to see her. So it was that Letitia coming home from Ireland reached Liverpool at exactly the moment when Henry arrived from India. Letitia invited Honoria to stay with the family at Clifton. She arrived in August, but it is not known what impression she and Henry made on each other at this first meeting. But we do know the impression she made about this time on another young man, Herman Merivale. Many years afterwards he wrote: 'Well do I remember the impression made on our circle by those fine features and the still more striking figure; the freshness, almost wildness of that natural grace; the frank unencumbered demeanor, and the step of an huntress Diana.'

Honoria Marshall was brought up by the Admiral and his second wife almost as an only child. Admiral Heath's children by his first marriage were much older and, though Honoria's brothers and sisters lived only a few miles away, she saw surprisingly little of them. She had very little formal education, running wild on the shores of Lough Swilly and on the mountains. Those northernmost shores of Ireland are mild and luxuriant, with fuchsias growing like brambles. The ever changing shadows of Lough Swilly remained in her mind's eye as a standard to compare with the exotic beauties of India. When she was a child, nature was her first teacher and she acquired a special love for wild flowers and all that grows, whether in Europe or in Asia. For the rest she taught herself by reading in Admiral Heath's library, and by listening to grown-up conversation. She knew English literature fairly well and had a reading knowledge of French, Italian and New Testament Greek; and she knew enough of science to follow with interest the proceedings of the British Association for the Advancement of Science at Bristol in 1836. She was sometimes excessively serious, but that too was part of the spontaneity and directness, which impressed her more conventional London acquaintances. Untamed by school or schoolroom she was intolerant; but not unkind.

Her family was religious, sensible devout Anglicans of the Irish variety. They were Evangelicals but of the kind that would later have been called liberal Evangelical. She, herself, had leanings which, if she had stayed in the British Isles, might have brought her near to Samuel Taylor Coleridge and the Broad Church of F. D. Maurice. Her cousins, the Lawrences, shared with her a devout but not dogmatic Anglican Christianity.

Henry was the first of the brothers to come back to gladden his parents' eyes. He was sick, and his mother's love was called out; he had shown himself a true soldier and his father was proud of him. On the second or third evening of his return he asked Letitia if she thought their parents would object to having family prayers. 'Not if you propose it.' So he fetched the Scott's Bible and said, 'Mother, suppose we read a chapter before we part for the night?' She agreed readily and he then said, 'Shall I ring and ask the servants if they would like to come?' There was a slight demonstration of surprise but no opposition. So Henry rang and said to his old friend, Ellen Moss, 'Ellen, we are going to read a chapter, and any of you who like can join us.' Ellen and one other came at once. And thenceforth there were family prayers, both morning and evening.

Henry's health took a long time to recover. Suddenly, while he was walking, reading or chatting happily, the fever would come upon him and he would have to be rolled up in blankets like a sick child. Gradually the attacks grew less violent and in the meantime he made himself the schoolmaster of his younger sisters, pronouncing their sums too bad to be endured and watching over their moral progress with a degree of care that would hardly be tolerated now. His sisters found it provoking, but they saw that he did it out of love and they put up with it.

The energy of his nature had greatly developed during his five years in the army and, as his strength returned, he soon passed into that restless activity which became his settled habit. He took drawing lessons, for in those days officers were expected to be able to draw and some of them were good artists. Henry was not good at drawing but he was impressed by Rippingale, his drawing master, struggling in poverty but giving to those who had even less than he.

In the spring of 1828 he was in London, where all the cousins met at the house of Admiral Heath's son, Josiah, in Bedford Square and at his villa in Twickenham. Honoria kept a day to day record of events in the letters she sent home to her Aunt Heath in Ireland. She copied these out for Henry nine years later when she was on her way out to India to marry him. At first Henry Lawrence came and went without apparently causing her heart to flutter. On 26th April 'Henry Lawrence dined here. I was too tired to do anything but lie on the sofa and read.' But three days later they went on 'our memorable walk in the city.' The weather had turned baking hot and at two o'clock 'Letitia and Henry came from Chelsea and I was glad to avail myself of Henry's services to escort me to a shoe mart.' And 'having made my purchases in Holborn, I proposed to go a little further to look at Newgate, and when there I recollected that I had never yet seen Father Thames. And as Henry said it was "not far", I thought I would go to one of the bridges. I have discovered that in London "not far" implies any space from three yards to three miles.' They arrived at St Paul's and were disappointed by the architecture, but more interested in each other. So they 'walked round it and gazed up at it, till we nearly assembled a crowd around us'. By now it was five o'clock so they went 'briskly on through such alleys and lanes and courts as I can hardly imagine human beings to exist in for an hour, till we got between Waterloo and Southwark bridges'. Here the pleasant scene gained added beauty from their feelings, but it was time to go home and neither of them knew the way. So they 'made rather a circuitous route till we came once more to Holborn, where I was so excessively tired that we got a coach to go home in, having excited no small surprise by our long absence'. But they were not scolded, Honoria ends her letter, 'My head is whirl, whirl, whirl.'

The next day they went together to the British Museum where Honoria found mineral specimens more beautiful than anything she could have conceived but she was puzzled by the Elgin Marbles and other antiquities, and felt ashamed going in among naked statues.

After that Henry's name 'somehow, comes in more frequently in my letters' and one day they all went to the zoo which had just been opened to non-members. Henry left London soon afterwards and there is no further mention of him in Honoria's letters. Yet those few days had changed both their lives for ever. Henry told Letitia that he was in love with Honoria; but with shattered health and no prospects, could he propose marriage? He consulted Angel Heath in the absence of Honoria's father and of Admiral Heath. And Angel firmly said 'no'. Looking back on this in after years Honoria judged Angel Heath 'a pearl of price' but thought her 'peculiarly unfitted to sympathise with her own sex'. Angel's 'no' sealed Henry's lips. So neither of them said a word to the other; but Henry confided in Letitia, who tactfully kept them in touch with each other's news, hoping against hope for them year after year but never going a syllable beyond what she felt justified in passing on.

Henry was at home for two and a half years, slowly recovering his strength. The time passed well in the austere but happy home of his parents, a serious time as was usual with him, but lightened by a little teasing from his sisters. He visited Paris and went for a walking tour in Wales with his brother John. And in the autumn of 1828 he joined the Trigonometrical Survey in the North of Ireland; the professional experience he acquired in the next few months proved to be the foundation of his career in India.

By now Henry's sick leave was nearly over, and it was time to look ahead. His parents were aged and his father was ill. His father's pension would die with him and his widow would be almost penniless. His father's life was uninsurable. Henry must get back to India where he and his brothers would establish a 'Lawrence Fund', saving every penny they could for their mother's old age. John would help; he had finished his course at Haileybury and was due to sail for Calcutta with Henry and their younger sister, another Honoria. When the day came for them to leave London, Henry took them all, including Honoria Marshall, to a shilling theatre in Regent Street. The show was *Tam O'Shanter*. Henry said goodbye without showing any emotion. 'Tam must ride' and that was all.

In India Henry nourished his secret love in letters to Letitia. In Ireland Honoria tried to forget Henry, but did not succeed.

CHAPTER 6

Lawrence's Confounded Zeal

It was a bitter wrench for Henry Lawrence to leave his family after those two years at home. He never saw most of them again except for a few months about twenty years later. He loved them all with undistinguishing regard, but it was Letitia whose letters he opened first, it was her that he missed the most and her opinion that he valued the highest. He wrote to her from the ship that bore him away: 'It seems to me as if I wanted little more on earth than your approved affection, and though to live and die under the same roof would be to me more than fame and wealth, I can rest me satisfied with what I have obtained; and when all earthly things passes away, may we not be separated in that dwelling from whence "there is no going out".'

'In the midst of my uttermost bitterness I regret not having come home. What have I not gained in that re-union with my family? More, far more than can be set against it in fevers, privations, fatigues or aught that may have obtained passport home. So strongly do I feel this that my advice shall ever be given to young invalids to pursue the same course, renew the affections of their childhood, and become acquainted in manhood with what in their youth they could not appreciate – the pleasures of a *home* and the beauties of their native country.'

A fellow passenger had 'a little cabinet of mineralogy. It is what I long wanted.' So on the long voyage out John and Henry studied mineralogy and Indian languages. On 9th February 1830 after a voyage of five months and a week, they reached Calcutta where John had to stay. Eighteen years old, John was continually ill in Calcutta and, uncharacteristically, so depressed by the climate and uncongenial life that, as he used to say, an offer of £100 a year in Britain would have taken him straight home. Meanwhile Henry was posted to a company of foot artillery at Kurnal beyond Delhi on what was then the North-West Frontier. At Kurnal he found his brother George who had recently married Charlotte Browne, the sister of the future General Sir Samuel Browne V.C., who invented the Sam Browne belt so that he could still keep his sword handy after he had lost an arm. Here for eighteen happy months Henry lived under George and Charlotte's roof, studying languages. As he had encouraged John to join him in his studies on board ship, so he encouraged George to join him at Kurnal. Henry was the more industrious but George, having served with native troops, could talk more Hindustani. 'George, however, soon got tired of this dry work and left his fatherly younger brother to plod on alone much vexed with all things: George for being idle, the language for being quite different from English and the *moonshee* for being stupid.'[1] For recreation there was a famous rackets court at Kurnal and after a battle royal with the *moonshee* and his language Henry worked off his exasperation in a furious game with George or some other friend.

George was adjutant of the Second Cavalry Regiment and in order to get into the better paid horse artillery, Henry went through the regimental riding school, and was gazetted to the Horse Artillery on 27th September 1831. This was the first ambition of every artillery-man. He was then sent to Meerut for further training in the manage-ment of horses and wrote to Letitia: 'Here I am a gay trooper bumping away in the riding school' and he added, 'I like the quiet humdrum of Kurnal better than the rattle and gaiety of Meerut.' He became an efficient rider, though not an elegant one. Afterwards a great part of his life was spent out of doors, often on horseback. 'His desire to see and explore everything, and his natural impetuosity of temperament' led him to ride distances which few other men could have endured. His horses were described by a comrade as 'thin, long tailed Sikh looking animals'. And henceforth they became familiar companions, being treated with much consideration. Having learned to ride he was posted to a troop of Horse Artillery at Cawnpore in February 1832.

Throughout his life Henry Lawrence dressed anyhow with 'his ill made clothes hanging loosely on his spare body'. He took no interest in 'rattle and gaiety' anywhere, and the music of the bands meant less than nothing to him. Both Henry and John Lawrence were apparently 'tone deaf'. There is a story that many years after, when they were together at Lahore, they were both at a reception. After a time John said to Henry, 'It is time for us to go. The band is playing God Save the Queen.' 'How do you know that?' 'The *syces* are getting the horses ready.' Writing his reminiscences, many years later, Colonel William Anderson, who was at Cawnpore at the same time, describes Henry as he was then: 'I almost see him in my mind's eye slowly walking home after parade, followed by a brown bay of this (Sikh-like) description, or again towards evening taking a severe gallop over the country, far from the haunts of beauty and fashion. He walked up and down the stables, musing I now suppose, and little noticing the various horses which he was supposed to watch over.'

His retired life was partly due to the urgent necessity that he and his brothers should save every penny they could for the 'Lawrence Fund'.

This was kept secret from their mother, Letitia being their confidante in England. All the brothers were generous but Henry was the moving spirit, though at first he was the poorest of the four. Eventually they succeeded in securing a comfortable old age for their mother. But in the meantime every penny saved by staying at home, when other men were amusing themselves, went to the fund; and every hour saved went in study to equip him for his career. But Henry was not morose, and Colonel Anderson adds: 'Though not sociable with us, we all entertained a high opinion of his honour and judgment. In case of a row or dispute, I am inclined to think all of us young officers would have deferred to his decision.'

John Lawrence had been appointed to Delhi, which was in those days the place above all others where great Indian careers began. He was still, of course, very junior but as a member of the Civil Service he started several steps ahead of his elder soldier brothers. By now they all had a foot on the first rung of the ladder, but in order to go up it they had to know Indian languages. Neither Henry nor John Lawrence had a turn for languages, but they were ambitious and both worked hard. After studying eight or ten hours a day in Urdu, Persian and Hindi, Henry took his examination on 17th July 1832 successfully, and the examiners begged 'to recommend him particularly to the notice of his Excellency, the Commander in Chief', which was most unusual. One of the examiners used to introduce joke questions; the last question he put to Henry in the colloquial test was 'translate "Go it ye cripples, Newgate's on fire".' To the general astonishment Henry answered at once, 'Chal chalai langra, Naya phatak jalta,' a literal but graphic translation. For years afterwards those who had known Henry Lawrence at this time, used to address these words to 'lazy boys, languid officers and unwilling steeds.' Which mystified all who were not in the secret.*

Henry Lawrence judged himself by a high standard and years afterwards complained that, though he understood the general sense of what was said to him, he had no precise grasp of native languages. But he must have improved over the years with practice and there is no indication that any linguistic deficiency impeded him in communication with Indians. His brother John also found Oriental languages difficult but learnt to use colloquial Persian very effectively. Persian at this time was India's language of culture and had penetrated deeply into Urdu, as Norman French penetrated Middle English in the course of the Middle Ages.

Promotion in the Indian Army was by strict seniority carried to such an absurd length that in Henry's words 'its subalterns are worn out veterans and its seniors dotards'. A heavy price was soon to be

*Recollection of E. A. Reade, who was one of the examiners.

paid for giving high command to generals who were already in their dotage. At this stage of his career Henry feared lest he should become one of those who are 'kept hanging on until our armour is too heavy for us'. But if regimental promotion was slow, there were great opportunities for a man who was seconded to the then political service, the canals or the survey, to mention only a few of the choice prospects.

Having qualified in native languages, Henry was now eligible for a wide variety of jobs, many of them interesting and some well paid, but he had no interest in high quarters, and his future was uncertain. An apocryphal but graphic story used to circulate that about this time Alexander, George and Henry Lawrence being together at Simla and all seeking openings for themselves, sought an interview with the Governor-General. 'But what shall we say, if he asks us what we can do?' asked Henry. 'Well,' said one of them, 'we can all stand on our heads.' And sure enough the Governor-General's opening words were, 'Well, gentlemen, what can you do?' They looked at each other and without a word each went in a different corner of the room and stood on his head.

Henry's enquiring mind and restless energy led him down many avenues. At Kurnal he became interested in canal building. The irrigation canals built by previous rulers had fallen into disrepair so that the crops depended almost entirely on the fickle monsoon. Three thousand years of spoliation had already destroyed much of India's original forests, leaving the bare land at the mercy of a climate that had grown arid in the absence of the cover of trees which had once filtered the sun and retained moisture. In the last one hundred and fifty years irrigation has been greatly restored and extended, but at this time the work was only just beginning and Kurnal was at its centre. Henry snatched time from his studies to spend a holiday month in 1831 on the great Doab canal with Colonel Cautley, the father of modern irrigation in India. Henry spent his holiday working with Cautley and liked the work. Writing to Letitia, on 1st March 1831 he describes it: 'This is a mingled operation of in-and-out-of-door, theoretical and practical, and altogether very much in the way of my pursuits.' Moreover the endless work of controlling the sluices, so that there was neither flood nor drought and everyone got his fair share after paying his appointed dues, brought canal officers into intimate contact with the people of the land. There would be endless complaints 'but all this I should consider a pleasing variety for, though the temper is tried, much is learnt, and with little trouble to oneself much kindness can be done'. So 'I have applied to be appointed assistant, in the event of Cautley being principal; but have little hopes, as I have not a shadow of interest and am not known.' He nearly got the job but was disappointed at the last minute. A year later he wrote to Letitia: 'I am glad to find that you expected me to fail in my canal application last year. The thing has long ceased to trouble me; for like other susceptible minds, mine is as quickly quenched as excited.' But twenty years later in the Punjab he turned to good account what he had learned about canals in his youth.

The man who did get the job with the canals for which Henry had applied was a young sapper officer, Robert Napier, the future Field Marshal, Lord Napier of Magdala. The two became life-long friends. It was Napier who laid out the canals and roads of the Punjab under the administration of the Lawrences. Henry called Napier his best friend and on his death Napier had buried with him an unsolicited letter of recommendation from Henry, extolling Napier's achievements in the Punjab. But their first meeting was hardly propitious. Napier's biographer relates that soon after his arrival at Cautley's headquarters 'a very odd looking visitor made his appearance there. His attire was astonishing even for the jungle – I think I never saw so disreputable looking a figure anywhere.' And his greeting to Napier was, 'So you are the fellow who did me out of the canals.'

Even before his transfer to the Horse Artillery, Henry Lawrence had begun to make himself known to the Government of India. In December 1830, when he was twenty-four, he wrote begging leave 'most respectfully' to draw the Governor-General's attention to some 'facts in reference to the late order for the abolition of horse draft for foot artillery, and the substitution of bullock draft in its stead'. The average rate of marching with bullocks was one and three quarter miles per hour or in difficult country one mile an hour at the utmost, 'as I myself witnessed during the war at Arracan . . . Whereas with horses an average of from two to four or even five miles an hour may be depended on, with the advantage of bringing the artillerymen fresh into action, as they are mounted on the guns during a quick movement' with horses, instead of being harassed and jaded by pulling at the dragropes, as they would have to do with bullocks. Moreover 'the difference of expense is but trifling'. He prefaced this letter by saying he understood that 'the Right Honorable, the Governor-General does not object to receive suggestions from individuals of however low a rank.' It is to the credit of both parties that the Government of India generally received with favour the ideas of this very junior officer.

Henry was zealous to serve where Providence had placed him but his thoughts were with absent loved ones. Writing to Letitia on 2nd May 1832, he enquires tenderly after all the family and tells her not to 'be zealous over much, and your precious strength will last the longer'. Letitia although very delicate was so strong minded that one forgot it. He adds, 'I often think that if two or three of you were gone,

I should scarcely wish to return home, though now it is my daily thought.' And then, in the same breath, 'Tell me what has become of Honoria Marshall?'

Honoria at this time was at the depth of her fortunes. Obliged to leave Fahan on the death of Mrs Heath, she decided to make her own way in the world, much to the annoyance of her family, who thought she should marry or, failing that, live at home doing little or nothing like other young ladies. She intended to become a teacher or a governess. But soon after leaving Fahan she fell into a long, severe and very depressing illness. It is not known where she was or who looked after her during this time.

By 1832 Henry Lawrence had reason to hope for promotion but hope was deferred, while his troop of Horse Artillery was ordered from Cawnpore to Dum Dum near Calcutta. They travelled by river down the Ganges and were struck by a severe storm, in which their fleet of boats was totally wrecked. No lives were lost, and much government property was saved by great exertions. But the officers and men lost everything they had with them. Lieutenants Grant and Lawrence and Assistant-Surgeon Serrell were, however, praised for their 'soldier-like disregard for their own personal property when so many lives were at stake'. Their conduct had been brought to the notice of the Government; and the Governor-General – Lord William Bentinck, 'the clipping Dutchman' as he was called for his economies – on hearing of their loss directed that 'a liberal compensation may be made'. Being fresh from his studies and so near to Calcutta, Henry Lawrence was able to appear before the examiners in the College of Fort William and on 6th December 1832 received the coveted letter P.C. (Passed College) as a final ratification of his knowledge of native languages.

In the meantime his brother George had been busy on his behalf with the Governor-General. 'What have you come for?' asked the Governor-General. 'Nothing for myself.' 'What then? I can tell you, you're the first man I have met in India who wanted nothing.' George then asked him point-blank that his brother might be given work on the Revenue Survey. The interview ended with Lord William saying to George, 'Well, go and tell Benson; and although I make no promises, I will see what can be done.' On 22nd February 1833 Henry Lawrence was appointed as an assistant Revenue Surveyor in the North-Western Provinces. He now had his foot on the second rung of the ladder, the Lawrence Fund had provided for his mother, and he could afford to marry. Six months later he wrote to Letitia about Honoria: 'I really think I shall be mad enough to tell her my story, and try to make her believe that I have loved her for five years and said nothing of my love.' But it was four more years before these two faithful hearts were united.

In the meantime Henry Lawrence spent eight months of the year in the fields and jungles getting to know the village people of India in their troubles and joys, settling their disputes about land, dealing with the one thing – the land tax – which affected their well being almost as much as the monsoon. Like others of his kind, he had to see through endless plausible stories, penetrating the motives of private interest, caste, kinship and feud, in order to find the core of unvarnished truth, which generally comes out when Indian villagers testify to what they know in the presence of each other and before a shrewd enquirer.

The five years, 1833-38, which Henry Lawrence passed in the Revenue Survey were years of great mental activity but still more of developing character. He had studied hard but now he passed from books to men and things. In the survey he was his own master. Given a certain work to do, the details of doing were in his discretion. He had to travel over wide tracts of densely populated country, whose inhabitants depended on his sound judgment for much of their prospects. As he got to know the people, the prejudices of a young English officer were corrected. The vastness and variety of the land came home to him. Things he had read about all fell into place. Day by day he explored the ways of Indian society and British rule. Year by year he became more thoughtful about British mistakes, more earnest to correct them and more clear about the direction that reforms must take. His ideas were his own but they were not flashes of genius, so much as painstaking conclusions dug out of the facts and then made original by forceful thought and practical application.

The Revenue Survey may sound like dull work. But to the Revenue Surveyor, in the words of Herbert Edwardes, 'If he has got any heart at all, come the greybeards of the village next to his camp, to tell their parish griefs, nine tenths which come under one head, – the corruption of their own countrymen in office, – and the other tenth the blindness of the white *sahib*.'[2] In India almost all the revenue came from land, and in theory the soil belonged to the Crown, those who lived from the soil being tenants rather than freehold owners as in Europe. In practice the Crown had simply the right to receive dues from the tillers of the soil or from intermediaries to whom rights in the soil had been granted. And so long as the dues were paid, the state did not interfere with those in possession. These dues were commonly called land tax and the prosperity of the country depended on the fairness of the assessment and the honesty of their collection. In the sixteenth century Akbar, the effective founder of the Mogul dynasty, had imposed fair taxation on the land throughout North India and for a time the taxes had been honestly collected. But this system fell into decay under Akbar's successors. More recently the collapse of the

Mogul Empire led to corruption at the best, and sometimes turned tax collection into sheer plunder.

As in Europe under the feudal system, there were often intermediate holders of rights between the Crown and the tillers of the soil, each with a right to exact his share of the dues, but in the prevailing anarchy those who had the power often exacted what they could get, without regard to any factor other than their own power or weakness. If peasants starved in consequence or were driven to robbery, that was their own affair.

It took the British some time to come to terms with a system that was unfamiliar to them and was often operating in conditions of such confusion that it was impossible to make sense of it. However they had to levy a land tax, if there was to be any government at all. Their methods were an improvement on those of their predecessors in that, once an assessment had been made, they exacted just that and no more – or no less. 'Native rulers might assess at a shilling and take either two shillings or only sixpence, according as their power or as their whim wavered.'[3] But in their first years the British often fixed the assessment impossibly high. Moreover, if a cultivator or other person responsible for paying the land tax persistently failed to do so, the British authorities sold his land to pay the taxes, a thing not sanctioned by custom, and which horrified all Indians.

The different measures taken by the British to bring order out of chaos and equity out of oppression are complicated and controversial but for the present purpose most of the controversy can be left aside. In the 1830s it was recognised that reform was urgently needed, and a remedy was devised by Robert Merttens Bird, a man who died unhonoured and unsung, but greatly admired by those who understood his achievement. Every year thousands of cultivators were sinking beneath the weight of the land tax and were in the words of James Abbott 'turned adrift from the lands which their fathers had cultivated time out of mind, to become vagabonds and beggars and swell the ranks of those robber bands, which were one of the plagues of India.'[4] Bird's remedy was to survey the whole land, reduce the assessments and fix them for twenty years in advance, so that every family would know where they stood; the value of money was stable in those days. Bird put forth all his might to convince the Government of India. Eventually he succeeded, and the Revenue Survey was put in hand.

It was no light task to survey such a vast area, and to ascertain with even approximate justice who was entitled to what land, after such a long period of violence and confusion. This made the survey expensive and the Government of India was short of money.

Herbert Edwardes describes Henry Lawrence as he was at this period. 'Time had subdued nothing in him. There he was in the vigour of early manhood, self-taught, self-disciplined, self-devoted, self-reliant, fiery of zeal to do the public work, hot of temper with reprobates and idlers, as hot to reward the diligent, impatient of contradiction, ignorant of the impossible, scorning compromise, resolute to do the thing, or die; in short, rough hewn, angular, and strong. Hundreds of manikins, high and low, had yet to pick and peck at him through life with their little chisels, and fret him smooth.'

He was fortunate in his chiefs. Bird was the head of his department. And James Thomason, though not yet the Lieutenant-Governor of the North-Western Provinces, where Henry was working, was very influential. James Thomason's father was Thomas Thomason, a famous chaplain in the East India Company's service, one of those devoted people who brought honour to the Evangelical name in the early part of the nineteenth century. James Thomason was a chip off the same block. Not being tried in war or war-like emergencies, like some of the great Indian proconsuls, he was a peaceful constructor, a pioneer of irrigation, education and other worthwhile achievements. James Thomason was deeply religious but never obtruded his beliefs where they might be unwelcome. He was the *Burra Sahib* but he was humble, and the friendship between this high official and the young Henry Lawrence was like a friendship of equals. It shows the older man in a consistently good light, thoughtful and considerate, with a light touch that was well calculated to encourage a junior, while Henry was sometimes inconsiderate to his older and very powerful friend.

James Thomason's character was noble and he had great gifts but his career remains a subject of controversy. He and Bird were levellers of a traditional hierarchical Indian society. 'The idea is too Londonish' was the shrewd comment on the survey of Colonel Gardner, the founder of Gardner's Horse, who had been in India since the turn of the century. Yet the Government of independent India has been more Thomasonian than Thomason himself. In his own day Thomason did much good and he laid the foundation for more good in the future but he may have pushed too fast and contributed thereby to the malaise that came to the surface in the Indian Mutiny. John Becher, one of Henry Lawrence's young men, complained to Henry in 1850 of 'this grinding, exacting, dead level Thomasonianism', introduced by Dalhousie who was Governor-General from 1848-56.[5]

Bird, his other chief, liked to have younger men working for him on the Survey. The work was hard and they had to show initiative. But having chosen them and given them a lead, he left them to work out their own salvation, much as Henry Lawrence was to do later in the Punjab. Henry responded to the challenge of the survey by working furiously and to good effect. This delighted the authorities but not all of Henry's colleagues were pleased. 'Colonel M.' told a friend that 'Mr

Bird had hauled them all over the coals for not doing more work. Lieutenant Lawrence had done twice the amount, and they must do more in the future or leave the department. And all owing to Lawrence's confounded zeal.'[6]

His hard work was indeed carried to excess and he gave no thought to meals. Sometimes he would return to dinner having invited guests but had forgotten to order anything for them to eat. Fortunately his neighbour at Gorakhpur, where he was surveying, was E. A. Reade, a lifelong friend. In his memoirs Reade writes: 'We used to rectify the omission by diverting the procession from my kitchen to his house instead of mine. My inestimable major domo had wonderful resource and an especial regard for Lawrence, who was in his estimation an Amir Kabir' (a great chief). His energy was to all appearance quite unorganised. As a surveyor he covered the floor of his tent with papers which seemed to be in complete confusion, but he had arranged them according to the pattern on the carpet in some way that he alone understood. Apart from his bouts of disabling illness his energy was unceasing and his friends feared that he would burn himself out before his prime. Major Robert Macgregor, a school friend, put it in a letter written on 25th January 1835: 'You must not measure *too* many villages nor *too* long remain abroad in the day; or else any promotion you get will not assist you long.'

He expected his native subordinates to work almost as hard, but he paid them above the going rate, claiming that nevertheless his work was cheaper. 'And,' he added, 'I do believe that the plunder they committed in the country was less.'[7] But they tried his temper and at this time of his life Henry was very hasty in his speech. Soon after his marriage, his wife diffidently reproved him. 'Darling, I do think you are not aware of the way in which you habitually speak to those around you . . . You scarcely ever address a man without an abusive epithet.'

He had his own way of imposing discipline. The following story is from *The Friend of India* for 25th November 1858. 'A native surveyor who refused to go back some ten miles to revise a serious error that had been discovered in his work was laid upon a bed by order of Henry Lawrence and carried by bearers to the spot, where he was turned out to rectify his error. The man was obstinate, refused to re-observe his angles, and returned to camp. Henry Lawrence ordered him up into a Mango tree, where he kept the recusant guarded by two *burkundazes* with drawn swords, until hunger changed the mind and temper of the surveyor.' This man ultimately proved an excellent worker.[8]

In 1837 Henry Lawrence surveyed 1400 square miles. To Mary Cameron, a friend of his wife, he wrote: 'I have now tents in three different places eight or ten miles apart and have two other encampments (making five in all) to look after; with such endless vexations and contretemps to encounter as he only can conceive who has engaged to furnish a geographical and revenue map of one sixth of Scotland in one year, showing not only the features of the country, but furnishing all the statistical details requisite for a land assessment. All this to be done, too, by men who, high and low, take bribes; so much so that it is perfectly useless discharging a man for it, as his successor will only perhaps be worse.'

CHAPTER 7

The Course of True Love

After his appointment to the Revenue Survey Henry suffered three years of agony. When Letitia received his letter of 1833, telling her of his love for Honoria and the improved prospects which made it possible for him to marry, Honoria had recovered from her illness, but losing all hope of Henry's affection, she had become engaged to a Mr Briggs, a clergyman. Letitia's answer told him that Honoria was lost and their father was slowly dying. After Honoria's engagement her correspondence with Letitia became less frequent. Moreover, an exchange of letters with India took at least six months. It was 1834 before Henry answered Letitia's letter, saying: 'Had I tried as one in his senses would have done, to have gained her heart, matters might have been managed. Such however was not to be; and if anyone is to blame, I am the culprit as I am the sufferer. The chances are very many against my ever being married. This I say, not as a boy of 17, but as one, though unattractive in himself, not easily captivated. Tell me always where and how she is, and keep up your correspondence with her.'

But almost as soon as she was engaged to the Reverend Mr Briggs, Honoria realised she could not go through with it. So she broke off her engagement, a bold step in those days. Despairing of married happiness, she then told herself stoically 'to leave love and take to learning', becoming for two years a school teacher at Prior Park school near Ashby de la Zouch. During this time her feelings were numbed. She ceased to take her customary delight in nature, but she enjoyed teaching. Honoria and Letitia had not altogether lost touch. And when Letitia learnt that Honoria's engagement was off, she decided that she was at last free to tell her of Henry's love.

Honoria's feelings after eight years were of deep gratitude for Henry's constancy, and acute regret for the pain she had caused him by an engagement to another man. First she felt pain 'as if of life tingling through a frozen limb', but she had enough confidence to write to Letitia saying that she would go to India and marry Henry, if he wanted her to. He wrote at once (in June 1836) telling her to come by the first boat sailing after February, but the letter did not arrive until 2nd November 1836. In the meantime she was with Letitia and the Lawrences at Lynton, where Angel Heath and Letitia had a cottage, and at Clifton where Henry's parents lived. During this time she became a member of that close knit family, new life flowed into her heart, and her love of nature returned at Lynton, a place which she came to love almost as much as Fahan. Honoria now knew her destiny but before she could sail for India there was much to do, saying goodbye to friends and relatives in England and Ireland and preparing for changes of clothes for a long sea voyage during which there would be no water for washing. Then there were family conclaves and obstructions, and no suitable boat for sailing. At last she said to herself, 'I'll go to town and see if *I* can't find a ship within a week. So to London I went and pitched on the *Reliance*' which sailed from North Fleet on 3rd April 1837.

In the meantime Henry and Honoria had been corresponding busily and she was now as deeply in love with him as he with her. On board ship her letters took the form of a journal addressed to Henry. 'How should I occupy myself but in pouring out my heart – first to God . . . and then to your beloved self?' 'I could not believe any man could so enter into a woman's feelings as you do . . . but your letters convince me that you are strung so that the cords of your mind will respond to that which wakens mine.' Honoria was, as James Abbott said, in an Oriental phrase, 'the female power' of Henry.

She was impatient of life in the confined space of a ship. 'I believe I am often, though unintentionally, brusque, and Letitia used to talk of my "knock me down manner".' But she thrilled to new sights and sounds. Everything was new to her. She had never seen a play till the ship's company put on some theatricals. As the weather got hotter, she sat in her cabin wearing nothing 'save a chemise, dressing gown and a pair of slippers. How am I ever to go clothed like a civilised being, in India is more than I can divine.' Years afterwards in the hot weather at Lahore she would go about indoors wearing only a petticoat and bodice, not the usual clothing of an early Victorian lady even in a tropical climate.

During this voyage she went through the 'records of past thoughts and feelings', tearing up 'heaps of old manuscripts, fragments of writing, scripture references, abstracts of mythology, grammar etc., etc.' which she had compiled over the years. 'They seemed to me belonging more to some other person than to myself, and gave me the impression of a young, ardent misdirected mind, striving after something better than it had attained, yet without stability of purpose . . . All, all begun, but scarcely anything ended. It reminded me of the feelings with which I have walked on the sea shore and looked at the broken shells, all of which wanted value from being imperfect.' But she was happy, very happy, as she looked forward to her marriage, adding characteristically: 'Do you know, my Henry, that the thought of death is most intimately associated in my mind with marriage. Is not our very vow till death us do part?' And 'But for a hope of full immortality, how could we endure the thought?'

Honoria and Henry had not seen each other for nine years, but 'it seems as if the last nine years were wiped away, and my heart as fresh and young as when we parted'. She made a record voyage of eighty days, and as the ship approached Calcutta she wrote: 'Oh Harry, we shall be up tonight. Will you be on board, dearest, this very night?' There was no Henry. The ship had outstripped the news of its expected arrival, and it was six more weeks before he came. They were married on 21st August 1837 and a fortnight later they embarked on the pinnace that was to take them up the Ganges to Revelganj whence they went overland to Gorakhpur where Henry was stationed. For them the reality of marriage was in no way short of their expectations. Honoria called their journey 'one long sunshine holiday of happiness', and a year later she wrote of 'a sense of bliss no words can tell, in loving one who loves so well'.

On leaving the pinnace they travelled on for four or five days by road 'if road it might be called, which road was none', sometimes together in a buggy and sometimes with Honoria 'in a *palkee* contrived from my sea cot in a most Robinson Crusoe like fashion'. Henry carried Honoria through water and got wet through. He took off his own clothes, girded Honoria's shawl round his loins, put on her cloak and proceeded like that to the great astonishment of the natives.

Gorakhpur, where Henry was in charge of the Revenue Survey, lay in fertile country in sight of the snowy range of the Himalayas with glorious mango groves all around and picturesque flowering creepers on every lowly dwelling. The monsoon was over and the newly wedded pair spent the next few months in tents travelling from place to place with their staff of assistants and camp followers amounting to almost a thousand souls, whom Henry ruled like a patriarch. Sometimes they went on expeditions by themselves into the deepest jungle, in Henry's words 'perhaps the first human beings, certainly of Europeans who have ever trod these wilds'. Saunders Abbott describes a chance meeting. 'We met in a tract of dense jungle . . . Tigers and wild elephants gave unmistakable signs of their presence. And, to my utter surprise, I found Mrs Lawrence with him. She was seated on the bank of a *nullah*, her feet overhanging the den of some wild animal, a portfolio on her lap, writing overland letters; her husband, at no great distance, laying his theodolite.' For Honoria camp life was an extension of her honeymoon, made more enjoyable by the chance to take part in her husband's work. To her life's end whatever he did was her affair as well as his. If she could help in it she helped. If not she sat by him in happy silence, supporting him with sympathy. In either case her enthusiasm never flagged.

Honoria describes the scene to a friend in Australia.

You would be much amused at the people who in the course of the day visit our tent. The 'potent, grave and reverend seignors' of the village came with all due etiquette, turbaned and belted, leaving their shoes outside, *salaaming* to each of us, and according to their rank standing or sitting during the interview. I have smiled at the contrast when one of these precise and solemn gentlemen conversed with Henry in measured tone, and with the proper number of 'Sahibs' and bows, while Henry sat without coat, waistcoat or jacket, and his legs over the arm of the chair or his feet on the table, and rattled away. Then, there are continual references from the villagers and the camp followers, who have frequent disagreements. There are the line-cutters and field measurers, coming in with their reports. The *moonshee* with his reed pen behind his ear, ready to read and write the Persian notes that are perpetually passing. And there is, never-to-be-forgotten, the little old *baboo*, with his broken English, large spectacles, and his shrivelled skin, looking very much like a bit of burned rag that one could blow away. *Baboo* is applied to those writers who understand English, and are to be found in every office. They are almost all Bengalese. This little man is a complete copying machine and a tolerable mathematician. He cannot endure that his book should be found fault with. 'Sir, you are my father and my mother. One, two thing I do, no mistake can make, multiply, sine, co-sine. Sir, you are my sucking father, Sir, I no mistake make.'

Henry's day is generally occupied with these people, but his work does not take him much away from home. Besides all these, our camp includes a carpenter, a smith, a bookbinder, a number of grain merchants to supply the camp, the wives and children of our servants and the other people, cattle of all kinds from elephants down to kids. In short a complete patriarchal establishment.

Before the arrival of Honoria in 1837 the Survey had run into further difficulties. The area to be surveyed covered 70,000 square miles with a population of twenty millions, and the revenue ultimately secured was four million pounds sterling. E. A. Reade, who knew well what was involved, said that 'the work would not have been completed throughout under a century'. 'What can be done?' wrote Thomason to Henry Lawrence, 'I much fear that the survey may drop or be done in so slow or bad a manner as to throw discredit on the measure.' He wanted Henry to come and work with him, saying, 'I will treat you like a prince, if I can only get you.' This was just before Honoria arrived in India. Soon after Henry replied to Thomason asking whether Thomason's sister in Calcutta could put up his bride on her arrival. Thomason answered confirming the plans for Honoria's reception and saying, 'I have some great curiosity to see the lady who is to rule your rugged destiny.' He continued that he would send Henry's letter to Bird and 'backing what you say with all the force I possess', and would request the Board of Revenue in their next annual report to 'furnish an estimate of the time in which the whole survey and settlement of the North Western provinces will be completed', suggesting himself that three or four years would be a reasonable time for this. In the same letter Thomason told Henry that Sir Charles Metcalfe, the Acting Governor-General, had authorised him to say that he was 'prepared to sanction any extension of operations which would ensure this'.

Thomason gave Henry his full confidence but warned him tactfully not to show confidential letters round when he wrote to the Board at Allahabad, and to be 'very *gurreeb*' (humble and respectful), 'for I half fear for the gunpowder in your composition'.

In the early months of his marriage Henry was experimenting with new methods and worked out a simplification of detail and a trebling of the native staff under one European Revenue Surveyor. Bird was delighted. As was the *Sudder* Board of Revenue. An official letter from the Board to Thomason on 1st September 1837 states that 'Captain Lawrence' – by now he was a captain – 'has conducted the complicated process of double survey more successfully perhaps than any other, and has certainly entered more entirely into the Board's views. Captain Lawrence is prepared to guarantee with the establishment stated a complete survey of 3,000 square miles per annum, where the villages average one square mile each.' Before that one thousand square miles had been the norm. This plan was agreed and put into operation and on the 15th May 1838 Thomason wrote to Henry: 'Bravo! hip hip hurrah! for the extended revenue survey scheme. It will be excellent to floor Bedford with a few round figures of four places of square miles.' But, taking nothing for granted, he added, 'I only hope Montgomery won't let you off cheaply but scrutinise your maps to the nth. Next to the pleasure of flooring Bedford, would be that of catching a crack surveyor tripping.' Robert Montgomery, married to a sister of Thomason, worked in the Survey at Allahabad where Henry and Honoria had now moved. Gentle and benign, he looked like Mr Pickwick but had a backbone of steel. Thomason observed to Henry, 'I am glad to find my proposition for interposing Montgomery between Bird and you like a slice of ham between the two crusts of a sandwich answers so well.' The gunpowder in Henry came out in his arguments with his chief. Montgomery was an ideal mediator now, and also twelve years later when he had to contain the friction between Henry and John Lawrence in the Punjab, when he compared himself to a tame elephant between two wild buffaloes.

Having completed the survey at Gorakhpur, Henry Lawrence was transferred early in 1838 to continue the same work at Papamao near Allahabad. Honoria described their time at Gorakhpur: 'It is a busy and wandering life but we both like it. Except during the rainy season, when we are driven in, we live wholly in tents, a week in one place, a month in another, a day in another. We rarely see a European face or hear a word of English.' By now Honoria was pregnant, and at Papamao they lived in a house. Paper littered and book strewn, it appeared uncomfortable to their neighbours, but they were happy. For a change, they were often with other Europeans, such as Bird and Montgomery. And they had as a guest 'a broken down surveyor', who had taken to drink, but whom Henry was trying to re-establish.

Honoria's baby, a son called Alexander or Alick (Tim was a pet name), was born on 6 September 1838 and from then on events crowded densely. Henry had become involved in a foolish controversy with a Captain McNaughton who had written in *The East Indian United Service Journal* in June 1837 an absurdly eulogistic memoir of a now forgotten General, Sir John Adams. Henry Lawrence took McNaughton's review to pieces in a subsequent issue, not it seems unfairly, but with the excessive zeal of an inexperienced writer. He signed with the orientalised pseudonym Hamil, formed from his initials: HML. McNaughton took offence and expressed this in print. Henry published a rejoinder. And so it went on, at intolerable length and with tempers rising, till McNaughton referred contemptuously to Henry as 'one, Lieutenant Lawrence' who, so he insinuated, had uttered 'calumny' and 'untruth'. Henry flared up and said he must challenge McNaughton to a duel. The army knew McNaughton well as an officer of great but misapplied talents and also as a bully. The year-long controversy between this veteran and an unknown young writer had attracted notice and the army had summed up the merits of the contestants. Henry's friends disapproved strongly of the challenge and one of them, Captain Macgregor, thought that all he needed to say was 'though I remain unconvinced by his arguments I cannot resist the language Captain McNaughton chooses to employ, and I am therefore compelled to decline any further discussion with him'. The cause was trivial, but Henry was adamant. He thought that his honour was impugned and he claimed 'the usual satisfaction'.

Honoria, knowing what was afoot, wrote to Henry:

Sept: 16th 1838 Allahabad.

My husband . . .

You did today what you never did before, when I came behind you, you snatched up what you were writing that I might not see it . . . On the question of duelling I will not dwell on the *reason* of it – all *that* you admit . . . I know that to a man the imaginary disgrace that attends an open declaration against duelling is bitter and agonising: but is not crucifixion the very word Christ applies to these mental sufferings and to which he calls us? You said a man who submitted to the charge of untruth would be spit upon. Was not Christ literally spit upon for us? . . . – Is your honour, your peace, your well being, less dear to me than to yourself? . . . To any other fault you may be harried; but there is deliberate sin, not only in giving or accepting a challenge, but in *intending* to do so. Oh! consider these things . . . if I have exceeded what a wife ought to say, you will forgive me.

Henry was deaf to this appeal from a wife who was still very ill after the birth of her first child. But at the last moment his friends dissuaded him from sending the challenge.

PART FOUR

AFGHANISTAN

1838–42

CHAPTER 8

War in Afghanistan

(i) At the Base

The first Afghan War which was brewing, nearly proved to be the Vietnam of the British Empire in India. Undertaken on a flimsy pretext, the operations were badly planned and executed far worse. And throughout, according to Sir John Kaye, 'a strange moral blindness clouded the vision of our statesmen'.

In 1838 the Government of India faced a new problem. The Russian Empire was advancing rapidly to a position which threatened India. Persia at that time was considered a cat's-paw of Russia. In Afghanistan the not very old Durrani dynasty had been overthrown almost everywhere but still had a toehold at Herat in the West. The Shah of Persia laid siege to Herat, and Herat was considered the gateway of India. If Russia succeeded in putting Afghanistan under the rule of one of her clients, as she had done in Persia, she would be in a position to destabilise India, whenever she wanted.

The new Governor-General, George Eden, Lord Auckland, was a conscientious public servant, who had been appointed by the Whig Government in a time of peace. When Henry Lawrence sat beside him at dinner in his glory at Simla, he summed him up as 'a quiet, frost-bitten chap . . . his conversation was soon expended, though not his appetite'. However, he judged Lord Auckland more charitably after he had been hit by disaster. In an emergency Lord Auckland failed, but the blame must be divided between London and Calcutta. The policy was worked out carefully between both Whigs and Tories. Their basic mistake was the unspoken assumption that in Afghanistan they could move pieces on the chess board as easily as they had been accustomed to do in India. The passes and roads had not been properly reconnoitred and, worse, it was not understood that Afghanistan was in every way a much tougher country than India.

The ruler at Kabul was Dost Mahommed of the Barukzye tribe,

who had replaced the Durranis. Born into the royal family but far from the succession, he attracted no particular attention as a boy and commenced a life of debauchery and depravity. However, he pulled himself together and became, and remained for a generation, one of the leading figures in central Asia. A series of royal murders brought him near to the throne and he took his chance. As a ruler he was ruthless and unscrupulous to the extent that was necessary in Afghan public life but he was not cruel and he righted injustices when he could. In foreign politics his life-long ambition was to live at peace with the British.

To forestall Russian intentions Lord Auckland sent Sir Alexander Burnes to Kabul. Burnes was able and knew Afghanistan but his judgment was erratic, and his instructions were to secure Dost Mahommed's friendship but to give next to nothing in return. The Dost wanted British support against Persian and Russian pressure and discussed terms with him. The Government of India in distant Calcutta then decided to depose Dost Mahommed and to replace him with Shah Shujah, the representative of the Durrani dynasty, who had lost his throne thirty years before and had been living ever since at Ludhiana in British India. The Government of India believed on insufficient grounds that the Afghans were ready to receive back the ill starred, vain and incompetent ruler whom they had expelled long ago, Shujah al Mulk, known to the Tommies as Sugar and Milk.

British India had no frontier with Afghanistan. Between the two states there lay the wide expanse of the Sikh Kingdom in the Punjab and, further south, the wastes of Sindh and Baluchistan which were under independent rulers. Ranjit Singh, the ruler of the Punjab, was a friend of the British and he could be persuaded to let a British army through if there was a prospect of suitable compensation at the expense of Afghanistan. And the Amirs of Sindh could be compelled to allow a British army through – and to pay for it, too.

In order to end the siege of distant Herat, which was not under Dost Mahommed's control, and, it was hoped, to consolidate a bastion against Russia, it was decided to send an army through foreign territory to dethrone the Dost and reinstate Shah Shujah.

There was no consideration of what was to happen if the aged and infirm Ranjit Singh died and his successors were less amenable. Accordingly a magnificent army was assembled on the Sutlej and divided into two columns, one to advance through the Punjab and the Khyber Pass to Kabul, the other to go by a circuitous and difficult route down the Indus and through Sindh, and the Bolan Pass to Kandahar.

On 9th August 1838 the Adjutant of the Second Brigade of Horse Artillery wrote officially to Brevet-Captain H. M. Lawrence informing him that orders had been received 'to prepare the 2nd and 3rd Troops immediately for active service in the field, to reach Kurnal or its vicinity on 31st October'. This was not a command for Henry Lawrence to join his troop. He was employed in civil duties under the Governor-General who must 'place him at the disposal of the Commander in Chief' before he could return to any military duty. Losing no time he wrote urgently to the Commander in Chief for permission to join the army, and while he was waiting for the answer, which came down from the cool Simla hills after a leisurely interval, he began at once to consider the work of the campaign and the share he might take in it. After three days of hard thought he boldly dispatched to the Quartermaster General of the Army his own plans to meet the new contingencies. The army was advancing into new territory inhabited by little-known tribes. Without eyes and ears it would be lost. The Commander in Chief would find Henry Lawrence a bad draughtsman but quite conversant with the duties of a reconnoitrer, rapid in his movements, and accustomed to judge of distances and put together field surveys. He knew India and its peoples and hoped that 'he would be found useful in ascertaining the position of the enemy, the resources of the country, the state of the roads, passes and fords and the numerous etcetera necessary to the success of an army'. For these purposes he proposed to raise a Corps of Guides 'as a temporary attachment to the Quartermaster-General's Dept'. The men should be 'selected *sowars* and *sepoys*, smart active men, who understood something of the Punjabi and Persian as well as Hindustani dialects; surveyors and surveying *clashees*, camel drivers, fruit and horse merchants, *shikaris* and such like men, who from previous habits would be both intelligent and willing instruments to handle'. He worked out the establishment of officers, n.c.o.s and men required for such a scheme and calculated the total cost at 4,168 rupees a month, to which he added 1,000 rupees a month for contingencies and in particular for 'spies who bring in authoritative information . . . a quarterly account of such expenditure to be furnished on honour'. Leaping to the imagined end of the campaign, he urged that 'if the passes of the Hindu Kush are to be fortified, they will need to be surveyed; and such work will require men who have been accustomed to think lightly of hardship, and to make the most of materials'.

It would have been well if he had left it at that but he went on to name the officers he proposed for the new corps. It says something for the Commander in Chief, Sir Henry Fane, and his staff that his scheme was considered at all. Indeed Sir Henry gave Henry Lawrence a personal interview at which he 'allowed the strong necessity for such a corps, entered in to all the details with great interest . . . and promised his warmest support but regretted that its adoption would depend on others'. It was turned down on the grounds that 'Sir Henry had already made all the arrangements', and that 'the whole of the passes through the Hindu Kush are now as thoroughly known as the passes of Kheree and Timlee leading into the Deyra Dhoon', which was far from the truth. Finally the Quartermaster-General, who was a kindly man, added: 'There will be ample opportunity for the employment of all that are like yourself desirous of making themselves useful.' And in a private letter to George Lawrence he wrote: 'I wish he had confined himself to the plan. But when it was followed up with the recommendation of three officers, one of whom he had never seen, I saw the thing would not do. Where Sir Henry [Fane] had so little patronage, giving away three appointments in a separate and distinct department, besides making your brother the head of his own scheme, was rather more than could be expected.' So the scheme was turned down then; and throughout the campaign the army suffered greatly from the lack of an intelligence corps. However eight years later when Henry Lawrence was uncrowned king of the Punjab, he established just such a corps.

On the same day that he sent in his plan for the Guides to the Commander in Chief (16th August 1838), Henry Lawrence sent a copy to the Governor-General's private secretary for the information of Lord Auckland, adding: 'I again entreat that I may not be prevented from going where my duty has clearly called me.' In due course Lord Auckland's private secretary answered very civilly that the Governor-General would make no difficulty 'should your services in any capacity be called for' by the army. But so far they had not been. Henry bombarded various authorities to send him to the war but was reminded by the Brigadier at Meerut that he was 'not yet at the disposal of his excellency, the Commander in Chief and, if it is intended that you should join, you will no doubt see yourself in General Orders'. Henry fretted for over a month. And on 16th September, ten days after the birth of his son, Alexander, he coolly wrote to the adjutant of the Brigade 'telling him that I did not deem an order necessary and would proceed to join on the 1st October'.

Honoria had been very ill, her baby was ten days old and she dreaded a separation from Henry, with the hazards of war in a savage country. Yet his honour was as dear to her as to him, and she had not married in expectation of 'the cloudless climes of fiction'. She was prepared, but none the less during these weeks her soul was pierced with agony. Henry in his obsession with the coming war saw nothing of this. He was determined to start by 1st October and Honoria was determined to go with him. So they started together but to her 'the whole journey seemed like a funeral procession . . . baby very ill, myself apparently sinking fast'. Sometimes driven in a buggy over rough tracks, sometimes carried in a *dhoolie*, she and the baby were jolted and rattled along for a full week. Then her misery reached its climax. Henry was riding ahead as he often did. Alick was crying and vomiting incessantly. In despair Honoria got out and walked up and down with her baby, sending a bearer on ahead to fetch Henry back. 'Oh the anguish of that hour,' she wrote a few weeks later, 'as I carried my baby about until I almost fainted. At last I laid him on my cloak by the roadside; but he cried so fearfully that I at once took him up again. I thought he would die there and then . . . Henry rode up. The bearer had never gone near him. He had only turned back from surprise at my not appearing.' By the evening they reached Cawnpore, where they had to stay for a full week before mother and child were fit to travel.

When the terrible journey was completed, Henry Lawrence joined his battery, leaving Honoria in Kurnal. He wrote to her several times a week, giving racy descriptions of camp life and ending one of his letters: 'I told you darling, your influence, your kindly and gentle influences, would probably prevail over me more in absence than in presence. You know it is not altogether obstinacy, for I have told you often how I've been led to do very absurd and violent things in others' presence, which alone I should hardly have done. Well, I . . . do but little now without saying "And what would her my love, my gentle love, say or think of it?" I told you I was getting on well with the servants. I have not given any a thrashing – scarcely touched one. In future you shall know each blow or angry word.'

When the army of the Indus was fully assembled news came to Simla that the Persians had raised the siege of Herat, which was the original pretext for the war. The expedition into Afghanistan was not, however, abandoned, but it was scaled down and Henry found himself among those who were to stay behind. He could have expected to return to the Survey but after thirty years of peace the frontier of British India had suddenly become a centre of activity. Sir George Clerk, one of the ablest and best of a great generation of Indian civilians, was in charge of the frontier as Governor-General's Agent for the Affairs of the Punjab and North-West Frontier. He needed an assistant to take over the civil administration of the small district of Ferozepore on the Sutlej. Frederick Currie, who had been the Commissioner at Gorakhpur when Henry was there, was now one of the Government Secretaries travelling with the Governor-General. He told his intimate friend, George Clerk, that Henry Lawrence was the right man for Ferozepore, and the appointment was soon arranged. In after years when Henry had risen to eminence on this very frontier, he used to recall how his friend, Currie, had announced his success in acquiring this appointment for him: 'Now I have helped to put your foot into the stirrup. It rests with you to put your foot into the saddle.'

Since the beginning of the century the Sutlej had been the boundary of British India. To the north were the Himalayas and to the south was desert. The intervening strip of flat, cultivable land was the route through which all previous invaders had come. Beyond it lay the Sikh Kingdom of the Punjab, then held in the strong hands of Ranjit Singh. He was a one-eyed little man and did not look impressive but as soon as he mounted a horse, he was seen for a leader.

The Sikhs were followers of a reformed religion which broke from Hinduism in the fifteenth century. At the end of the seventeenth century Moslem persecution drove them to arms and in the confusion following the fall of the Moguls they had become a power to be reckoned with in their native province, the Punjab. Ranjit Singh was a minor chief who by courage and consummate ability had in the course of a lifetime become the ruler not only of the whole Punjab but also of Peshawar and the Derajat beyond the Indus and of a large part of the western Himalayas, including the fabulous vale of Kashmir. He was utterly unscrupulous and avaricious, but not bloodthirsty. He shrank from inflicting the death penalty and preferred to gain his ends by stratagems and deception rather than by war, though he had a large, well-equipped and well-trained army. His court was dissolute and he exercised little control over his wives. It was supposed that only one of his putative sons was really his, but Sir Lepel Griffin, who knew the Punjab well, wrote that 'the bazaars of Lahore . . . were not so shameless as Piccadilly in 1893'.

About a sixth of his subjects were Sikhs. The rest were Moslems and Hindus, whom he often promoted to high office, but the Sikhs were the ruling element. Before Ranjit Singh many chiefs and adventurers had carved out domains for themselves across the Sutlej and Ranjit Singh was almost ready to absorb these in 1805, when the British established themselves in Delhi. Three years later he was ready to strike but, perceiving that he was up against a strong force, he abandoned his claims across the Sutlej, and entered into a treaty with the British which he kept loyally up to his death.

Ferozepore, which Henry Lawrence was sent to rule, was one of the smaller Cis-Sutlej states which had come under British protection at this time. It had lapsed to the British three years before on the death of its Rani. Its nominal extent was 100 square miles but not one tenth had been in the undisputed possession of the Rani. In his novel *Adventures of an Officer*, Henry Lawrence describes the town as it was in her day. Though of great antiquity, it 'was little more than an assemblage of *Zamindars'* huts mixed up with a few *banyas'* shops, and overhung with a crumbling old fortress, crammed to the throat with dogs, filth and old women'. The Rani's palace was 'a couple of little rooms, each about fifteen feet by nine and as many high'. From the roof there was 'a good view of the surrounding country, of its desolation, of its endless bare plain, varied only by a few and single trees, and by fewer wretched village sites, which at large intervals covered rather than ornamented the country . . . There was an air of poverty and of squalidness all around Ferozepore; scarcely a thriving shop in the town and not one acre in thirty of the land under cultivation.' The people were of the Dogur race and 'their appearance struck me; their immense noses and large, strongly marked features, their spare but athletic frames, and their bold independent bearing'. The *dogurs* divided their time between breeding cattle and stealing them, as did many of their neighbours. And since eight or nine small territories with independent jurisdictions met about that point, thieves and murderers could easily slip across the border.

There were continual frontier disputes and raids, which cost about 500 lives a year. Even this was an improvement. A few years earlier, before Ferozepore came under British protection 'no man dug his well without erecting his tower of defence beside it, and no traveller or trader thought of moving with less than a score of men to protect him'.[1]

At the end of 1838 this godforsaken place suddenly became important, as the frontier post through which all troops and supplies for the Afghan War must pass. And Henry Lawrence was for three years in charge of its fortunes. He set to with a will, completing the rebuilding of the town, straightening and widening the streets and introducing some elementary drainage, which the inhabitants undertook to keep up. The insecurity had been such that the subjects of the Rani, huddled for safety into her puny capital, could only cultivate those fields which were near the town. However the presence of British Indian troops at Ferozepore now made it safe to go farther out and Henry made plans to remodel the tumbledown fort which would in the words of the government inspectors 'when finished and armed be capable to resisting a considerable force with field artillery'. New settlers were encouraged and long streets of shops were built for the traders who were now attracted there. The inspectors reported that 'the town, when finished, will be as airy convenient and well built as any in Hindustan'. And George Clerk noticed that Ferozepore was already rivalling Amritsar as a trading centre.

The army had brought security but among its innumerable camp followers there were many who, 'though nominally following some occupation useful to any army, proceed with it for the sole purpose of plundering when a suitable opportunity offers', he wrote to Honoria. Therefore it was necessary to build a new court house and to establish a reformed jail for these more or less professional criminals. Care for prisoners was a life-long concern of Henry Lawrence. Using the experience gained in the Survey he settled the disputed boundary between Ferozepore and the neighbouring state of Faridkot. First, 'they nearly killed me by yelling', he wrote, 'and keeping me out in the sun' but it was necessary to 'hear all there is to hear and see all there is to be seen'. In the end Henry's settlement gave great satisfaction to all parties. Soon he was asked to settle other boundaries and the local causes of crime were greatly reduced. His method was first to read the papers in a dispute and then to fling himself into the middle of the quarrelling parties, spending days on end riding over all the ground with them. He then applied common sense, an independent judgment and a knowledge of Indian ways so that even those who lost declared themselves satisfied with the decision.

These local affairs were by no means the whole of the responsibilities that fell on him. He had to negotiate with Lahore for the passage of troops and stores to the war in Afghanistan. Ranjit Singh died six months after the beginning of the war and his successors made difficulties, fearing with some reason that these proceedings placed their independence in danger. Relations were not easy but it was in these negotiations that Henry Lawrence acquired his unique knowledge of the Sikh Kingdom and its personalities. He also had to organise commissariat and transport, and there were innumerable financial transactions that threatened to become an active banking business. He did not have the help of a clerk to do the work. Finance was always his weak point and this was a great bother to him, but the post office was also a severe burden. Most of the correspondence to and from the army at the front came through Ferozepore together with 'the letters of all unknown persons in India',[2] but the Government provided no clerk for this work either. Henry and Honoria, knowing how important letters are to soldiers on active service, used to spend 'six, eight and ten hours in the post office in the day or rather during the night'.

Henry's pay as civil administrator turned out to be only 700 rupees a month instead of 900 rupees in the Survey, and when he protested, Lord Auckland ruled perversely that 'there is a great deal of difference between knocking about with a theodolite all the hot weather, living in tents nine months out of the twelve and sitting with one's heels on the table, playing civilian'. So it was 700 rupees. In conveying this to Henry, J. R. Colvin, the Governor-General's private secretary, wrote: 'You must, therefore, determine whether you will remain at Ferozepore on that, or go back to the survey. I suspect you will remain, for you are in the way to future promotion and distinction in the political line, which you could not be in the survey.' He remained, though Ferozepore was not the bed of roses that Lord Auckland imagined. When he met Henry the Governor-General had asked him

Above: Henry Lawrence as a young man.

Below: The Reverend James Knox, Principal of Foyle College, in his 89th year.

Above: Letitia Lawrence.
Below: Honoria Lawrence.

Left: Ranjit Singh. Below Left: Dost Mahommed Khan, painted on ivory by an Indian artist c. 1840. Below Right: his son Akbar Khan, by the same artist.

Above: Kabul from the
Jalalabad Road, during
the First Afghan War,
1838-42. *Centre:*
Afghan soldiers in win-
ter dress. *Right:* a sowar
of the cavalry.

Left: General Sir George Pollock. *Bottom Left:* George Lawrence in Indian dress during the First Afghan War, *Bottom Right:* Lord Ellenborough, Governor-General of India 1841-44.

Above: The Residency in Nepal. The two small boys are Alick Lawrence
and Lawrie Pemberton, his playmate, with Henry Lawrence standing.
Honoria Lawrence is standing in front, with my grandfather in the arms of
an *ayah. Below Left:* Honoria Lawrence *c.* 1850, and *Below Right:* her sons
Alick and Harry, *c.* 1848.

Above: Henry Lawrence in his bath tub with his son Harry on his shoulder, by Herbert Edwardes. *Below:* the Lawrences' cottage in Koulia, above Katmandu.

Above: Maharajah Dhulip Singh (1838-93), sketched by Queen Victoria, July 1954. *Below:* Maharajah Gulab Singh (1792-1857).

whether he liked the Survey work and knew so little about it that he asked him whether he had any natives under him.

On 15th April 1839 Honoria wrote from Simla to an Irish friend: 'This bleak spot is now become of importance . . . You would be amused, could you see the two little pigeon-holes we live in. There is a large fort of mud and bricks, the lower part of which is a network of filthy narrow lanes; going up a flight of steps in the wall, we come to the state apartments' – evidently the Rani's former rooms – 'one on each side of a little court. They have neither window nor fire-place, and doors that close very badly; so we were obliged either to keep out the light or let in the wind, which was always blowing and bringing either rain or dust. We suffered much from cold for three months, and then the heat was excessive. By next year I hope we shall have a house, and the pleasure of seeing some verdure near our doors. My baby got the ophthalmia from the glare reflected from the barren ground.'

The next year, 1840, they spent the hot weather together in Ferozepore, and Herbert Edwardes tells us that they had 'a house, a real house . . . in the cantonment and they were able to escape from their fiery furnace in the fort. Poor souls, it never was their lot to build very snug nests under very safe eaves. Their destiny was on upper boughs that rocked in the wind; and a few soft thorns and hard scraps of wool were all they ever wove into a home. But they got the first of the sun up there, and were thankful.'

Henry complained repeatedly about the terms of his appointment, first to Colvin and then to Thomason. Lord Auckland was adamant and Colvin could do nothing, but their correspondence was uniformly friendly. In writing to Henry, Colvin referred to Honoria as 'your queen', and, when he had occasion to write to her, addressed the letter to 'Her Most Gracious Majesty the Queen, Ferozepore'. Henry's letters to Thomason are lost but their nature can be inferred by the replies. These intimate letters give a moving picture of one of those close friendships between men which the Victorians were not ashamed to express.

On 8th March 1840 Thomason replies to Henry's 'affectionate letter' of condolence on the death of his wife. 'The spirit rose as the body sank . . . She knew what was approaching and . . . cast all her cares upon God.' About himself: 'I am lame and always shall be for one leg is one and a half inches shorter than the other, but I suffer no pain and am able to walk about.' 'I am sorry you have been so badly treated in the matter of allowances. What can be done? Don't injure yourself by overwork and let us hope for better days.' But Henry's grievance festered. He was entitled to more pay and he needed clerks to help with the financial transactions and the postal work. He thought Thomason, as Secretary to the Government of the North-

Western Provinces, could put these things right. On June 8th Thomason answered:

> I am exceedingly amazed at the charming simplicity displayed in yours of May 6th and June 1st. You address me as if I were a king or at least the Prime Minister of one, bearing the dispensation of rewards, emoluments – almost crowns. Don't you know that I resigned my crown when I left Azimgarh [where he had been collector]? I might then . . . have brought a worthy Revenue Surveyor under the shadow of my outstretched wing, but all that is changed. In little Pocklington itself I am but the cipher of a cipher. In the political world especially I am a nonentity. The appointment at Ferozepore is specially exempted from the jurisdiction [of the Lieutenant-Governor of the North-Western Provinces]. Now you see my dear Lawrence, how useless it is to pour your sorrows into my friendly ear. You only harass (I mean harrow) my soul with the thoughts of the ingratitude of princes who could admit claims such as yours to pass unacknowledged, merits such as yours to remain unrequited. We did you more justice in the survey department. Next time you write don't forget the wife and child who ought to be mentioned even when political appointments are on the tapis and a tiger has been killed.

The Indian hot weather makes people testy; Henry took this gentle mockery in bad part, his reply showed that he did not yet understand the frustrations that often go with high office. Henry thought that Thomason could easily put all right with a word to Colvin and he pressed his point angrily. Thomason replied on 20th June:

> [Colvin] is my friend certainly [but] so far from correspondence between us being regular, the only way I can ever get an answer to even my demi-official notes on business is by writing in half column and either Lord Auckland or he fills up the blank column. The simple state of the case then is that I know nothing of the footing on which you stand, or on which your office is constituted and it is quite out of my power to help, rejoiced though I should be to do so . . .
>
> By way of apology, I do hope you will believe that to hurt your feelings was the furthest possible from my thoughts. You unconsciously touched on a tender subject, the powers of the Lieut. Governor, which have been the cause of some sore feeling here. Perhaps I wrote under that impression a little more unguardedly than I ought.
>
> By way of thanks, I am indeed obliged to you for giving me your

feelings on receipt of my note, for it has opened my eyes to what I should never otherwise have guessed, and will put me more on my guard in future even to my bosom friends.

By way of caution, you might have told me your mind a little less tartly. You risked by your haste the loss of a very sincere friend. The risk is passed but do not again answer angrily on the spur of the moment . . .

I am very sorry you find your position at Ferozepore so uncomfortable, nor do I know how to advise you or help you. I cannot help directing your attention to one alleviation of your lot, for which I would gladly exchange all I have. Your wife and child are with you and well. Is that nothing? . . . I do not jest with you, I do not laugh at you. I beseech you as your best friend to look more thankfully at the blessings that are left to you and to be less fretful under the trials and mortifications to which you may be unjustly exposed.

Things were soon put right between the two friends. Already on 14th July Thomason was writing to Henry: 'a second cordial and most welcome letter from you.' The two men exchanged happy family news and Thomason concludes: 'You see I have pleasure even in my solitude with which a stranger intermeddleth not and I ought also to be more thankful and less downcast than I am. You may fairly read to me the same lesson as to social dejection, which I read to you regarding official dejection. We should be happier and better men, if we both looked more thankfully to the hand that blesses us, and less repiningly to the hand that chastises us.'

On 16th November 1840 a dearly beloved daughter was born to the Lawrences and christened Letitia Catherine after Henry's sister, Letitia. And in the hot weather of 1841 Honoria went with her two children to the Simla hills, where Henry joined her part of the time. They stayed first at Sabathu, where there was a cantonment but afterwards they built a cottage on the nearby hills of Kasauli, high enough to be cool in summer but near Simla and easily reached by the Sutlej from Ferozepore. This cottage and the house they built later at Lahore were the only real homes they ever had. At first there was only one other European family at Kasauli but they loved the beauty and solitude of the hills. The Lawrences' cottage is now, by the generosity of its Indian owners, a rest house for the parents of children at Sanawar, with furniture and pictures on the walls that have been there since the Lawrences first came to Kasauli.

All went well until the end of July. In Honoria's journal we read: 'Tuesday August 3rd 1841. Let me record the power and goodness of God in supporting those He sees it needful to try. Tuesday. She was full of mirth. How she crowed and sprang almost out of my arms! On that last Monday evening Henry had collected all the children about him on the parade ground and was playing at leap frog with them.'

Then the children became ill, first Alick and then Letitia. Henry asked whether he should go back to the plains when the children were ill but the doctor said he should go and Honoria was left alone. The next day the children were worse and Honoria began to be alarmed for Alick. When the doctor came he examined both children and said 'Yes, Alick is very ill but it is about *her* you need to be alarmed.' 'When Dr Steele on the noon of Sunday told me she was in danger, it was like a thunder clap but when he said that nothing more could be done and I took her in my lap to die, a holy calm came over me . . . When my darling ceased breathing, I thought she said to me, "Mother, you are often afraid of this dark valley. See how easily I have passed through it". I longed to be able to tell the poor natives around me of all that comforted me.'

'Sunday August 8th. A week today since her departure. Oh what she may in that time have learned! All that we are darkly striving to know may be unfolding itself to her unclouded faculties.'

(ii) To Rule the Unruly Afghan

'The Chief may sleep sound in his grave,
Who would rule the unruly Afghan'
Verses Written in India by Sir Alfred Lyall

Most people expected that the campaign in Afghanistan would be easy and Henry Lawrence was no exception. At the beginning all went well. Kabul and Kandahar were occupied and Shah Shujah was placed once more on the throne of his not very many ancestors. Distance, lack of water and a very rough terrain were greater obstacles than any resistance from the Afghans. But there were ominous signs. George Lawrence describes meeting 'a well dressed Afghan, who told me he had visited our camp and seen our troopers, saying with much contempt, "You are an army of tents and camels; our army is one of men and horses." "What could induce you," he added, "to squander *crores* of rupees in coming to a poor rocky country like ours, without wood or water, and all in order to force on us a *Kumbukht* (unlucky person)

[80]

as a king who, the moment you turn your backs, will be upset by *Dost Mahommed* our *own* King".'

The political leader of the British invasion was 'the Envoy', Sir William Macnaghten, and George Lawrence was his Military Secretary. Macnaghten was a very experienced servant of the Government of India, a brilliant orientalist with a warm sympathy for the peoples of India and liberal ideas about their treatment. Some called him 'almost a great man'. But he had spent too much time at a distance from scenes of action. Having convinced himself that the Afghans would be delighted to welcome back their former ruler, he had a blind spot for any evidence to the contrary. Before long some of his staff were warning him of widespread dissatisfaction but he dismissed them as 'croakers'. His chief assistant was the still-young Alexander Burnes who hoped to succeed his chief before too long. Burnes had distinguished himself by adventurous journeys in Central Asia before he was thirty and it was his misfortune to become famous before his judgment had matured. At Kabul he had a position of prestige but not enough to do, being at every point subordinate to the Envoy. Sometimes he described approaching danger and was dismissed as another croaker. At other times he shared the optimistic illusions of the Envoy.

In Afghanistan political power lay more with the Pathan tribes than with the central government. Tribal and personal rivalries are intense and no coalition stays together for long. Since ancient times Afghanistan has generally shared a common history with Persia, Persian has been the language of culture and there is a large Persian and therefore Shia element in the towns, which is always somewhat at odds with the Pathan, Baluchi and Turki tribes of the countryside who belong to the Sunni branch of the Moslem faith. It was not and is not difficult for a disciplined European force to occupy the chief towns and to move in force between them. But it was and is very difficult to control the mountains and deserts or to make the roads safe enough for small detachments to move freely between the towns. In a pitched battle the army of British India, when properly led, had no difficulty in beating an Afghan army several times its size but then, as the Duke of Wellington foretold, the difficulties began. The Afghans took to the hills, they seemed able to disappear behind the smallest rock and they were armed with the *jezail*, a long muzzle-loading rifle fitted with a rest beneath the barrel so that a marksman could take steady aim. The Afghans had a much longer range than the Brown Bess musket with which the *sepoys* and Tommies were armed. The Afghans knew every stone of their barren hills; whereas the Indian army was accustomed to fighting only on plains and in jungle.

As already stated, the British army advanced in two columns, one

going through the Punjab and the Khyber to Kabul, and the other
with Shah Shujah by a circuitous route through Kandahar where one
of his sons was made Governor and then on to Kabul where Shah
Shujah was duly enthroned. Only a man who is strong, wily and
ruthless with a strong sense of direction can rule in Afghanistan. He
must know how to appeal to many and diverse human feelings and to
build up fragile combinations in such a way that, when one card house
falls down, he can quickly reshuffle the pack and put a new one in its
place. But Shah Shujah, though intelligent, was pompous, weak and
short sighted. He continually offended those who should have been
his friends and he appointed worthless ministers. At first he was
welcomed with modified rapture in Kandahar, if not in Kabul, but
this did not last. He did not know how to rule as the British would
have ruled and they did not allow him to rule in the ruthless manner of
Afghanistan.

His rule was weak, as well as corrupt and oppressive. He soon
became very unpopular and the British who had put him there and
kept him there shared his unpopularity. Most of the country was soon
in revolt but Sir William Macnaghten refused to believe that the
restored King was not proving a success. There were some tiresome
local troubles but all would soon be well. The two races liked each
other. Who can resist the manly open faces of the Afghans with their
twinkling eyes and those firm handshakes? The Afghans are good
company and they enjoyed the society of their visitors. Both peoples
shared the same love of sport and the Afghans enjoyed the horse races
and all the new sports which the British taught them. The British said
they came from a cold country but the Afghans laughed at that. They
had seen them come from India. But when the lake froze and their
visitors made skates, gliding gracefully where others could only slide,
the Afghans opened their eyes in wonder. That first winter in Kabul
must have been fun. The European officers began to build houses and
bring their wives. So were they going to stay? That was not what had
been said at first. But not all the officers were married and it soon
became clear that the Afghan ladies liked the company of British
officers as much as their husbands did. Kaye remarks discreetly,
'those temptations which are hardest to resist were not resisted by the
English officers'.

Before long the misgovernment of Shah Shujah and the misbehav-
iour of some British officers made most Afghans regard the British as
hated invaders, but human emotions are subject to sudden gusts and
the feelings of the Afghans were various and changeable. George
Lawrence, reflecting afterwards on the British mistakes, points out
that the Afghan tribes lived 'in a state of chronic civil war. As these
tribes had failed to coalesce as a nation to oppose our entrance into

Afghanistan, and had apparently acquiesced in our policy of imposing upon them a king who had been an exile for thirty years, we were
unfortunately led to conclude that the Afghans were indifferent on the
subject and so divided by mutual jealousies and blood feuds, that they
could never be induced to act together for any national purpose.'
Besides 'there was something in the Afghan individual character
which also tended insensibly to put us off our guard. Possessing many
noble, natural qualities, such as individual courage, hospitality and
generosity, of fine and commanding appearance and presence, good
horsemen capable of enduring without complaint much exposure and
fatigue, fond of all manly sports and frank and social in their bearing
and manners, there was much calculated to prepossess us in favour of
the Afghans as a people on first acquaintance. Further experience,
however, proved them to be destitute of all regard to truth, treacherous, revengeful and bloodthirsty, sensual and avaricious to a degree
not to be comprehended by those who have not lived among them'.

Those self-appointed religious warriors, the *ghazis*, no doubt felt an
intense and constant hatred for their Christian invaders and perhaps
even more for the Hindu majority of the *sepoys*. But the powerful
Persian element in Kabul, the *Kyzilbashes* or red heads, so called from
the red turbans of the Shias, saw advantages in a British connection
and were markedly friendly towards them. And in the shifting intrigues of the Pathan tribes there were generally elements ready to
make common cause with the British against their tribal enemies.
Moreover British subsidies to potential friends were a powerful per-
suader. Both before and after the disasters that befell the British-
Indian army it was the settled opinion of the best judges that with
reasonably good management the British position in Afghanistan
could have been maintained. But it would have been expensive. The
long line of communications with India had to be kept open and this
was most easily done by paying agreed subsidies to the tribes who
controlled the Khyber Pass and other approaches. These tribes regarded such payments as their natural prerogative, and Sir William
Macnaghten had perforce been open-handed to them. But the
Government of India became increasingly restive about an expense
which was becoming an intolerable burden on the Indian budget. And
there was no immediate prospect that the army could be withdrawn. It
was unjust to the Indian peasants, who provided the revenue, to
saddle them with the cost of occupying Afghanistan. It was doubly
unjust to impose an unpopular King on the Afghans but Sir William
Macnaghten, Lord Auckland and those who had advised the invasion were not prepared to recognise that fact. Yet from 'the other
side of the hill' things could not have looked too good. Kabul,
Kandahar and other strategic points had been occupied and there had

been no prospect of dislodging the invaders. And after various discouraging adventures Dost Mahommed Khan gave himself up to the British at the end of 1840, and went into an honourable exile in British India, where he was greatly impressed by much that he saw. All the same, after the Dost's surrender resistance did not fade away, but was organised by his son, Mahommed Akbar.

After careful thought the Government of India decided in the course of 1841 that the existing policy must continue but that there must be economy in the way it was implemented. The economy chosen was to cut the subsidies to the Afridi chiefs who controlled the Khyber Pass. The result was to cut communications between Kabul and India. This put the garrisons in Kabul and Kandahar into difficulties but there was so far nothing in their situation that could not be remedied by firm action carried out with reasonable competence. Sir William Macnaghten rose to the occasion and behaved with courage and good sense, but could not, of course, take military decisions. Major-General Elphinstone, who had fought at Waterloo, was in command. He was universally loved but he was old and his health was failing rapidly. He had become unable to trust his own judgment, listened to everyone and was influenced by the last person who had spoken. His second in command, Brigadier Shelton, a one-armed veteran, was brave but had no judgment and his 'cankered vanity and dogmatical perverseness' (Kaye's phrase) made him impossible to work with. Moreover he seemed unable to master that degree of organisation which is necessary for the success of even the simplest military operations. The combination of Elphinstone and Shelton was the haphazard result of promotion by a combination of seniority, and jobbery. Endless counsels of war led nowhere. Among the junior officers there were heroes, such as Vincent Eyre and Colin Mackenzie, but under such superiors their best efforts came to nothing.

No one at this stage foresaw clearly the 'signal disaster' that was being prepared but in June 1841 Henry Lawrence who, as Herbert Edwardes puts it, 'like all thoughtful and imaginative men often caught prophetic glimpses of coming things, had published in the *Delhi Gazette*, half in jest and half in earnest, what he called *Anticipatory Chapters of Indian History*'. The Prophecy of Darby Connor runs as follows: Darby Connor is Henry Lawrence under a thin disguise. In 1855 he has retired from service in India and lives at Letitia's holiday cottage at Lynton. He casts his mind back to 1845 when 'Shah Shujah having died of horror at the Envoy's having in a moment of forgetfulness seated himself in the royal presence, Timoor Shah was murdered by his brother, who having put out the eyes of Sir Alexander Burnes and impaled Captain Rawlinson, drove the British troops before him and proclaimed himself sovereign of Kabul, Kandahar, Herat and

Peshawar.' Having suffered a disastrous and unlooked-for defeat, the demoralised British troops suffered most severely on return to India. 'Few officers, indeed, recrossed the Attok, and the harassed and skeleton battalions that did return to Hindustan told frightful tales of misery, and talked in a strain long unknown in British India of the superior prowess of the Afghans . . . All Hindustan was in a blaze; the cry of "The Feringhee raj is over!" resounded from one coast to the other.' Henry then described 'the blaze' in terms that looked forward prophetically to the Indian Mutiny.

In 1855 'Lord Jamaica . . . was by the blessing of Providence then our Governor-General'. Lord Jamaica is obviously Sir Charles Metcalfe who was also through George Lawrence's wife connected by marriage with the Lawrences. 'Lord Jamaica', perceiving that 'the very foundations of British rule were shaken', sends out a confidential circular 'calling on every man who bore a commission' to state on half a sheet of foolscap his view of what should be done. Darby Connor then takes half a sheet of the largest size of paper he can find and writes out his prescription which is at once accepted. Anyone establishing a brewery would choose honest, active and thoroughly competent people to head the business and run it. 'Down to the errand boy, no working berth is filled by a mere brother, son or cousin.' But in 1838 the army of the Indus started 'clogged with infirm, home sick and aged men and retarded by want of information and arrangement'.

Darby Connor, who is thirty-seven, proposes that an army of 6,000 picked men be sent, that no officer above the rank of captain should be permitted to go and that the officer in command of the expedition should have supreme political as well as military authority with full power to weed his battalions, leave incumbrances behind and to make all staff appointments. Lord Jamaica accepts all this without quibble and puts Connor in command. Half the Irishmen in India apply at once to be Adjutant-General or Quartermaster-General of the force but Connor rejects all but one, who reminds him that they once ran away from school together. All the senior officers chosen are between twenty-seven and thirty-eight; among the native troops, where the system of promotion by seniority was pushed to absurd lengths, half the native officers are invalided and their places filled by the promotion of young and active men.

Henry continued his spirited story for six chapters until a continuation would have seemed a criticism of his brother George's chief. On the way he had lightheartedly sketched in most of the principles he was to apply a few years later in ruling the Punjab.

In Kabul the obvious place to garrison was the Bala Hissar, the Black Fort. It was easily defensible, but it was also the residence of Shah Shujah and, in deference to his feelings, the army built for itself a separate cantonment outside the city. The site was ill chosen and much too large to be defended; and the commissariat stores were kept outside the cantonment.

Sir Alexander Burnes lived in his own house in the city. Suddenly on 2nd November 1841 an armed mob surrounded his house and set it on fire. Burnes sent a message to the Envoy asking for help. He showed it to George Lawrence who came in at that moment and found the Envoy in earnest consultation with General Elphinstone, Brigadier Shelton and other officers. Being asked for his opinion George said that not a moment should be lost in sending a regiment to Sir Alexander Burnes' house, whence strong parties should then go to the houses of the two leaders of the insurrection and seize their persons. 'My proposal,' George says, 'was at once set down as one of pure insanity.' After much delay Shelton came with a large force to the Bala Hissar, where George Lawrence had already gone. He describes the scene:

Brigadier Shelton's conduct at this crisis astonished me beyond expression . . . I knew he was unpopular with his own corps, but I did not attach much weight to the fact . . . He was apt to condemn all measures not emanating from himself, and call in question and depreciate the merits of others, after alluding to what he would do in their position. I confess to a doubt having crossed my mind before then, as to whether, if tried, he would not be found a failure, but I as often dismissed it as unjust to the man. Added to all this, he was dissatisfied with his position, a great croaker, and anxious to return to India . . . Shelton on my joining him seemed almost beside himself, not knowing how to act and with incapacity stamped on every feature of his face. He immediately asked me what he should do, and on my replying "enter the city at once", he sharply rebuked me, saying "My force is inadequate and you don't appear to know what street fighting is." "You asked my opinion," I rejoined, "and I have given it. It is what I would do myself."

Finding further expostulation vain, I begged that two guns might be placed on a platform in an elevated spot of the Bala Hissar, so as to fire down effectively on the very limited portion of the city to which the disturbance was *then* confined, and which was fully exposed to artillery fire from where I was standing. To this Shelton assented, and directed Captain Nicholls to take up the guns. Nicholls however, represented that his horses were unequal to drag the guns up such a steep ascent. At this I lost patience, and turning to the Brigadier, exclaimed, "Really, Sir, if you allow your officers to make objections instead of obeying, nothing can be done. We had better unharness the horses, and two companies of the Shah's own

Native Infantry will soon put the guns in position." This was done, and fire opened. The king [Shah Shujah] at this time asked me more than once why the troops did not act.

The mob burnt Sir Alexander's house and another house where treasure was kept, they 'cut in pieces Sir Alexander and his brother, Captain Burnes and Captain William Broadfoot' and stole £17,000 out of the treasure. Intelligence came that 'Captains Trevor and Mackenzie, who both held detached fortified posts in the city, were holding them with great determination and gallantry, though each had only a handful of men. Both officers sent urgent and repeated messages for aid, and I proposed to General Elphinstone to order out two companies immediately to reinforce Mackenzie and throw fresh ammunition into his fort, volunteering to lead them by a way passing through only a short street, so that they would be very little exposed to the fire from the houses. My proposal was condemned by the staff as most imprudent.' Trevor and Mackenzie had to cut their own way out, 'proving by their successful resistance . . . the weakness of the mob at that time and how easily we would have quelled the insurrection had we only firmly and instantaneously used the powerful force at our disposal'.

Yet nothing was done either to rescue Burnes and his companions or to exact retribution for their deaths. So an accidental *émeute* became overnight a formidable insurrection.

Of those in authority [George Lawrence continues] the Envoy alone comprehended the gravity of the crisis, and showed his usual resolution and energy of character. But as a civilian he was powerless against military paralysis. Things went from bad to worse. The commissariat was plundered while the army looked on with folded hands. Efforts to obtain further supplies were bungled and every sally turned into a defeat, till our friends were afraid to sell us food. The army went hungry and began to be cold, an unfamiliar affliction for the Sepoys and the vast numbers of camp followers who went with the army. By degrees brave and disciplined men, who had at first clamoured to be led against the enemy, became numbed and cowed. The leaders of the insurrection taunted the British openly and with complete impunity. The Envoy could do nothing. The military would agree upon nothing, except that they wanted to go back to India.

Cold and hunger increased, and the rebels grew ever more insolent till the worst period of winter was at hand. Sir William Macnaghten was reduced to negotiating for an unopposed return to India, well though he knew that the chance of plunder would be an irresistible temptation to the tribes on the long rough way back to Punjab and that no reliance could be placed on the military to organise a difficult retreat successfully. As much as anything this unfortunate army was destroyed by its complete lack of *bundobust*.

On paper Macnaghten came very near to agreement with Mahommed Akbar and the other chiefs that the British would evacuate Kabul and proceed to the Punjab, that this retreat would be unimpeded and that they should be given all necessary supplies, but the negotiations were spun out by the Afghans, who never performed any part of the various bargains they made, until snow was on the ground and the British Indian Army was reduced to extremity.

On the morning of 23rd December George Lawrence with two other officers was summoned to accompany Sir William to a conference with Mahommed Akbar and the other chiefs to discuss the latest tangled proposals for a treaty. As they left the cantonments, General Elphinstone expressed some fears of treachery. Sir William answered, 'If you will at once march out the troops and meet the enemy, I will accompany you and I am sure we shall beat them; as regards these negotiations, I have no faith in them.' The General replied, shaking his head, 'Macnaghten, I can't. The troops are not to be depended on.' Later, as they were on their way, George Lawrence asked again if there was not some risk of treachery. 'Treachery!' said Sir William, 'of course there is; but what can I do? The General has declared his inability to fight, we have no prospect of aid from any quarter, the enemy are only playing with us, not one article of the Treaty have they fulfilled, and I have no confidence whatever in them. The life I have led for the last six weeks, you Lawrence know well; and rather than be disgraced, and live it over again, I would risk a hundred deaths; success will save our honour and more than make up for all risks.'

They met the Afghans who were more numerous and crowded nearer than seemed right for a confidential meeting. The small British party were invited to sit. Suddenly George felt his pistols snatched from his waist, his sword drawn from its scabbard and his arms pinioned by one, Mahommed Shah Khan, who raised him from the ground saying, 'If you value your life, come along with me.' He turned and saw the Envoy with horror and consternation on his face, struggling with Mahommed Akbar, and the two other officers in the same predicament as himself. Resistance was useless, so George said, 'Lead on. I will follow you.' His captor and his retinue kept off a blood-thirsty mob with the utmost difficulty and eventually brought their prisoner to a place of safe but dismal captivity. He afterwards learnt that the Envoy had been killed by Mahommed Akbar and his mutilated remains shown in the centuries-old covered market which was the pride of Kabul. Nothing else is certain about the Envoy's death. On the whole it seems more likely that the original purpose was to seize him but not to kill him and that the killing took place in one of the sudden surges of emotion to which Mahommed Akbar was subject.

Again nothing was done either to avenge the Envoy's murder, or to rescue the captives. With the Envoy gone, General Elphinstone turned to Eldred Pottinger, as the most senior political officer, to continue the negotiations. Pottinger who had, single-handed, animated the defence of Herat earlier in the war, was a modest man built in a heroic mould, who seemed marked for a great destiny. He survived the perils of Afghanistan to die of fever in Calcutta. After the Envoy's murder the troops were in a mood of furious anger and Pottinger urged Elphinstone to lead them at once in an attack on Kabul, but the General would hear nothing of it.

So negotiations went on through a very cheerless Christmas Day. The Afghans presented a curt draft treaty. The British were to evacuate all their positions in Afghanistan, and their 'going would be speedy', all the cash in the British treasury must be handed over and all but six guns must be surrendered. Dost Mahommed and his family were to be restored to Afghanistan and hostages must be given for their release. All that was offered in return for this humiliation was a promise of safety on the retreat to be secured by an escort of chiefs, chiefs who had repeatedly broken the most solemn obligations. Pottinger saw that these disgraceful terms were a trap to lure the army to destruction, and urged refusal. Reinforcements from India were known to be on the way. The Bala Hissar could still be seized and held till the spring. Pottinger urged this, but Shelton's obstinacy barred that solution. The only other course practicable was for them to abandon their baggage and all encumbrances, and fight their way back. Pottinger thought that 'this was perilous but practicable. However, I could not persuade them to sacrifice the baggage; and that was eventually one of the chief causes of our disaster.'

There had been confidential warnings that the true intention of the Afghan negotiators was utterly to destroy the army but Pottinger was as powerless as the Envoy to bring Elphinstone and Shelton to their senses. This left Pottinger no alternative. Finally on New Year's Day an agreement was signed but the chiefs continued to play cat and mouse, putting off the departure from day to day, so that the misery of the British Indian Army might be greater as the weather got colder and their hunger increased. Finally on 6th January 1842 the whole force moved off in one unwieldy mass. There was little organisation and no sense of urgency. Everything was mismanaged. Soon there developed a monster traffic jam. Afghan marauders saw their chance.

Nearly all the baggage and most of the commissariat stores were lost on the first day; the snow was stained with blood and the corpses marked the passage of the army for many months. Each day was worse than the last. Those who escaped the knives and the bullets of the Afghans succumbed to hunger and frostbite. A few ghastly, crippled men, women and children hid in caves and some of the *sepoys* straggled back. Out of the British fighting men none but an assistant surgeon, Dr Brydon, got through to Jalalabad, where 'the illustrious garrison' was defending itself stoutly against heavy odds. With all his companions gone Dr Brydon defended himself until his sword broke. He then threw the hilt at an assailant. He had no pistol but, as he dropped his left hand, his enemy rode off, evidently thinking that he was drawing a pistol from his holster. Dr Brydon struggled on to Jalalabad to bring the news that he alone had escaped. His horse lay down at once and died. Fifteen years later Dr Brydon went all through the siege of Lucknow and lived many years afterwards in retirement in the Highlands where his professional service to his neighbours was greatly valued.

(iii) At the Front

Henry Lawrence at Ferozepore was the first person in India to hear of the disasters in Afghanistan. When the despatch arrived describing the murder of Burnes and the fearful extent of the insurrection, Henry and Honoria were sitting at table with two other officers. Honoria describes how he was called out of the room, but returned immediately 'and merely gave me a *look* to go into the next room, where I found the letters just come, with his direction to copy them. I made the requisite copies, and left all ready, merely requiring his signature . . . I returned quietly to my seat at the table, there to play the agreeable while Henry left the room, sealed and sent off the letters. And then we sat with the guests until they went, and left us at liberty to speak to each other.'

Clerk acted at once, vigorously and on his own authority. Neither the Governor-General nor the Commander in Chief seemed to know what to do, but in ten days Clerk had assembled four native infantry regiments under Wild on the Sikh bank of the Sutlej and proceeded to move them across the Punjab to Peshawar.

Ranjit Singh had died on 27th June 1839 and, once his masterful hand was gone, the Sikhs became increasingly restive at the British Alliance. The British reverses robbed them of their respect and the Sikhs became insolent to the British troops. Brigadier Wild's brigade would be in an exposed and delicate position at Peshawar. Clerk had established a unique influence at the court of Lahore but he needed to be backed by the best diplomacy at Peshawar if his unwilling allies, the Sikhs, were not to become open enemies. If this had happened the British force at Peshawar might well have been destroyed, as the army at Kabul had been. And then the brigade at Jalalabad, the army at Kandahar and separate units cut off elsewhere in Afghanistan would be in desperate straits. In Asia failure was very contagious. One or two more reverses on this side and the crisis would have been as grave as the Indian Mutiny. Major F. Mackeson, Clerk's Agent at Peshawar, was likely to have his hands full with the affairs in the Khyber, and beyond. The new man now to be sent to Peshawar must have tact and judgment and be able to think quickly. For this delicate diplomatic task Clerk did not choose the smoothest operator, but Henry Lawrence, the man with the hottest temper on the Frontier. As Herbert Edwardes puts it: 'This was not a time for phlegm.' So Clerk 'passed his fingers over his arrow heads and drew the sharpest from his quiver'. On 5th December 1841 he wrote to Henry: 'I shall send you some brief official instructions for your own satisfaction, but I do not think it necessary to say much to you, who will anticipate all I could wish to do, on occasions which, after all, must be dealt with by you at Peshawar as they arise . . . I feel much confidence in your knowledge of the Sikh authorities – in their reliance on your fair dealing – in your experience as a district officer and a people's protector – and in your activity and decision, to meet emergencies of every shape.'

Henry arrived at Peshawar on 28th December. Rumours were abounding. One day the story was that every *Feringhee* at Kabul had been murdered, except Sir William Macnaghten who had turned Moslem, then that Akbar Khan had been killed by his own troops; the Moslems at Delhi were said to have given thanks for a British defeat, and so on. But soon the ghastly truth became clear. Among so many rumours and tragedies George Lawrence's fate remained uncertain. At one moment he was said to be a prisoner with the Afghans. At another Honoria's brother, James Marshall, had been killed on the retreat, which was true.

Wild's brigade was a scratch corps, not properly integrated and unbalanced in composition. Sir Jasper Nicholls, the Commander in Chief, had sent with them some foot artillery men who were on their way to Afghanistan as a routine replacement, but they had no guns. He told them to borrow guns from the Sikhs. But the Sikh gunners refused to give up their artillery. Wild's first aim was to break through the Khyber Pass and relieve Jalalabad, but Sir Jasper justified the absence of guns by observing: 'I have yet to learn the use of guns in a pass.' Yet experience taught that guns were particularly useful in mountain warfare, they bridged valleys and reached to the top of precipices, they reached difficult strongholds, they covered the exposed advance of infantry up mountain sides and they pursued a routed enemy faster than he could fly.

A disciplined and properly equipped force could go anywhere. But the Khyber inspired a legendary terror. So Wild's troops lay paralysed without guns on the wintry plains beyond Peshawar, looking at the snow-clad peak of the White Mountain, the black shadow which marks the yawning mouth of the defile. And the longer they looked, the less they liked the prospect. They were already demoralised and now the Sikh soldiers 'strode insolently among our tents and derisively asked our Eastern soldiers if they ever expected to return from the darkness of these passes'.[3]

Henry Lawrence was one of the two officers at Peshawar responsible for relations with the Sikhs. He had direct access to George Clerk but Mackeson was his senior. The Sikh Governor of Peshawar was General Avitabile, one of several European soldiers of fortune who had entered the service of Ranjit Singh and raised the brave but disorderly Sikh soldiery to the warlike standards of a European army. Avitabile, a cunning intriguer, was well able to hold his own in the scheming of the Sikh court. He also had a talent, almost a genius, for civil government which induced Ranjit Singh to put him in charge of Peshawar, an Afghan province which the Sikh generals had conquered but could not rule. Henry described him as 'coarse, vulgar, cold blooded and illiterate' but also 'bold, active and intelligent with great resourcefulness and tact'. He spoke a mixture of languages which was not fully intelligible but 'his grimaces and gesticulation and the play of his hands are not bad interpreters of his meaning'.[4] His methods were cruel, unscrupulous and effective. He hanged men right and left, caring little whether they were innocent or guilty, as long as they belonged to the right clan. The jeering atheism of this civilised savage horrified Moslems, Sikhs, and Hindus alike. But he 'knocked down crooked streets and created broad thoroughfares and squares shaded with trees, and established a thoroughly continental system of police, which made human life a little safer, even after dark'. His Afghan subjects spoke of him 'with the admiration of a troop of jackals for a tiger'. But his own troops treated his orders with contempt. To suffer this with the British officers looking on was – Honoria thought – fit punishment for his proud satanic nature.

Avitabile had amassed a large fortune and was vainly seeking permission to visit Europe with a chance to convey his hoarded wealth out
of the Punjab. But the Sikh government 'had an awkward habit of
using its provincial governors as leeches; allowing them in silence to
suck out the wealth of the people and then, in a fit of well dissembled
indignation, passing them through the finger and thumb'.[5] The arrival of the British solved Avitabile's problem. He lent them whatever
money they needed to finance the current expenses of the army in
return for drafts on British India, which quietly put his wealth out of
reach of Lahore. He kept open house for the British officers and was
always ready to meet British wishes; but neither he nor anyone else
had much control over the Sikh troops.

Between them Henry Lawrence and Mackeson had to deal with
Avitabile and the other Sikh generals. Henry found Mackeson was a
man of outstanding ability, but too cold for his liking, and there was a
lasting friction between the two. Mackeson was a difficult man and
Henry wrote to Clerk that he had 'a manner which is not pleasant from
having been so long out of the world and is better versed in Oriental
than in European fashions'.[6] Henry felt every slight, enduring in
silence for two years but eventually, protesting to Mackeson, 'the
service we have done has not been small, but you have not been kind
or friendly'.[7] His considered opinion afterwards was that Mackeson
was 'an excellent soldier, a first rate linguist, a man of such temper as
no native could disturb. His life was spent in discoursing day and
night with false Sikhs and false Khyberees at Peshawar, or treading
almost alone, or attended by an Afghan escort, the paths of the
Khyber. A road that Avitabile would not have passed with a brigade
was probably traversed fifty times by Mackeson with a few Afghan
horsemen.'[8]

Henry's work was never properly defined and he wrote to Honoria:
'I have . . . no charge, no anything but always busy at something, one
minute to listen, another to write, another to talk; not very satisfactory
but Pollock, Mackeson and Shakespeare are all proper fellows.'[9]
Henry told her that at first he half expected that affairs at Peshawar
would be taken out of Mackeson's hands and transferred to him but he
admitted that this would have been absurd, for Mackeson 'knows all
the people about here well'. But he could not get answers to letters out
of Mackeson who was 'industrious but desultory; more so than
myself'.

Eventually some not very satisfactory guns were borrowed from the
unwilling Sikhs and there was talk of preparation for advance. Effective control of the Khyber throughout its whole length was in the
hands of the tribes but the fort of Ali Masjid five miles from the

entrance of the Pass was held by 'a mixed set of Afghans and Punjabis, whose fidelity is uncertain' under the command of Captain P. Mackeson, a cousin of Major F. Mackeson. Ali Masjid stands on a small hill at a strategic point amid the sternest roughnesses of that dread defile. The first need was to supply and hold it.

John Becher, at that time a young subaltern, used to meet Henry Lawrence at the same mess at Peshawar. 'We all recognised in him the leading man of the camp. He was always sanguine and ardent for an advance.' With hindsight it is clear that it was useless to attempt anything in the Khyber until morale had been restored. This is shown in a story told by Becher. One evening the adjutant of the 64th Regiment came into the mess and said that his troops had been refusing their pay, they demanded not only increased allowance, but also fur coats and gloves to protect them from the cold of an Afghan winter. Throughout the day they had grown more presumptuous and were now in open mutiny. Just then the officers heard the bugles sounding a general assembly. Henry, surprised, went off at once to find Brigadier Wild, while the men fell in and waited in pitch darkness. The order came for the gunner to light the port fires. The troops stood in great suspense, just able to 'see Lawrence on horseback, dark and prominent against the sky, vehemently urging, and riding here and there. At length we were ordered back.' Wild had wanted to use the other *sepoy* regiments to coerce the 64th, but at that time and place this was suicide. With great difficulty Henry had persuaded Wild to wait till the morning, when 'the matter was arranged under Lawrence's counsel, and the Sepoys accepted their pay'. In after years Henry spoke with horror of the dangers of that night[10] when the troops at Peshawar stood on the brink of another signal catastrophe.

Wild was in a pitiable situation. Ali Masjid must be supplied now at all costs, and Jalalabad must be relieved as soon as possible. All his four native regiments were composed of young soldiers whom the mutinous Sikh troops had filled with horror of the Khyber. His cavalry consisted of one troop of Native Irregulars and his artillery was four elderly Sikh guns. For these Henry had brought eighteen camel loads of ammunition and small stores from Peshawar, but Wild was short of musketry ammunition. The camel men ran off with their camels but Henry bought up 1250 camels and 527 bullocks. Wild had no commissariat but Henry organised one for him, gathering grain and fodder from the surrounding country.

The Afridis who controlled that part of the pass would come to no terms for a free passage and Avitabile warned Wild not to try to force his way with so inadequate and demoralised a force. But Sale at Jalalabad cried 'Come on!' and at last the tribes attacked the little force at Ali Masjid so fiercely that they, too, called loudly for help.

Clerk, again on his own responsibility, had moved a second brigade under Brigadier MacCaskill across the Sutlej on 4th January 1842; and behind him General George Pollock was making his way. But Wild felt that he must advance now, at all hazards without waiting for reinforcements. Two regiments seemed enough to get to Ali Masjid. On the night of the 15th January they surprised the Afridis and got through without opposition. Three hundred bullocks had been laden with grain but only sixty-three arrived; the rest had been unaccountably left behind. There should have been supplies for a month for the whole half brigade, but instead they were shut up in a perilous situation without sufficient food for a week. It was bitterly cold, the besieging tribes were in great number and they fired all night. The men who held the surrounding hills that were necessary for the defence were much exposed but they held their ground.

To remedy this new disaster Wild needed to follow at once with the rest of his brigade and supplies for the whole force. He wanted to take a contingent of Sikhs who could garrison Ali Masjid and keep open the communications with Peshawar but they had no stomach for that. Day after day excuses were made, excuses that they had not been paid, that they had no carriage or no grain. On the evening of 18th January the half-disciplined *Nujeeb* regiments of the Sikhs mutinied and drove out their officers. The British had to go forward without the Sikhs and an unsuccessful attack was made the next day. Henry wrote to Honoria: 'I'm quite well but I've witnessed a shameful sight today – our troops behaving ill before a handful of savages.' But some had fought properly. In all 112 had been killed and wounded. The net result was that two regiments were 'locked up in Ali Masjid short of provisions, without a possibility of (us) reaching them until General Pollock reaches us'. To Macgregor, the political officer with the garrison cut off in Jalalabad, he could only write: 'I grieve to say you can have no assistance from us for at least a month. Yesterday we were beaten back from the Pass, our guns breaking down at the first discharge, and the Sepoys of the 60th behaving ill. The Sikhs marched back to Peshawar as we entered the Pass . . . We cannot even relieve . . . Ali Masjid . . . Reckon therefore on nothing from us for a whole month. I say it with real grief.' During the fighting Henry said he had been 'general, artilleryman, pioneer and cavalry at different times . . . and doubt I'll be well abused by all . . . Our people, when they see ten men call it a hundred, and I'm in bad odour for contradicting it.'

Sir Jasper Nicholls had opposed the Afghan entanglement from the first. When the Kabul disaster happened, he could well say, 'I told you so,' but having done that he felt no obligation to do more. Enough troops were eventually sent, but Sir Jasper seemed to grudge every man who was sent to the front. Decisive action taken in time could have averted the disaster but Sir Jasper dawdled in a manner that seemed deliberate.[11] Lord Auckland was dumbfounded at what had happened. He was also conscious that his successor, Lord Ellenborough, was on the way to India to relieve him and he was scrupulous not to do anything that would limit Ellenborough's choice of policy. He did, however, see that in any event a good general would be needed. He chose 'not the first major-general on the roll, nor the oldest alive in the Army List, nor him who had most grandfathers in England; but . . . the man best suited to the service in hand . . . An artillery officer was chosen not more than fifty-five years old who had not yet been forty years in the service, whose descent was merely from Adam.' Major-General George Pollock was 'taken from his quiet command at Agra, a plain unassuming man, remarkable for no shining qualities', yet distinguished 'by strong common sense, sound judgment, patient determination and conciliation, amounting to a high order of management, foresight and preparation for things coming, crowned with equanimity in the midst of gloom and a public spirit far above that of his Government'. By steady use of his one talent, he rose to greatness. And when he became a national hero, he remained the same modest, considerate human being he had always been.

Pollock could not reach Peshawar till the beginning of April. In the meantime Wild was blamed for not doing what could not have been done. When he was famous and Wild forgotten Henry wrote: 'Few officers have been worse treated than the gallant and unfortunate Wild. As brave a soul as ever breathed, he was driven broken hearted to his grave.'[12] The half brigade at Ali Masjid and Captain Mackeson, who received little credit for his gallant defence, cut their way back to Peshawar, but not many came out of those days with credit. The *sepoys* behaved badly but there were excuses for them. As for the officers, Henry wrote to Honoria: 'With a few exceptions there is not a man with head and heart in the force.' Morale went from bad to worse with the *sepoys* making bitter reproaches against their officers, and bad morale showed itself in illness. When Pollock arrived in February, something like half the force were in hospital.

Pollock saw at once what was wrong. He did nothing dramatic, but spent much time in the hospitals seeing to the comfort of the men and sympathising with their troubles. Morale improved at once and the hospitals began to empty, though the most unhealthy season of the year was upon them. The garrison at Jalalabad was defending itself successfully but its position remained precarious. Time pressed but Pollock was not going to attempt the passage of the Khyber until he was ready. He needed a balanced force in sufficient numbers to keep the communications open and it would be some weeks before troops who had gone to pieces could be risked in hard fighting.

Pollock sized Henry Lawrence up at once, and took him into his confidence, but not entirely so. Henry had hopes of becoming the General's military secretary but Pollock appointed Sir Richmond Shakespeare. Shakespeare was a cousin of Thackeray with whom he had for a time shared a nursery. He had earned his knighthood as a very young man by a daring diplomatic journey into Central Asia in which he persuaded the Khan of Khiva to free some Russians, who had been seized on slave raiding expeditions, and escorted them home to St Petersburg before returning to service in the East. Henry felt jealous but he was too busy to let it prey on his mind. He told Shakespeare that he was 'a good man to do business with', indeed the only man at headquarters who answered letters and he told Clerk that Shakespeare was 'a fine fellow, really the only one about worth listening to'.[13] On the whole Henry got on well with General Pollock but he was by no means uncritical of him, thinking rather unfairly that Pollock was afraid of responsibility and that Pollock had unaccountably 'thrown him overboard'. Pollock was criticised for being in the hands of the political officers and he may have wanted to show his independence by distancing himself from Lawrence. This and other grievances against Pollock still rankled ten years later.[14] Yet much kindly feeling remained and the Pollock and Lawrence families became hereditary friends.

The Sikhs were bound by treaty to help the British with 5,000 troops in aid of Shah Shujah who was still the ostensible object of British concern. This obligation had not been pressed so long as things went smoothly, but now it had become vital. The Afghans needed to see that the Sikhs were Britain's allies. But the Sikh soldiery were very unwilling allies. What would happen if not even one regiment would march with Pollock into the Khyber? Or, if the Sikh army barred Pollock's communications and his line of retreat at the crossing of the Indus? 'The happy solution of these terrible questions was due mainly to the tact and influence of Mr Clerk at Lahore, and next to the exertions of Lawrence at Peshawar.'[15] Clerk had somehow persuaded the Sikh government to order Rajah Gulab Singh to Peshawar with instructions to coerce all mutineers and cooperate with the British. Gulab Singh was one of the three 'Jammu brothers' who were then in the ascendant in the politics of the Punjab; Dhyan Singh, another of the brothers, being Prime Minister at Lahore. Gulab was Rajah of Jammu in the foothills of the Himalayas. He had the smoothest manners and the fiercest nature of the three brothers, and his ambitions lay in the direction of Tibet. At Peshawar he was not in a hurry to carry out his instructions, nor, it may be supposed, were his masters. Day by day fresh news of the disaster came down from Kabul and was magnified in the bazaars. Henry received an indiscretion from an 'American' adventurer (or at least from one who tried to conceal his own past by pretending to be an American), which indicated the mood fairly accurately. 'It is the opinion of all that you will never set foot in Kabul again; and this is the time to break your strength, to raise insurrection here and there, draw off force in different directions and then act.' But it might be wiser to wait before committing oneself to either side. 'The Sikhs wear a mask', which the Afghans do not; in the opinion of General Avitabile that was the only difference. Before the arrival of Gulab Singh the Sikh forces at Peshawar were commanded by General Mahtab Singh. When Henry offered to call on him, he rudely answered that 'he would send word when it was convenient'. It was never convenient. Henry said that he had eaten so much dirt that it would take seven years to get the taste out of his mouth. But he would have been the first to say that the Sikhs, too, had their grievances. While those in charge of British policy were studiously correct in their behaviour, some of the Anglo–Indian newspapers and some junior officers talked openly of the advantages of annexing the Punjab.

When Gulab Singh arrived at Peshawar, Mackeson and Lawrence asked him to make an example by disbanding the regiments which had mutinied. Gulab Singh, who was a Hindu, answered coolly that the Sikhs bore him ill will enough already and that he would not be supported in coercion. It was commoner at this time for mutinous Sikh troops to punish their officers, rather than *vice versa*. During 1840 and 1841, while pretending to be completely occupied with Sikh affairs in the plains of the Punjab, Gulab Singh had extended his power to Skardu and Gilgit in the Himalayas and had seized Gartok in Tibet which gave him a monopoly of the valuable trade in shawl wool. But in the depth of winter the hardy Tibetans had surrounded the invaders and, when they were sufficiently demoralised by starvation and cold, massacred them, as the Afghans massacred the British, almost at the same moment. The Grand Lama then prepared to drive Gulab Singh's forces back whence they came. It was now Gulab Singh's turn to beg the British that 'the news might be made as little as possible'. After this he lost all interest in helping his allies. Lawrence wrote that everything 'has served to confirm us in the opinion we had already formed, that no assistance is to be received from the Sikhs'.

On 20th February the British decided to bring matters to a head. 'Mackeson was the spokesman; and those who can remember his [Gulab Singh] commanding countenance and stately form . . . can well picture the scene as *"ore rotundo"* he advanced through all the preliminaries of courtesy and the exigencies of the situation' before allowing himself to be asked 'for what purpose the Sikh army had been sent to Peshawar, and what order had been received from the

Durbar. As easily can those whose lot it has been to parley with that Ulysses of the hills, call up before them the sweet deference of attention, the guileless benevolence, the childlike simplicity, and the masterly prolixity of fiction, parenthesis and anecdote, with which the Rajah Gulab Singh stroked his silver beard while listening to the question, and then charmingly consumed the hours in avoiding a reply. Much had he to say about the past . . . but as to the future and what has now to be done to save the British garrisons still in Afghanistan, Rajah Gulab Singh . . . got no further than to remind the English that the great Dost Mahommed Khan was a prisoner in their hands, and might very conveniently be set up again. Or if that was disagreeable, there were other Baruckzyes, brothers of Dost Mahommed, in the hands of the Sikhs, quite ready to be used (and one of whom was his own sworn friend . . .) It was humbug to talk of Shah Shujah, who was our enemy.'[16] Worn out with discourse, the British officers impatiently reverted to their opening question . . . But time was up. The Rajah's "opium hour" had arrived: and if detained he might even be so rude as to fall asleep. Hurriedly he produced a paper which, he said, was instructions from the Maharajah at Lahore, whereupon the master of twenty thousand allies yawned and took his leave.

Henry had already concluded that the Maharajah in Lahore was a cypher and that all power now centred in the Jammu brothers and the Sikh army. If the British wanted their help, they had to make it worth their while. He proposed to the Government that the Sikh troops should be given the same *batta* as the British, that the Rajahs should be 'secured in their territory, even with additions; General Avitabile guaranteed our aid in retiring with his property; and any other *sirdars* aiding us cordially, be specially and separately treated for'. Henry developed these views as time went by, and about three weeks before the interview described above had proposed that the British should assist Gulab Singh 'to get possession of the valley of Jalalabad and endeavour to make some arrangement to secure it and Peshawar to his family . . . We are surely bound to no faction or party in Afghanistan; but after retrieving our character punishing our enemies, are free to make such future arrangements as will most conduce to the future tranquillity of our Indian Empire.' Mackeson pressed the same views on the Government but Clerk, watching affairs from the frontier, 'took a calmer, no doubt, juster view' than the two young men at Peshawar 'receiving urgent appeals from Sale in Jalalabad and putting up with insults from the Sikh soldiery'. It would be wrong 'to assign suddenly and directly to the Jammu Rajahs any territories as a compensation for services demanded of the Sikh durbar.'[17]

The mood was slowly changing. On 4th March 1842 Henry reported to Richmond Shakespeare that 'Mr P. Mackeson (Ali Masjid Mackeson) heard people talking yesterday in the *hammam* to the effect that our army was mutinous and that the enemy knew it'. On 9th March he wrote to Honoria: 'I am so puzzled to know if our Sepoys will advance . . . Of the Sikhs I have not a hope' but on 21st March wrote: 'No desertions have taken place for many days, and the troops seem to have recovered their spirits.' March was a wet and cold month, with camp followers of the Kabul force straggling back week by week 'with fingers and toes bitten off by frost, their caste destroyed, and their friends dead or in slavery'.[18] Morale was still shaky, but European reinforcements were on the way. Sale's force held out at Jalalabad but was short of food, eating salted camels and horses, killed to save fodder. Pollock could only answer his appeals by saying that 'without more white faces' the *sepoys* would not move. Finally, on 5th April everything was ready for the advance.

In the meantime Henry had been in hot water. He wrote very freely to his chief, George Clerk, making most damaging criticisms of his superior officers. While Clerk was away from his base at Ludhiana for a few days one of his assistants had opened Henry's caustic dispatches and had, as he confessed, been 'indiscreet and thoughtless enough to have the whole of these copied indiscriminately and . . . the contents went down word for word to the Commander in Chief at Calcutta'. Sir Jasper had ordered an enquiry into the conduct of the officers mentioned and, Clerk continued, 'the Government . . . has thought proper to reprimand you severely for telling the truth so unequivocally'. In replying officially to Clerk, Henry indicated that if, after enquiry, the reprimand still stood, 'I shall request to be relieved from the duties of a situation, the nature of which, it would appear, I do not clearly understand'. Mackeson, too, got a share of the reprimand, and it seems that there was even talk of a court martial.[19] Their offence was being too free with their military advice. Yet, said Henry, 'If we had not been pretty free, I wonder what would have happened to the two regiments at Ali Masjid.' Henry was cut to the quick and even thought of giving up the political service and going back to his regiment. It was, as Edwardes commented, 'the old Indian story. Military defeated . . . and vexation vented on the politicals.' Anglo-Indian opinion in its sorrow and rage was blaming the political officers for everything that was wrong. Some of the politicals had, indeed, shown lack of judgment, but less so than the military and there were among them other men of sterling worth in addition to Mackeson and Lawrence. The reprimand seems to have petered out. Perhaps it was an indirect way of getting at George Clerk who had pushed to the limit his right to advise the Commander in Chief and the Governor-General.

In preparation for the campaign Henry had made his will, appointing Thomason as one of Alick's guardians. Thomason had accepted the office with warm-hearted affection and Honoria, contemplating the possibility of her husband's death, had expressed a faith that was growing steadily stronger and simpler. 'Oh may we feel, whichever goes first, that it is but going home a little before the other.'

Pollock, cautious and thorough as always, chose his moment admirably. He spent days patiently explaining to his officers just what each was to do, and it looked as if the Sikhs would help by forcing one mouth of the Khyber while the British forced the other. Scarcity of baggage cattle was met by reduction of baggage. Two or three officers shared a tent and the General set the example, by reducing his baggage cattle to one camel and two mules. For once an Indian army went stripped of its impedimenta.

Mackeson's diplomacy had opened the Khyber in the usual way. 'The Afridi clans of Khyber have their own hereditary jealousies, splitting them up in peace into as many interests as there are pastures and running streams, just strong enough to paralyse each other and betray the fastnesses which nature has made almost impregnable. With one of these factions the invader treats; and obtains, if not a free passage, at least the disunion of his enemies.'[20] On this occasion the price for a free passage had after lengthy negotiations been agreed at 5,000 rupees and the chief had given hostages for clearing the whole length of the Pass. But on 2nd April Mahommed Akbar Khan, seeing that the crisis of the war had arrived, detached a strong party with two guns to Ali Masjid and the Afridi chiefs told Mackeson that all hope of a free passage was gone.

Henry Lawrence and Mackeson then fell out about which of them was to go forward with the army. Pollock wrote to Henry: 'Your going with me was one of the things I had set my heart on.' But Mackeson was the senior and he had local expertise. So the choice fell on him but Henry got round Pollock by offering 'to take a couple of guns up on the little hill inside the defile', a proposal that proved irresistible to an artillery General. After that Henry managed to go on at intervals all the way to Kabul.

While Mackeson was negotiating with the Afridis, Henry had spent his time visiting the sick and wounded in hospital and devising means for supplying the troops with water. This was needed during the long hot days when the heat reflected from the rocks could become unbearable, even causing death from heat stroke. He obtained hundreds of earthen jars, brass vessels and water skins. Some were carried by *bheesties*, others were slung on camels, some pots were carried on men's backs and a number of men in each company carried water pots slung on belts round their waists. The 5th April was a hot day, and General Pollock testified that these precautions saved great distress.

The night of 4th April was tense. There had been no time to give the troops practice at fighting in these conditions and against the Afghans. There had been no skirmishes to give them confidence. All was staked on one throw. The camp bells seemed to strike the hours louder than usual as the men lay down by their arms. Orders had been given that 'no fires were to be lighted under any circumstances; no drums to beat or bugles to be sounded'. The force was to be in arms at half past three.

Pollock describes the defence: the Afridis had blocked the pass with 'a high, thick stone wall in which was laid long branches of trees, projecting towards us many feet, thereby preventing approach'.[21] They expected a frontal attack and had relied on throwing the attackers into confusion by a galling fire from behind this formidable obstacle and from breastworks in the hills on either side. But Pollock held his main column in reserve, while skirmishers under cover of the grey light of dawn stole up the hills on either side, surprised the Afridi pickets and drove them before them in a long and gallant struggle. At last the heights were crowned. The clans broke up and 'with their hideous wild-cat yell', in Edwardes' phrase, rushed to those crags and points of vantage from which they knew so well how to fight with rifle and knife. Meanwhile the centre column quietly made a passage through the barricade. 'The artillery swept the hill in front with shrapnel; and before the sun . . . was a spear's height above the horizon, the whole British force . . . was moving inch by inch to a hard but certain victory.'[22]

Henry was to go with the Sikh column which was to enter the Pass by its other entrance. Pollock remembered to his dying day how he went to his tent at three o'clock in the morning, so that they might start together, and found him sitting up, deadly sick and vomiting, apparently down with cholera. He wrote to Edwardes: 'I did not ever expect to see him again alive', but when he reached the front of the Pass, there was Henry Lawrence helping to get the guns into position. He dashed about from one part of the battlefield to another, finding out what had happened, taking any necessary measures and, above all, seeing that the men had water. The troops had improved in spirits and several 'voluntarily addressed me with such speeches as "We will go all the way to Kabul, *sahib!*" All the Sikhs fought well under their French General, Court, clearing one entrance of the Pass and then returning to guard the other. We are all now very affectionate,' wrote Henry to Honoria in a letter dated 7th April 1842.

Clerk wrote to Henry: 'Don't be disheartened that Government has been cross and stingy. All along this frontier praises are loud of your exertions, alacrity and spirit. The whole of this I knew and reckoned on, and hence I sent you.' Retelling this to Honoria, Henry commented: 'It is wonderful what soft snobs we are and how we like butter better than bread.' But the praise he liked best of all was being told by Clerk that he had been patient. 'Think of my being patient in my old age!'

It took a slow and tedious week to get through the twenty-eight miles of the Pass without further loss but the defenders were staggered by their initial defeat and, seeing both plunder and blackmail escape them, drew off to the hills. Organised opposition had ceased with 'half the enemy bought over and many others wavering'[23] but the Khyber is never safe and General Pollock went forward cautiously.

In the meantime the garrison of Jalalabad had sallied forth and won a decisive victory. They left the walls of Jalalabad and met the relieving force at Lalpoora near the Khyber's northern exit where the local chief was friendly to the British. Lord Ellenborough, newly arrived in Calcutta, issued eloquent congratulations to Pollock and his army and to 'the illustrious garrison' of Jalalabad, by which name they have been known ever since.

Henry's letters to Honoria purr with contentment. 'What odd fellows I have to deal with', and he describes the wild bandits who went round with him. 'One of them yesterday regularly hunted me, because his matchlock was burst and I would not mend it. He followed me all the morning and then sat looking at me at the tent door during the day. But I am a man of wonderful temper. I don't recollect maltreating anyone since I came here, except, once pulling an ear and another time boxing it and once pitching into Davee Singh who is never present when he is wanted. However they are all now warriors.'[24] Adapting himself to his surroundings, he was now dressed in semi-oriental clothes with 'a large white muslin piece twisted round my hat into a graceful turban'.[25]

Henry Lawrence returned to Peshawar but soon found a pretext to go back through the Pass. He got on well with Pollock but in his letters to Honoria he said more than once that Pollock was 'a rum one'. He did not know in full what instructions Ellenborough had given, how often they were changed or how difficult they were to interpret. Pollock saw clearly that nothing in India would be safe until retribution had been exacted for the treacherous massacre of a whole army, and the captives still in the hands of the Afghans had been delivered. But Ellenborough blew hot and cold. After the relief of Jalalabad he felt his oats. Nothing could stop him. Then the first attempt to bring relief to Kandahar through Sindh and Baluchistan received a check. Ellenborough lost his nerve. Pollock must retreat as soon as possible, but Pollock kept his own counsel and played for time, intending to go on if he had a chance. He had no transport and for the moment could neither advance nor retreat. Henry at Peshawar was not in the secret, but Pollock quietly sent on supplies, so that the enemy could not guess what orders had been given. Ellenborough kept changing his mind with each change in the wind. Neither he nor the Commander in Chief cared for the fate of the captives but public opinion in Britain cared very much; Henry, whose brother George was among them, cared still more. Akbar Khan threatened to take them beyond the Hindu Kush and sell them as slaves in Turkestan. But then he would have lost a valuable bargaining counter.

The only key which fits Lord Ellenborough's ambiguous orders during the summer of 1842 is that he wanted Pollock at Jalalabad and Nott at Kandahar to advance to Kabul if they could, and to reassert British power before withdrawing again to India, but he did not want to take the responsibility of saying so. He would take the credit, if they succeeded, but he wanted them to seem to be disobeying his orders if anything went wrong. If they could recover the captives, that was their affair. Honoria expressed the thoughts of many concerning the highest authorities in India: if the prisoners were to be left to their fate, 'the Commander in Chief ought to be gibbetted', and she might have added the Governor-General. Looking at this confusion in retrospect Pollock seems always to be in command of the situation but at the time Henry thought him 'frightened out of his wits at his responsibilities, pestered, bothered, shoved into a corner by his political fire eaters and shoved out of it again by his military about turns'. If he was frightened, that did not deflect him from his course.

Among the captives was George Lawrence. George was a burly little man, unlike most of the Lawrences who are tall, and was called 'Cocky' Lawrence. He was swift of foot and kept himself fit by running races with his captors. It was he who had to divide supplies fairly, whenever there was anything to divide; and he gave generously when he had anything to give. He seems also to have been an unofficial chaplain, conducting the services on Sundays. For a few days, when George was sent on a mission to Jalalabad to try to negotiate their release, the brothers met. When the time came for George to go back to captivity, Henry offered to go in his place, but George refused this. In Genesis 44 v. 18-34, Judah had done the same for Benjamin and the passage is underlined in the Scott's Bible given to Henry by Padre Craufurd so many years before. Henry never told Honoria of the offer he had made, but George told her.

During all this time Henry and Honoria were busy with their literary plans. They had contributed to the *Delhi Gazette* a serial novel, *The Adventures of an Officer in the Service of Ranjit Singh*. They now enlarged this for publication in book form, adding copious notes about the Punjab. *The Adventures of an Officer* can still be read with enjoyment and has been recently reprinted. Henry poured forth a stream of news and comment for Honoria to edit and place in the *Delhi Gazette* anonymously or under various pseudonyms. It is surprising how far a serving officer could go in reporting a campaign. There were limits, and Henry evidently transgressed them and could have got himself into serious trouble if his pseudonyms had been penetrated. He wrote a savage attack on the Governor-General, saying to Honoria, 'I feel almost as if Lord Ellenborough was a personal enemy.' Here he realised he had gone a bit too far and authorised her to tone it down.

He wrote a long article on Lord Auckland published in three successive issues of the *Delhi Gazette*, and concluded that 'in all matters connected with the internal management of the country he has been eminently successful . . . He possessed all the qualities required to form a good man but was deficient in some that constitute a great one; . . . striving to acquire the good opinion by kind offices, he seemed to dread censure.' And 'there was a want of magnanimity displayed in his war policy throughout, but more especially in attempting to cast the blame of all failures and disasters, which ought fairly to rest with the Government, on Local Agents.' This was almost praising with faint damns, but Lord Auckland was down and Henry Lawrence was always on the side of the underdog.

His most original contribution to journalism at this time was a series of articles about this and that signed 'Crude Notions'. He had thought much about the tragedies of the war. Sorrows are not good in themselves but the unfolding of human potentialities needs troubles. He quotes that creative, if unorthodox, Scottish divine, Erskine of Linlathen: 'The happiness, which God intends for men, consists in a particular form of character; and that character can only be brought out by trials, and difficulties and afflictions', not that afflictions necessarily produce this character that contains a 'greater proportion of the constituent elements of happiness and glory.'

At length Lord Ellenborough gave Nott at Kandahar instructions to retreat, if he liked, through Kabul. This was going to 'Edinburgh by way of Brighton Pier'. At the same time Pollock felt that in his repeated instructions to retreat, Ellenborough had left sufficient uncertainty to allow him to advance on Kabul before retreating, provided that Nott did the same. It took some time for the two Generals to make sure that they were of the same mind. The only way for them to communicate was through *cossids*, professional messengers (or spies) who were great characters. Their romantic trade was very risky and they were paid danger money. In this campaign recorded payments to *cossids* varied from 20 rupees to 500 rupees. As soon as messengers had got through and they had reached an understanding Nott and Pollock advanced simultaneously. It was a race which Pollock won, arriving a day or two before Nott. Henry went forward with the Sikh corps who had become thoroughly pleased with the campaign. Some of the British would not believe the change that had taken place in them. Indeed as late as the end of September Lord Ellenborough wrote to Pollock that he was to treat the Sikhs, who were holding the communications at Jalalabad, as enemies or very doubtful. Henry said they 'may be friends or enemies according as they are treated. The fellows will and have behaved well, though had I not been here they might have been treated in such a way as to send them over to the enemy.'

As the Afghan resistance crumbled, the European captives with George Lawrence among them were taken to the Hindu Kush for security, but they then negotiated their own release in return for a handsome payment to their head gaoler. As they returned to Kabul from the Hindu Kush, they were met by a party of cavalry under Sir Richmond Shakespeare. They were well and several went on to distinguished careers, among them the young John Nicholson, who was introduced to Henry by George. He became a close friend of all the Lawrence brothers and also of Honoria. Many *sepoy* prisoners and camp followers were also rescued. Not all thought them of so much consequence as the Europeans, but Henry did. Neither class nor race made any difference to his feelings.

Pollock carefully protected the people of Kabul from the vengeance of his own troops who had been enraged during the advance by seeing the corpses of so many of their comrades and of the camp followers and their families still lying by the roadside. Nott, on the other hand, found it hard to believe that any Afghans were innocent of treachery and murder. Pollock tried, not very successfully, to make him restrain his men. It was decided, however, that some mark of vengeance must be left in Kabul but not such a mark as to injure the innocent. After destroying the centuries-old covered market, the army retreated in its own time to India. On his passage through the Khyber Pollock crowned the hills on both sides of his route and suffered no loss. Nott was less careful and his column suffered accordingly.

The campaign was over, and Henry described how at the beginning of November they 'bowled through the Khyber as if it had been the road between Hammersmith and London'. He then told Letitia how 'like a bright particular star I shot past the army at Peshawar and reached the river Ravi . . . when I heard that my dear wife had arrived at Ferozepore. So, turning my horse's head this way, I rode straight in and happily found her at the ferry' – waiting just where he had told her five months before – 'all well . . . She was a good, *most* good wife before, but I'm innocently told by her that she will try and be better now.'

PART FIVE

NEPAL INTERLUDE

1843–45

CHAPTER 9

Resident in Nepal

At the end of the First Afghan War Henry felt that he had been passed over in the distribution of honours and promotion.

Three times he was appointed to a job and then moved. His health worried him and he was talking of going home to Britain, though he could not afford it. He complained of his work, he complained of his pay and his lack of recognition and, above all, he complained of the Governor-General. At the beginning of September he received one day a thick, heavy and carefully sealed packet from the Governor-General addressed to 'Major Lawrence C.B.' Here at last was recognition, or so it seemed, but when the packet was undone layer by layer, out tumbled no Order of the Bath but just a Kabul medal, looking very like a half crown. Lord Ellenborough apologised handsomely for his mistake. He had supposed that Henry Lawrence was already a C.B. which made Henry think that a C.B. was what he ought to be.

Lord Ellenborough's handling of the last phase of the Afghan War was greatly lacking in moral courage and his bombast alienated Anglo-Indian society. But in most other respects he was a good Governor-General. He was the most erratic of those who held that high office over 190 years, but he knew far more about India than most of them, having been President of the Board of Control, an office that corresponded roughly with that of Secretary of State for India.

A close friend of the Duke of Wellington, he saw himself as a soldier *manqué*. So he cherished the Indian Army but regarded the Political Officers, quite unfairly, as the cause of the disasters in Afghanistan. Fortunately he made an exception for Henry Lawrence, whom he held in high esteem. Presumably no one told him the bitter criticisms that Henry was making about the Governor-General.

Ellenborough tried to find for Henry some work worthy of his capacity and in a climate where his health could be restored and appointed him to Dehra Dhoon, that most favoured valley at the foot of the Himalayas, only to find after Henry had taken up his post and 'traversed the Dhoon from Hopetown to Hurdwar', that by a law of the Medes and Persians it was reserved for members of the I.C.S. John Lawrence might have been appointed but not Henry or George, since they were soldiers by profession, albeit seconded to civilian duties. So Henry had to be shifted to Ambala and then to the State of Kaithal which had recently lapsed to the Company, as Ferozepore had a few years before. Kaithal was next door to Ambala and in each case Henry entered zealously into his new duties, but with a good deal of muttering and complaining. When his complaints became too loud, Thomason, who had become Foreign Member of the Governor-General's Council, checked him, saying in a letter written on 1st May 1843:

It is intended that you should have charge of Kaithal and that you should not at present have more than 1,000 rupees. It is not for me to discuss whether it would or would not be reasonable for you to expect more. But it is for me to represent what I think should be your course in such a state of things, with reference to what becomes you as a public servant and what is most for your own interests. I trust that you will cheerfully and zealously perform your duty in this post and bide your time. I can only say that you at present stand well at headquarters and that you have a sincere friend there watching your interests. Disinterestedness and public spirit on this occasion may do you much good; any hasty or intemperate action will greatly prejudice your cause and put it out of the power of your friends to serve you. I entreat you still further; put a bridle on your words as well as your actions. Tell your grievances to your wife but to no one else. Do not call yourself, nor affect to consider yourself an aggrieved person. Do I ask too much? I hope not. By neglecting my advice you can gain nothing: by following it you may gain everything.

So Henry bided his time through the hot weather and the monsoon, complaining of his lot, but greatly enjoying family life. While his father was at work, Alick ran in and out of the *kutchery* making cocked hats of the police reports, riding astride on the sword of a captured robber, and generally treating the office as his playroom. Henry always liked his children about him while he worked.

The great breakthrough of his career came on 16th September when he was appointed Resident at the Court of Nepal. This placed him at once in the front rank of India's public servants, with duties that were important but not onerous, in a climate where his shattered health could be restored and on a salary of 3,500 rupees a month which was far in excess of his modest needs. In a letter written on 3rd October Thomason said: 'I hope you like your new appointment in Nepal. I happened to know Lord Ellenborough selected you for it in a great measure because he hoped the climate would agree with you and enable you to stay in the country. If all the speeches you have made regarding each other during the last years were noted down, whose would read best?' Two years later Henry wrote in his private diary that his appointment was 'most unexpected and not as welcome as it should have been', but later he wrote 'I like this place more than ever . . . I thank Lord Ellenborough more daily'.

Henry had set his heart on a career in the Punjab which was now in an extraordinary state of commotion. 'One ruler after another had been swept away by the hand of the assassin,' and the army was out of control. 'Its lawless praetorian bands had long been vapouring about marching down to the sack of Delhi and the pillage of Calcutta,' and it was being taken for granted that before long they would have a try.[1] The British for their part were beginning to think about what should be done with the Punjab after the inevitable clash. Henry Lawrence disliked being away from the scene of action at such a time. However, his opinion on Punjab affairs was sought by the highest authorities in India, so that he kept in touch even from Nepal.

Henry was asked to be at Katmandu, the capital of Nepal, by 1st December 1843. That left six weeks before he need start, which gave him just enough time at Kaithal to complete a 'summary settlement' which would let the cultivators know where they stood for the next two or three years while a more deliberate assessment was made, designed to last twenty or thirty years. Later the name of Henry Lawrence became a watchword for those who would save the native aristocracy of India. When his duty was 'to prop native states, battle for the faithful observance of British treaties and soften the fall of conquered chiefs, that is what he did.'[2] But in Kaithal he had to report that under native misrule 'the estates had been year after year deteriorating, and that much of the territory was in a fair way of becoming perfectly desolate'. Edwardes observes that 'the same report has, in truth, to be made in nine cases out of ten, where British succeeds native rule, though exceptions may be found both ways'. Henry Lawrence liked the Indian *ryots* better than their rulers but each had his rights based on custom and he did not think it right for foreign rulers to disturb those rights without grave reasons.

He instituted radical reforms in the short time that he was at Kaithal. The tax farmers lost their contracts and the land was leased direct to the owners and cultivators of the soil; forced labour and many vexatious taxes were abolished; sometimes the revenue was remitted altogether to give time for recovery but in all such cases the *zamindars* were bound in return to dig new wells or repair old ones and to bring in a certain number of ploughs; he 'endeavoured by all means to encourage the growth of potatoes, sugar, cotton and useful trees'. Thousands of acres were overgrown with small jungle but there was not a single timber tree in the district. The Sikhs were great destroyers of trees but Henry planted some miles of roads with trees and gave out large quantities of seed for plantations. The population started to come back and in six months the number of ploughs increased by a half.

Kaithal had not passed smoothly into the Company's jurisdiction. The Rajah being dead, some of his retainers saw an opportunity of loot if the transfer could be put off for a time. They therefore invited the Kaithal troops to attack a small British detachment encamped outside the walls. Being overpowered, this small force withdrew and, after some delay, a larger force was sent to enforce compliance. But plunder had begun and the troops sent to stop it caught the contagion. The Rajah had no heirs, so his property seemed fair game. On hearing of the plunder, George Clerk ordered Henry Lawrence over from Ambala. He found British officers plundering, as well as *sepoys* and camp followers. One detachment broke open the treasury over which they stood guard. When Henry heard this he is described by an eye witness as seated on a marble throne in the royal loggia in great excitement, wearing an Afghan *choga*, like a dressing gown. With 'his thin locks and goat beard streamed in the wind' he looked like 'some sort of pythoness on her tripod under the afflatus'. Reporting what had happened to the commanding officer, Henry demanded that all the officers should be called on 'to give up every article of property that they may have taken since their arrival'. In after years he often related with indignant humour that he saw one party lowering a gig over the walls to another down below. The gradual erosion of discipline in the Bengal Army was one of the factors leading to the tragedy with which this book must end.

The Kingdom of Nepal, in which Henry and Honoria spent the only peaceful years of their married life, was founded between 1757 and 1770 by the Gurkha leader, Prithi Narayan Sah, who carved out an empire with the main chain of the Himalayas as its backbone. His domains were divided from the rest of India by the *terai*, a strip of land between the foothills and the plain of Hindustan. The *terai* had once been a fertile garden, and is now so once more, but was then an unhealthy jungle of swamp and marsh which malaria rendered impassable for half the year. Prithi Narayan gained an ascendancy over the previous Rajput princes partly by keeping a regular army based on European models but still more by treachery and cruelty. At the court of Nepal political murder took the place of elections, but the common people were not ground down.

Early in the nineteenth century the Nepalese had tried conclusions with the British and had been worsted, losing much of their territory, including the future site of Simla. After that they maintained distant but peaceful relations with the paramount power, permitting no British to enter Nepal except for the Resident, his doctor and the captain of the guard who were allowed only to enter and leave by a prescribed route – and not the most convenient. No British woman had ever set foot in Nepal, and contact between the Residency and the Nepalese was discouraged, so that the Resident could only learn about the people he was among 'as he would learn about a swarm of bees', in Honoria's phrase, 'by observing, comparing, noting down'. All communication between the Resident and the Court had to go through the chief minister, if there was one.

The magnificent Gurkha regiments were already serving with the British but they were away from their home for years on end, and wider communications between Nepal and British India hardly existed. The Lawrences are the only source for what happened in Nepal during the two years when they were there.

The previous Resident, Brian Hodgson, was a distinguished scholar but he had allowed himself to be drawn into the Court intrigue of Katmandu, which for artistic duplicity surpassed all other Asian Courts at that time. But the Government of India was determined to interfere no more, and Thomason put their policy into a personal letter to the new Resident:

We profess to leave the Nepalese entirely to govern themselves; and the only cases in which it is incumbent upon us to advise, remonstrate or dictate are when our own interests require such interposition. But the Government would be ill represented if every valuable opportunity were not used to prompt to that which is good, and to deter from that which is evil; to express abhorrence of acts of cruelty, perfidy and injustice; to give full approbation to all that is benevolent, honest, high minded, and just. The main object is to identify oneself with the real and best interests of the State. When we feel that such is really the case, and that the object is worked out in a kind, conciliatory and single minded manner, considerable influence will probably be obtained.

But all must be open and above board. We can never match the natives in intrigue; and when we attempt to meet their machinations by counter-intrigue, we shall be foiled and discredited.

Herbert Edwardes summed this up as follows: 'The public work of the Resident of Nepal consisted of studiously doing nothing but observing everything.'[3] This forced inactivity gave Henry Lawrence 'what is seldom brought to busy men except in sickness – a pause in the mid-career of life – a smooth stone, halfway up the hill, whereon to rest and look round, and think . . . to judge their earlier errors and reflect on their principles of life'. By nature Henry was one of the scholar administrators who played a great part in the British Empire. He read hard, not systematically, for that was not in his nature, but omnivorously; and everything that he read fell into place in that living structure of thought and feeling that grew in him throughout his life. India was his sphere, and as he read he would ask himself: 'How does this bear upon our position in India – upon the government of subject races – upon a mercenary army – upon barrack life and soldiers' wives and children – upon the treatment of prisoners in jail – and upon our relations with native states.'[4] And as he read, he wrote about what he had been reading.

It was uncertain whether Honoria would be allowed in Nepal but on 5th November they set off together and the first night's travel brought them to Kurnal, which had been one of the finest military cantonments in India, but had been abandoned a year or two before for reasons of health. In this deserted city they found John Lawrence with his newly-wed wife, Harriette Hamilton, the daughter of an Irish clergyman from the familiar shores of Lough Swilly. Aunt Harriette was a worthy helpmeet of the redoubtable John Lawrence. Here they spent a few happy days before Henry went on, leaving Honoria behind till he discovered whether she would be allowed to join him in Nepal. During these days Henry wrote his *Defence of Sir William Macnaghten*, in the opinion of John Lawrence the best thing he ever wrote. Public opinion had made Macnaghten a scapegoat for the disaster in Afghanistan, and his widow had asked Henry to put the record straight. Pollock and others supplied the material, and George Lawrence helped explain events, as he was in as good a position as anyone to know what had passed in Sir William's mind during the last fateful weeks. In defending Macnaghten Henry was also vindicating the political officers, of whom he was one. He wrote the *Defence* in one burst of energy while he was at Kurnal and sent it to England for publication by the next mail, but it was lost in a shipwreck. He began to rewrite it in Nepal, by which time fresh evidence had made him change his mind to some extent, but there were still gaps which he could not fill and the project began to go bad on him. The revised manuscript was sent home but for some reason unpublished, and has now disappeared. More than five pages were, however, printed by Herbert Edwardes and they contain a clear-sighted analysis of the mistakes which had such disastrous results fourteen years later in the Indian Mutiny.

The general scope of the *Defence*, as summarised by Herbert Edwardes, was 'to show that whether the policy of the Afghan War was right or wrong, its failure was purely a military failure, and Sir William Macnaghten was in no way responsible for it. On the contrary, when the insurrection broke out, he stood alone in advocating those soldierly measures, which would at once have put it down.' The passage quoted by Edwardes has become famous.

Henry Lawrence never ceased to remind his contemporaries that 'our chief danger in India is from within, not from without', that the 'basis of British power in India is a well paid, well disciplined army, relying from experience, on the good faith, wisdom and energy of its leaders' and that 'our army is composed of men, like ourselves, quick sighted and inquisitive on all matters bearing upon their personal interests'. The Indian Army was wonderfully faithful, but they were men and their fidelity must not be taken for granted. Henry Lawrence's influence on his Indian contemporaries was primarily one of example but the example would not have been so influential if he had not also been a prolific journalist, drawing attention year after year to the strength and weakness of British power and to its defects, both material and moral and above all to its precarious nature. The British were like people who scattered gunpowder around while continuing to strike matches freely.

Before they went to Nepal, Henry and Honoria had been actively planning to publish a serious magazine on the lines of the *Edinburgh Review* and the *Quarterly Review*, but devoted entirely to Indian affairs. The same idea occurred to J. W. Kaye, another artilleryman of the Bengal Army who was living in Calcutta. So he founded that remarkable journal, *The Calcutta Review*. 'It was a bold and seemingly a hopeless experiment,' he wrote in his life of Sir Henry Lawrence, which is one of the best portraits in his celebrated *Lives of Indian Officers*. 'I expected that it would last a few numbers and then die, leaving me perhaps a poorer man than before. Its success astonished no one more than myself. That it did succeed was in no small measure due to the strenuous support of Henry Lawrence. It was precisely the organ for which he had been wishing for the expression of his thoughts.'[5]

Henry contributed to the second issue of *The Calcutta Review* 'a long and very interesting chapter of Punjab history'. Thereafter he contributed two, three or even four major articles to each number. 'His fertility, indeed was marvellous.' And his contributions were gravid with 'important facts accompanied by weighty opinions and wise suggestions'[6]. He was a trial to editors because he thought faster than he could write. Sentences were left unfinished and sometimes a word or a phrase would stand by itself in the middle of a page, but Honoria always knew how to link the disjointed fragments and straighten out Henry's sentences. His handwriting was a trial to his friends in his lifetime and is now a trial to historians, 'and as the copyists whom he tried only made matters worse, there was sometimes ludicrous confusion in his sentences as they came from the hands of the native printers'.[7] But Honoria and Sir John Kaye were admirable sub-editors and Henry was a very cooperative writer, enjoining them eagerly to cut and prune. 'There was, indeed, a charming candour and modesty about him as a writer: an utter absence of vanity, opinionativeness, and sensitive egotism about small things.'[8] This contrasts with his touchiness in all that concerned his career. His inner struggle with concern for the bubble reputation was unceasing and he was only finally victorious in this when he lay on his deathbed.

Henry Lawrence was not a great writer but he almost had the making of one, and his literary merits have hardly been sufficiently recognised by previous biographers. With a powerful mind and a warm and vivid imagination he had an Irish gift for finding a telling phrase. Moreover he combined a powerful memory with that capacity to discern structure in a great jumble of disparate facts, which marks a first-rate scientist or historian. If he had concentrated on the writing of history, he could have become a great historian. His account of the Punjab at the time of Ranjit Singh's death is worthy to be compared with Tacitus's famous account of Rome on the death of Tiberius. His articles in *The Calcutta Review* on the contemporary history of the Punjab attracted the interest of the new Governor-General, Sir Henry Hardinge, who 'saw at once that the writer possessed that practical knowledge of men and things that, in the conjuncture then approaching, would render him an invaluable auxiliary, and he longed for an opportunity to call Lawrence to his presence'.[9]

Before long news came that Honoria had permission to join Henry at Katmandu. She answered in her joy: 'How delightfully snug we shall be! How much we shall read and write and talk and think and *pyarkurro* one another! How strong we shall become! How we shall teach Tim and grow wise and good ourselves.'

Early in the nineteenth century effective power in Nepal had passed into the hands of Bhim Sen, the chief of the powerful Thappa clan. The ruling family continued to enjoy the wealth and glory of monarchy but without power or responsibility. In 1837 Bhim Sen fell from power and two years later he died. The Maharajah was well disposed to the mass of his subjects but his conduct was 'detestable as regards the chiefs' and he apparently believed himself to be under a spell of enchantment as regards his son, a brutal, half-insane boy who demanded a share of power which was conceded by his father in such a way that it was impossible to say where authority lay. Henry Lawrence called these two 'Mr Nepal' and 'Master Nepal' but there was also 'Mrs Nepal', the Rani, a silly, self-centred woman who was ruled by violent passions of avarice, hate and ambition. The great aim of each of these three was to oust the others and murder all his other opponents. There was, however, another actor in this sordid drama. A few months before Henry's arrival Matabar Singh, a nephew of Bhim Sen, had been brought back from exile in India where he had been living at Simla on an allowance given by the British Government. His ostensible purpose in returning was to side with the Queen but his true aim was to dominate all as his uncle, Bhim Sen, had dominated. He was brave and determined but he was as unscrupulous as the rest. He thought nothing of eliminating his opponents by wholesale proscriptions, but lacked judgment in carrying out this dangerous operation. For two years he was in and out of office, failing to consolidate his position partly because he murdered so many of his enemies that the rest combined against him out of fear for their own lives, and partly because he was too vain to realise that the Maharajah, while heaping him with honours, was also plotting his downfall. At midnight on 17th May 1845 the King sent for his minister on urgent business and had him murdered in his own presence, the Queen's lover being one of the principal executioners. Henry summed up the resulting situation in a letter to Thomason: 'Mr and Mrs Nepal are very good just now; the youth rather grumpy, the lady on the stilts; the papa rather frightened at his own heroism in mangling the corpse of the dead lion. He writes and says he killed him, but he only hacked at him when dead.' Edwardes summed it up: 'This slow murder of the minister . . . took . . . two long years. The victim was in exile and had to be enticed. He was a Gurkha and his suspicious nature had to be lulled. He was ambitious and he had to be fooled with power. He had an uncle to avenge and he had to be fed with human blood. He was as brave as a lion and he had to be killed by cowards.' 'Twelve hours after the murder, not a voice was heard in favour of the man who the day before had been everything,'[10] said Henry in a letter to Lord Auckland. A few weeks later Henry met two of the murderers riding in one buggy with Jang Bahadur, Matabar's nephew, who was strongly suspected of complicity in his uncle's murder. Eventually Jang Bahadur restored the Shogunate established by Bhim Sen, an arrangement which gave Nepal a century of peace and independence.

Before that the story reads like a mad nightmare. It is recorded in great detail in the Lawrence papers, but is very hard to understand. At times it baffled even Henry Lawrence, and his judgments were not always consistent. His official duty was to witness events without trying to influence them except by an occasional tactful warning, which was usually disregarded. For the most part his handling of these affairs was approved by the Government of India, but occasionally he received a mild rebuke for slightly exceeding his instructions, and once he was told that his official letters to the *Durbar* were too 'dictatorial'. He was not by nature a good career diplomat but eventually he acquired a high degree of diplomatic skill, in his relations with Indians if not always with his own countrymen.

The court life of Nepal had a polish which made its barbarism the more revolting. But the *Journals of Honoria Lawrence* show a happy and smiling peasantry and Henry, writing to Lord Auckland, testified that he had neither witnessed nor heard a single act of oppression since he arrived. Writing to John Nicholson Honoria went further: 'I do not believe that in Nepal one man out of a thousand lies down at night hungry or rises without knowing where he will get his day's food,' a state of affairs which she contrasted unfavourably with London. Kaye adds that 'the Henry Lawrences were not among those who could see nothing good in native Indian institutions and nothing defective in our own.' Henry's letter to Lord Auckland continues: 'The Gurkhas will always intrigue and will generally be as insolent as they are permitted to be but they know our power too well to molest us, unless in some such catastrophe as would cause a general insurrection in India. They would then be quick enough in stirring themselves, but they have no means of acting in the plains . . . The country is a magnificent one. Thirty thousand men could take it in two months without fear or failure. The strategic and other advantages would be enormous. I see the advantage of *us* taking the country whenever the Gurkhas oblige us to do so but I have no wish to hasten the measure.'[11] This judgment is made more explicit in a letter to George Clerk: 'The fair and honest way of dealing with the Gurkhas is to let them distinctly know our power, so that they may not commit themselves, for hitherto their vanity has been so flattered that they are up to any absurdity.'[12] Eventually, they sent Jang Bahadur to London to see British power for himself. He advised the Gurkhas to stay in their hills. Which they did, both in 1857 and ever after.

During their time in Nepal the Lawrences felt a great need of people of their own kind whom they could look up to and who would advise them about the education of their children. However they had only three companions. Captain Smith, the Captain of the bodyguard, though no doubt plucky, was 'bullying and overbearing and crouching with a zig zag up and down notion of truth'. Dr Christie was so stupid and full of fixed ideas that he often misunderstood what was said, and if he read a newspaper often took it to mean the opposite of what it said. When Smith went he was replaced by Captain Ottley who brought his wife with him. They were no improvement. 'In the trio who form our sole society . . . inanity, prejudice, apathy, selfishness and falsehood are all I discern,' wrote Honoria. She added unconvincingly, 'Yet this is the stuff that respectable, worthy, excellent people are made of.' Both Smith and Ottley had blazing rows with Henry and, reading between the lines, it seems that Dr Christie was so frightened of Honoria that he would say anything that came into his head. It must have been an ordeal to be marooned in a Himalayan valley with that formidable pair, but Smith, Christie and the Ottleys do seem to have been made of very coarse clay. Try as they would, Henry and Honoria could not help despising them. Smith was an incorrigible liar, grossly insolent, up to his ears in debt and not straight with his creditors; and after the first two months did no work. When he was recalled he stole the Lawrences' cook and still expected them to feed him.

Later in his career Henry Lawrence was unrivalled at getting the best out of fellow countrymen. But these were men he had chosen himself. He had inherited Smith and Christie, but Ottley was his own choice. We do not know how he analysed what had gone wrong, but he made no more such mistakes. As a replacement for Ottley he asked for Harry Lumsden, 'Lumsden of the Guides'.

Henry and Honoria were, however, very happy in their own company and with their children. Alick had some psychological obstacle which prevented him learning to count properly. This was treated by Honoria as naughtiness and there was a dreadful conflict of wills between mother and son. Freud was not born but the Lawrences were right to think that even without him wise advice from outside would have helped them to bring up their children. Victorian attitudes to children are now sometimes hard to understand and this may lead us to misjudge our ancestors. There was much happiness in Victorian childhood, as well as troubles, which are sometimes over-publicised.

The Lawrences had a summer cottage at Koulia, 1,800 feet above Katmandu, where many very happy family days were passed. Once Henry was there for a few days with Alick and Lawrie Pemberton, a playmate for Alick whom the Lawrences were looking after while his parents were in the plains. When it rained Henry read to the boys and they recited hymns and *The Lays of Ancient Rome*. Then he told them stories of Joseph and his brothers, and of Nelson – not concealing his 'political atrocities' and his desertion of his wife. Big tears rolled down Alick's cheeks when he heard of the Hero's death and of Joseph's recognition of his brethren. It rained hard but they played as contentedly as if they were out and, when it cleared up, they went out 'skipping like little lambs'. 'A delightful day,' wrote Henry in the diary which by a great effort of will he kept spasmodically for about four months. And at the end of a long letter to Thomason about public affairs he added: 'I divert my mind from the sweets of politics by tumbling on the green with Tim and young Pemberton, teaching them to read, write, and jump; and my admirable wife says I understand the philosophy of education to perfection.'

On 24th January 1845 a second son was born, Henry Waldemar

Lawrence, the first white baby born in Nepal, my grandfather. Honoria, who had been seriously ill during her pregnancy, was recovering when suddenly she became desperately ill, an illness attributed to Dr Christie's incompetence but later skilfully treated by a German doctor in the suite of Prince Waldemar of Prussia. The Prince was a noted traveller and explorer who had been given permission to visit Katmandu. Henry found him 'modest and unassuming . . . an excellent specimen of royalty'. When Honoria got better, she wrote that she felt 'as if I had been buried for twelve months . . . Everything I tried to understand was like writing on blotting paper . . . I thought the time was passed for my ever being of use to anyone and that, if I lived, it would only be as a burden, a sorrow, even to him who loves me best.'

When Honoria was not ill, the days passed pleasantly. After breakfast, there were prayers, and then the beggars came. About eighty lame, blind, aged and lepers were on their list for daily help. Henry made it a rule to give away one-third of his income and sometimes much more. He and Honoria hardly noticed what they ate or what they wore and, though they had to keep up a certain state, from this time on they always had much more money than they needed for themselves. Henry's great charity was the foundation of the hill schools which he began to plan in Nepal. The barrack children of the British forces in India, and especially the girls, were growing up in dreadful conditions, so dreadful that nearly all of them died in childhood. Henry planned to establish hill schools for them where boys and girls could be brought up together in a good climate, properly fed and educated and started in life. He solicited gifts for this purpose and gave generously himself, but it was a hard struggle. The Government of India did not answer letters and many of those canvassed privately were unenthusiastic. There were bureaucratic difficulties and it was thought that the soldiers would not part with their children. To his friend Havelock, Henry wrote: 'I have met with so many rebuffs that even my audacity has been insufficient.' The Lawrences did not give in, all difficulties melted away and in a few years Sanawar in the Simla hills was a flourishing school looked back on with warm affection by those who were its pupils. 'Send him to Sanawar and make a man of him' was one of the options for Kim a generation later. Sanawar and its sister foundations the Lawrence School at Lovedale in the Nilgiri Hills and Lawrence College at Ghora Gali in the Murree Hills are now among India's leading public schools, using the phrase in the English sense and India in the old sense as including Pakistan.

At the end of 1845 both Henry and Honoria felt that it was time to leave Nepal. Honoria had to go home for her health and Alick had reached the age at which European children no longer thrived in

India. Henry was thirty-nine, he had had time to look before and after, and he was ready for a move. In his own words he was 'more aged in constitution and appearance and yet I often feel very young in all respects, ignorant of much I ought to know, frivolous, unsettled and uncertain . . . I have seldom been idle but always desultory and distracting my attention from any continued course of study or action.'

Desultory and erratic he was, but no one else would have thought him frivolous. His reading was wide, though he had a habit of skimming and was generally reading several books at once. As an author he was very fertile and energetic but he was not satisfied. Typically he entered in his journal on 29th July 1845: 'A busy but not very profitable week has passed. Desultory habits, thoughts and occupations are my bane. Try.' A few weeks later he wrote: 'I should like to make rules for myself but having often done so and broken them, I will simply write that I'll try to look after myself as to Anger, Tidiness, Procrastination, Regularity. To do as far as possible any Nepal work before breakfast and to devote Saturday to bring up all arrears of Nepal work and letter writing. Sunday to be kept holy as the day of rest and preparation for heaven.' After leaving Nepal he wrote on 7th January 1846: 'We have had two most happy years here . . . We have gained some experience and, I trust, will both be the better for our seclusion.'

The years of preparation were over. The war drums were beating, and eight strenuous years of conflict, military and political, lay ahead.

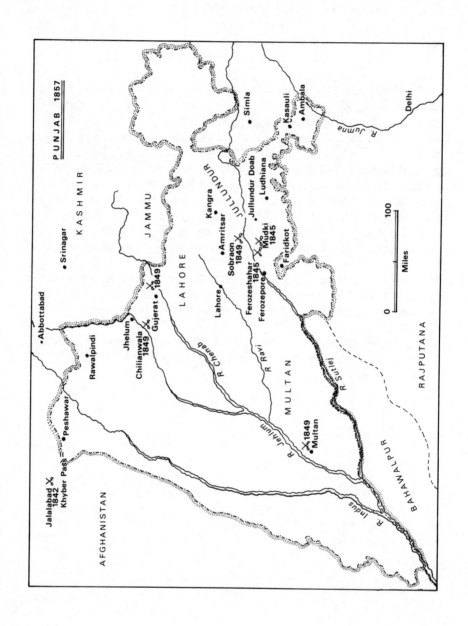

PUNJAB 1857

PART SIX

THE PUNJAB

1846–52

CHAPTER 10

The Uncrowned King of the Punjab

(i) Before the Treaty of Bhairowal

While Henry Lawrence was regaining his strength in Nepal, the heirs of Ranjit Singh were tearing each other to pieces in the Punjab. With each act of violence among the rulers the soldiery found themselves less subject to political control. The *Khalsa*, as the Sikh army was called, was an extraordinary institution. It ran its affairs through committees of soldiers, and therefore has been compared to Cromwell's army, but it was more like the Cossacks, splendid fighters, egalitarian of a sort, but lacking the rudiments of political organisation. In effect, the *Khalsa* fixed their own pay, increased their numbers and ordered more cannon, till the state was on the verge of bankruptcy. The soldiers had been trained by European officers but their own Generals were not trained in European warfare. They did not, for instance, use maps. The soldiers, on the other hand, were well trained and had excellent artillery, better than anyone on the British side appreciated. Henry's first estimate of the Sikh artillery had underestimated it, but he had to some extent revised his views. In battle the *Khalsa* were well disciplined but in politics they had no discipline at all, and even as soldiers, when they were not in the firing line, they were volatile. General Allard, a French General serving with Ranjit Singh, had said, '*Les nôtres se battront bien, mais une fois*' (Our people will fight well, but only once.) Unlike Ranjit Singh, the *Khalsa* had no sense of their own limitations. So they spoke openly of advancing to Delhi and beyond, and a conflict with the British was generally assumed to be mainly a question of time. On the British side there had long been many who looked forward to a fight with unbecoming eagerness, but the higher authorities, though firm, were conciliatory. Sir Henry Hardinge, the Governor-General, quietly strengthened his defences to the north-west without doing anything that could seem to threaten the Sikhs. Although he did nothing to precipitate the clash, he could not postpone it for ever.

Ranjit Singh had in effect no heir, so that the Sikh magnates were left to fight it out among themselves. After a number of political murders they became understandably frightened of each other, but still more frightened of their army. They did not want to try conclusions with the British but they could not control the *Khalsa*. It was said that if there was a war with the British, the Sikh rulers would gain in either event. If they won, their dominions would be enlarged, and if they lost the *Khalsa* would be curbed. The nominal ruler was Dhulip Singh, a little boy whom Ranjit Singh had accepted as his son, though everyone knew that his true father was a low-caste Hindu. His mother, the Rani Jindan, was beautiful, high-spirited and ambitious but her view of politics did not extend beyond a short-sighted concern for her own interests. And even in the court of Ranjit Singh she was notorious for her loose morals. Altogether the Sikh state had become a ship without a rudder, when on 13th December 1845 the Sikh army lurched into an invasion of British India. The British Commander in Chief, Lord Gough, was a fine old warrior of Anglo-Irish stock, who was immensely popular with the troops, but an uncertain tactician. When his Irish blood was up, he would attack regardless of reconnaissance or artillery preparation, but at other times he was capable of near fatal delay. When the test came, the Sikhs turned out to be more formidable than anyone on the British side had foreseen. The invaders were held – but only just held – at the drawn battles of Mudki and Ferozeshahar at which last battle George Broadfoot, George Clerk's successor as Agent to the Governor-General, was killed.

Frederick Currie, now secretary to the Government of India, sent an urgent summons to Henry Lawrence: 'Lose no time in coming, you are a long way off.' This message arrived when Henry and Honoria had just reached British territory on their way back from Nepal. Henry started at once and rode headlong to join the army, leaving Honoria and the children to make their way back to England. He stayed with John on the way and astonished everyone by arriving riding a camel and wearing John's leather breeches, which did not fit him. Before he arrived, Hardinge had appointed Henry to be Broadfoot's successor as his Agent for the Affairs of the Punjab and the North-West Frontier. An Agent in Anglo–Indian usage was a definite rank in the hierarchy, one who exercised not merely the powers usually possessed by an ambassador in the days before telegrams when an ambassador really did represent his sovereign, but plenary and discretionary powers which enable him to make decisions and effect military dispositions in a fashion which would have startled any representative of Britain in Europe 'save Stratford Canning himself' (Morison's phrase).

Henry took on his new functions with zest. He already knew the people he would have to deal with and the precise circumstances of their various inheritances. At this stage of his career he was particularly fortunate in his chief. Lord Hardinge, the hero of Albuera, had as a young man been one of Wellington's most trusted lieutenants in the Peninsular War. He was the best type of soldier. Conservative in politics and no genius, he had an enormous amount of common sense. Very brave and skilful in war, he was yet a man of peace. Completely unpretentious, he was quick to recognise merit and generous in his appreciation of it. Henry and he took to each other at once and became close friends, so much so that Hardinge was accused of relying too much on the Lawrences.

It is at this point that John Lawrence entered the mainstream of Indian history. Henry and John were very different but at the same time more alike than was first apparent. Both had immensely strong independent characters with a power to penetrate to the heart of a situation which amounted to genius. Both were born with retentive memories, and had developed uncommonly good powers of judgment. Both were brave and both had an immense devotion to duty. For John duty was 'the stern daughter of the voice of God' but for Henry she was more like a muse. Both were deeply Christian but John hid his faith from prying eyes even more than Henry did.

Henry was less predictable and very touchy, often taking disagreement for personal antagonism. He was correspondingly sensitive to sympathetic treatment from those in authority over him, such as he received from George Clerk and Henry Hardinge, but not from Dalhousie. John by contrast was rough, gruff and imperturbable, with the skin of a bear. He had a warm heart but he hid it from all except those who were closest to him. John was a slave driver, asking indeed nothing that he could not do himself, but slow to praise, believing that praise 'puts wind in a man's head'. He was unshakably fair to all but grew increasingly dour. So he was greatly respected but not much loved. Henry was full of fire and imagination. He loved all men, even some dreadful villains, and was loved in return. And as John was the first to point out, he had a firmer grip on men. It was well said that Henry was a poet whose material was the lives of men.

John had now been ten years in India, thoroughly learning his trade in the district of Delhi, then India's school of statesmanship. As a junior but still responsible officer at Panipat he had been on his own, wearing semi-oriental clothes, talking his rough but effective Persian and Urdu to all and sundry, and seeing so few Europeans that, when he did, he could not always find English words. Quick and thorough in all he did, he acquired an extraordinary reputation as a detector of crime. The saying was 'Jan Larens *sabh janta*' – 'John Lawrence knows everything'. His rough manners and boisterous humour were disconcerting but he was accepted as a man of good will.

In 1845 John was Commissioner of Delhi, which was not merely the historic capital, but also the base from which all fresh supplies must reach the army on the Sutlej. John did wonders in bringing up the heavy artillery, in requisitioning and loading carts with other supplies, and in making sure that everything was paid for and arrived on time where it was needed. In consequence the army was well supplied for the crowning victory of Sobraon just sixty days after the opening campaign. As an old soldier, Hardinge served in the campaign and made an important contribution to the victory, usually but not always respecting the authority of Gough as Commander in Chief. Henry Lawrence was at the heart of the battle of Sobraon, standing beside Hardinge and, characteristically as an artillery officer, seeing to it that the guns did their part. Comradeship in arms was the foundation of the friendship between Henry Hardinge and Henry Lawrence. At Sobraon after a hard fight the Sikhs were decisively defeated, but still formidable. The war could have dragged on for a long time but the Rani and her advisers at Lahore, learning that the Governor-General had decided against annexation, shut the gates against their own army and asked the British for terms.

It was rumoured that the Sikh Generals had all along had a secret understanding with the British. It is true that if they had pressed their advantages in the early stages of the campaign, they stood to win a signal victory. But Henry Lawrence and Hardinge, who were in a good position to judge, agreed that the Sikh generals had done their best. They were however not very good generals and, as they did not foresee victory, they made themselves in Hardinge's phrase 'as little obnoxious as possible to the English'.

The British terms were moderate. Hardinge had rejected annexation of the Punjab and its dependencies as impracticable. The Jullundur Doab, the land between the rivers Sutlej and Beas, was however annexed and John Lawrence was placed in charge of it. The British were to receive an indemnity of 15,000,000 rupees; there was to be a Council of Regency until the Maharajah came of age in 1854; British troops were to remain in the Punjab till the end of the year; and Henry Lawrence was to be British Resident at Lahore. The Sikh *sirdars* 'now found it to their interest to re-establish some kind of authority for the little Maharajah, and his vixen mother under the protection of the victors of the war'.[1]

On Henry's arrival at Lahore in early 1846 one of his first actions was to invite everyone he met to dinner. But there was no light. So he said 'someone must drink a bottle of beer'. He then produced a pound of tallow candles and placed one in the empty bottle. As more bottles were drunk the party ended in a blaze of light. This remained one of Henry's favourite means of illumination.

The British Government did not propose to interfere in the internal administration of the Punjab beyond advice and good offices. Hardinge's instructions to Henry were to give 'such friendly counsels as those which passed between the two governments in the time of Ranjit Singh'; but then the Sikhs were unbeaten and there was no British army at Lahore. So Henry Lawrence's influence was decisive, even if his direct power was strictly limited both by treaty and by his instructions. He was to work through the Sikh *sirdars* whom he knew intimately and understood. But the survivors of the murderous intrigues of recent years were a poor lot. The Rani's influence was powerful among them and her lover, Lal Singh, had more character than most of them. So he was the obvious choice as Chief Minister. There were pressing problems which had to be decided by someone. The swollen army was still under arms and had to be paid, reduced and reorganised, but Henry Lawrence thought that provided they were handled sensibly, any danger from them would pass. He wrote to Currie: 'No very strong ties bind them. While actually in arms they hold together from that strong feeling of fidelity to their salt, and to each other, which so generally prevails from one end of India to the other. But once subdued and broken up, the materials are too incongruous to be easily brought together again.' It must be remembered that the Sikhs were only about a sixth of the population of the Punjab, there were many Moslems and Hindus of various kinds in their army, and communal rivalries could be bitter.

Ranjit Singh's Kingdom had known little government of any kind since the great Maharajah died, and that remarkable man's methods of rule had been unusual. Reporting to the Government of India, Henry Lawrence wrote: 'For many years Ranjit Singh kept no accounts at all, and men now alive tell tales of his conquering a hundred villages one day and giving them away *viva voce* the next, keeping neither a record of the fact nor granting a *sunnud* for the gift. In the same way he trusted to his memory for many years complicated accounts of expenditure to his troops (generally in grain and kind). And periodically he allowed the rough memoranda of those who were responsible to himself to be destroyed.' Many of the administrators appointed by Ranjit Singh were still in office and it was understandable that they were perplexed by a new system which required 'an application to business, a division of labour and minute superintendence in all branches'.[2] So anyone who had occasion to refer his case to central government was likely to apply directly to Henry Lawrence whose word was known to be final. At this early stage, and with every wish to govern through the Durbar as far as was possible, he found himself the *de facto* ruler. His purpose was to combine the personal nature of oriental rule with British standards of government, which were at that time unknown in the Punjab. At this stage of his career 'the peculiar genius which he had for human relationships and decided action found full expression'.[3]

Throughout the countryside every official, high or low, accepted office almost entirely for what might be gained by bribes. Henry had no illusions about the men through whom he would have to rule but he did not consider them irredeemable. In *Adventures of an Officer* he put his own views into the mouth of the hero, Bellasis: 'the true philosophy then is to cultivate their better qualities, and make the best of their defects; treating them with what indulgence is possible, respecting their religious prejudices, but at the same time obliging them to respect yours, and not to treat you as if you were an unclean animal'; and to inculcate a good routine as the best safeguard in time of need.

Appeals to the Resident were more than one man could hope to hear, but Henry's eye had been caught by a young man, Lieutenant Herbert Edwardes, who had made a reputation by a series of witty and penetrating articles in the *Delhi Gazette*, signed under the pseudonym Brahminee Bull, a supposed brother of one John Bull, a Director of the East India Company. One day Henry looked up from his papers and said to Edwardes: 'Would you like to be my assistant?' The reply was affirmative. Henry said, 'Well that's settled,' and went on writing. The Governor-General gave Henry a free hand to choose the best Europeans in India to work with him in the vast new provinces for which he had required sudden responsibility.

From this time he always carried a little notebook in which he wrote down everything he heard about any promising young man and, when the right berth for him was there, he asked for his services. In this way he gathered round himself 'Henry Lawrence's Young Men'. Leaving aside his brothers John and George, the greatest of these was John Nicholson. Herbert Edwardes, Henry's first biographer, was a typical member of this group. Henry explained his work to Currie at this early stage of British indirect rule:

> The native letters alone which are addressed to me require several hours daily attention . . . Nine men out of ten who come to me need not, or ought not to come; but until all have been patiently heard, I have no means of ascertaining who should, or who should not, have come . . . At present Lieutenant Edwardes' chief duties are hearing complaints and talking to complainants, gaining and condensing intelligence and translating papers; but there are a hundred little matters that can hardly be detailed, but which may be easily under-

stood when I say that from early dawn till 7.00 p.m. – fourteen hours, he is, with scarcely more than an hour's exception for breakfast, more or less employed in public duty. We ride together every morning for two or three hours, but it is not for pleasure, but invariably to see places and persons connected with business. We are then seated at our table till dark.

Henry's touch never failed with those British or Indians whom he had himself chosen. But he had his difficulties with British officials inherited from a previous administration. Mackeson, a very able man, who had been a difficult chief in the First Afghan War, was now a very prickly subordinate.

The central provinces of the Sikh Kingdom were quiet but trouble brewed on the periphery. And quiet was relative, even in the more settled areas near Lahore and Amritsar. At the time a great part of the Punjab was desert. There was a thin green strip of cultivation along each of the five rivers, but down the middle of each *doab* or mesopotamia there was a wedge of wasteland up to fifty miles broad. The only inhabitants of this desert were untamed nomads who raided the cattle of their settled neighbours at night, driving them off into the wilderness where no one could find them. There might be abundant water in the rains but for the rest of the year life depended on water holes which were toilsome to make and therefore few and far between. At the centre of each *doab* water was not found at less than eighty or ninety feet or sometimes much deeper.

In May 1846 trouble broke out at the fort of Kangra in that part of the foothills of the Himalayas which had been ceded to the British as part of the Jullundur Doab. This place was in the hands of a chief who with his garrison of three hundred men declared that he would not give up his charge, unless Ranjit Singh returned from the dead to demand the keys of Kangra. This was not out of character for that time and place. Curiously enough the rock of Kangra was the centre round which Henry's novel *The Adventures of an Officer*, had revolved. The hero Bellasis, on being invested by Ranjit Singh with the charge of Kangra, had been instructed by the crafty old Ranjit to admit no one, neither 'my son, minister or servant, bear they my seal or not – no one gains admission, not even myself, until thrice I have thrust my head in at the wicket and thrice thou hast thyself examined my beard'. This is an order which Ranjit actually gave to one of his governors.

The fort of Kangra stands on a precipitous and isolated rock four hundred feet high and is defended by strong walls. The only access is by a winding passage defended by seven gates, and though often attacked, Kangra had never been taken. The other hill forts, with which the upper part of the Jullundur Doab is dotted, submitted to their new rulers but Kangra held out. John Lawrence, who was immediately responsible, saw that if Kangra was not quickly reduced the war might break out again along the hills. So he sent some heavy guns and deputed young Harry Lumsden – Lumsden of the Guides – to find a way of getting guns to a roadless place in rough country where no siege guns had been seen before.

Hearing what was happening, Henry Lawrence rushed at once to Kangra bringing with him Rajah Dina Nath, an able, avaricious and influential member of the Sikh Durbar in the hope that he could persuade the garrison of three hundred veteran Sikhs to surrender quietly. On this occasion he promised the rebels their arrears of pay, a safe conduct, and travelling expenses to their homes. But in vain.

Yet within a week Harry Lumsden, most ably assisted by Robert Napier, had constructed a temporary road for the guns to travel on and brought them forty miles to the foot of Kangra. John Lawrence describes the scene:

> In the evening a deputation from the Sikh garrison came out . . . the members, three greybeards, were quiet and courteous but determined. At last, as . . . they were on the eve of departure I suggested that they should stay and see the guns at break of day ascend the hill. They listened and agreed but with a gesture which denoted incredulity. At four a.m. they were awakened by vociferous cheering. They started from their rough beds and rushed out, believing that it was a sally from the garrison. They were soon undeceived; for a few moments later there appeared a couple of large elephants slowly and majestically pulling an eighteen pounder, tandem fashion, with a third pushing from behind. In this manner gun after gun wound its way along the narrow pathway, and, with the help of hundreds of *sepoys*, safely rounded the sharp corners which seemed to make further progress impossible. The Sikh elders looked on with amazement, but said not a word. When the last gun had reached the plateau, they took their leave. In an hour the white flag was raised.

The affair of Kangra passed off quietly but here and elsewhere the ground was strewn with tinder; and sparks fell on it from time to time. Henry's personal relations with the Sikhs and other Punjabis might be of the best, but it was not to be expected that vigorous people, who had suddenly lost much of their independence and seemed likely to lose more, should not have bursts of resentment. These were apt to break out suddenly and for unexpected reasons. And they had to be quelled quickly if they were not to spread. On 21st April 1846, a few weeks after the end of the war, a British sentry in Lahore thought he was being impeded in his duties by a herd of cows and 'in self defence, as he says, he cut at them', brutally using the sharp side of his sword. Three or four animals were wounded and in protest the shops were closed. Henry 'sent word to Lal Singh that the sentry should be punished but that he must desire the shops to be opened; and I further requested that he would punish those who tried to create a disturbance by inducing people to shut their shops.' Henry went into the city with two assistants and a dozen *sowars* to explain to the people what had happened and to assure them of protection. They were about halfway through and 'had quite satisfied the owners of two of the animals, and were still in the house of the second talking to him, when we heard a disturbance outside'. They went out, found a scuffle going on and were plentifully assaulted by brickbats from the neighbouring houses. 'Scarcely a man or horse escaped unhurt and Lieutenant Edwardes was severely struck on the head.' Henry had the gates closed immediately, put the guards on the alert and sent for Lal Singh and Tej Singh and told them 'to hand over to me the owners of the houses from which we had been pelted, as well as any armed men found in the streets'. After some prevarication the instigators, who were Brahmins, were handed over and their ringleader was later hanged, but no other life was taken and the ebullition subsided quietly. This ended the event known to history as the Lahore Cow Row. Henry's final comment was: 'Had I been aware of the extent of the excitement that prevailed, I should not have gone into the city; as it was I acted, as under somewhat similar circumstances I had some years ago done at Ambala, when I found that a few kind words very soon appeased the mob.' Sparks continued to fall on the tinder but it never burst into flame if one of the Lawrences was there.

Friendly relations with a strong independent state in the Punjab had served British interests well for nearly forty years, and it was hoped to keep the Sikh Kingdom in being. But it did not follow that all the conquests of Ranjit Singh should be kept in one piece. Moreover there was a problem of finance. Under the terms of peace, as already stated, the Sikh Government undertook to pay to the British an indemnity of one and a half *crores* of rupees, approximately one and a half million pounds. Only a third of this was coming from Lahore, but among Ranjit Singh's conquests were vast tracts of hill country, including the fabulous vale of Kashmir. Gulab Singh, the Hindu Rajah of Jammu in the Himalayan foothills adjoining Kashmir, and an influential feudatory of Lahore, had long cast covetous eyes on this alpine kingdom. He had been astute enough to keep out of the way at the time when the inheritors of Ranjit's power were destroying each other; his two brothers and his nephew fell victims, but Gulab survived. He had stood studiously aloof in the Anglo–Sikh War, neither taking part in the invasion of British territory nor quarrelling with the other magnates of the Sikh Kingdom. Thus he was in a strong position to take a leading part in the peace settlement. He offered to pay two-thirds of the war indemnity, namely one *crore* of rupees, if he was made Maharajah of Kashmir. Henry advised acceptance. Gulab Singh had the money and was well pleased with his purchase. So the matter was agreed.

Nothing in the Punjab was straightforward. The existing governor of Kashmir was Sheikh Imam ud din, a Moslem servant of the Sikh state. The Sheikh's attitude to his new master was ambiguous and he refused to surrender his charge, being secretly encouraged in this by Lal Singh, the Queen's lover, who was also Chief Minister. Gulab Singh, though a very successful politician in the then oriental style was not an effective general, being too miserly to equip his troops properly or send them in sufficient numbers. So he was unable to take possession of Kashmir. How then was he to be put on the throne? The Durbar were unwilling to bestir themselves. However under British pressure they allocated what would now be called a task force, numbering ten thousand men, to take Kashmir from Imam ud din and give it to Gulab Singh; but the men were reluctant to move, in order to hand on the jewel of the Sikh Empire to a man who was cordially disliked by the *Khalsa*, or to move at all. Eventually John had to tell the officer that their *jaghirs* would be confiscated and they would be imprisoned unless they obeyed their orders. Thereupon Henry put himself at the head of the unwilling army. He knew that Lal Singh was acting treacherously against him. So he left John in charge at Lahore and let Lal Singh know that if anything happened to him John had instructions to arrest Lal Singh.

John, left behind in Lahore, was in two minds about his promotion to acting Resident. He wrote to Letitia: 'My new appointment is a splendid, an honorary and responsible berth, but I can't say I like it. I prefer roaming about in tents and riding about the country. Here I am living in the middle of a native town with queens, princes, and such cattle to deal with, and find them a disgusting set.' But he carried out his duties with zest, writing to Henry that he had told Lal Singh that 'if anything occurred to you or the other *sahibs* we would *sefku* him to a certainty. The Rajah has looked quite green ever since.' The Sikh force, with Henry at their head, advanced in spite of hunger and unaccustomed cold, taking orders without demur from the British officers against whom they had been fighting eight months before. Two years later John wrote that it had been 'touch and go whether the Sikh surrendered or the troops went over to him'.[4] In the event Imam ud din, by now thoroughly frightened, surrendered himself personally to Henry, who wrote in a letter to Kaye that he 'trusted to carry the thing through by expedition and by the conviction that a British army was in our rear to avenge us', if anything went wrong. It was a cardinal principle with the Lawrences that in an emergency quick action was essential, but they did not act rashly or precipitately. The Indians said that when Henry Lawrence *Sahib* had looked twice up to heaven and once down to earth and stroked his beard, 'he knew what to do'.

Gulab Singh, who had now been placed on the throne of Kashmir, had a bad reputation among the British, partly due to the unfavourable portrait drawn of him by Henry Lawrence in his writings. In *Adventures of an Officer* he had written that Gulab Singh yearly added to his territories 'by conquest or the terror of his name. He had overrun the whole district between Kashmir and Attock: and inflicted such terrible vengeance on the people of Sudan, a large district southeast of Mozaffarabad cutting up, maiming, flaying to the amount, it is said, of twelve thousand persons, that the men of Dundi and Salti, two adjoining territories, sent in their submission, but begged not to see his face'. Gulab Singh remains an enigma to this day. There is no doubt that he was avaricious and that his avarice could lead him to be oppressive, that he was unscrupulous and cruel, and that he was a past master of deceit and concealment, but it hardly seems that what he concealed was always bad. Henry describes his *persona:* 'In manner Gulab Singh is highly mild and affable; his features are good, nose aquiline and expression pleasing, though rather heavy. Indefatigable in business, he sees after everything himself; hardly able to sign his name, he looks after his own accounts, and often has the very *gram* for his horses weighed out before him.'[5]

In 1846 the immediate practicality was that Henry had to use all his skill and determination to place Gulab Singh on the throne. Henry did not pretend that Gulab was anything but a bad man, yet he said he was no worse than other native rulers. And he never ceased to point out that all native rulers of that time had been brought up in the school of treachery and violence, so that it was hardly reasonable to expect nineteenth-century standards of conduct from them. Moreover, there must have been something about Gulab Singh that appealed to Henry, who had a strong personal influence on the Maharajah, continually urging him to exercise 'justice, mercy and moderation', to make female infanticide a crime in his dominions and to use all his great influence to stop *suttee*. At all times polite to the Maharajah, Henry could on occasion speak very plainly to him. Judging others by himself, the wily ruler trusted no one in his own entourage, but he had boundless confidence in Henry. And remarkably the Christian symbol IHS began to appear on the coinage of Kashmir. There is no conclusive evidence about how this came about, though it is clear that it was in some way connected with Henry Lawrence. An anecdote which I have heard (from the late Mrs Willie Holland) provides a possible explanation. One day the Maharajah was watching Henry at work, and interrupted him with the question, 'Why are the British always successful?' 'Maharajah Sahib, I cannot answer that now. I am very busy.' But after a few minutes he took a piece of paper, wrote on it IHS, and gave it to the Maharajah, who took it to be a talisman. Gulab Singh's gratitude to Henry soon took tangible form in the gift of a *lakh* of rupees to Sanawar school. And a few years ago one of his descendants, a daughter of Dr Karan Singh, the present titular Maharajah of Kashmir, was a pupil there.

Gulab Singh consistently saw his interest to lie in friendship with the British and paid at least some attention to their advice. On his first arrival in Kashmir the people were astonished at his good behaviour. Reporting to the Government of India Henry wrote to Currie that having invited the two British officers in Kashmir, Vans Agnew and John Nicholson, 'to tell me all the good and all the bad they could discover in the Maharajah's character, I have not been able to discover in these reports or in those of two news writers I employ in Kashmir, that his Highness has committed any act of overt oppression. I consider his avarice to be his one great vice.' Later at the crisis of the Indian Mutiny the Maharajah threw his weight on the side of the British, sending a contingent of troops to fight at the siege of Delhi under the leadership of Richard Lawrence, the youngest of the brothers.

Henry had taken great pains to make it clear to all that the new ruler of Kashmir was to be master in his own domains. For the time being two British officers remained with him 'until affairs are brought into some order . . . but,' Henry added, 'I doubt the advantage of permanently leaving an officer with the Maharajah, though perhaps it may prove useful to depute a respectable Native Agent, who can keep government informed without being an incubus on the local authorities and detracting from their credit without himself having any real authority'.

On returning to Lahore Henry had to deal with a new crisis that was the direct result of his success in Kashmir. On surrendering to Henry Lawrence, the Sheikh Imam ud din had placed in his hands three letters showing that in his resistance to Gulab Singh he had been acting on treacherous instructions from no other than Rajah Lal Singh, the *Vizier*. The Sheikh to his credit made it a condition on handing over the letters that it should do 'no injury to Maharajah Dhulip Singh and the independence of the Lahore state'. There was little doubt that the letters were genuine and, if so, it was impossible for the Rajah to remain in office. But first his guilt must be established in open court. At this prospect Lal Singh and his mistress, the Rani, 'were in great distress; the former holding private interviews from morning to night, the latter consulting the astrologers and sacrificing to the gods in favour of the Rajah'. A court of enquiry was established with Currie as President, Henry and John Lawrence and two senior officers also being members. 'The court was to be perfectly open to all and the Sirdars of all degrees were invited to attend.' The hearings, which took place on 4th December 1846, were well attended, the evidence was 'most conclusive, the defence miserably weak, and the court pronounced a unanimous sentence of guilty.' When this was communicated to the Sikh magnates, they acknowledged unanimously that Lal Singh could no longer be *Vizier* and, that being determined, they seemed to dismiss him from their minds, except as a large *jaghirdar* whose income must be recovered to the state without delay. In office he had dismissed as many of the old Sikh soldiers as he could, replacing them with his own creatures: he had reduced the *jaghirs* of the *sirdars* on the plea of public poverty while appropriating enormous grants to himself, his relatives and his servants. 'As a minister therefore he failed to conciliate with either the chiefs or the army and, as a private character, he was personally odious to the Sikh people for his intrigue with Ranjit's widow, or as they regard her, the mother of the *Khalsa*.' Henry had given Lal Singh repeated warnings that his conduct was calculated to rouse implacable opposition, but he had ignored this. A few days after his trial, Lal Singh was escorted to Ferozepore in British territory. Reporting all this officially to Currie, Henry concluded by saying these 'monstrous events . . . have been enacted in perfect peace; perfect quiet reigned in the city and the country. Not a shop was closed or a plough laid aside during the trial, deposition or removal of the *Vizier*; and those who are acquainted with the past history of this unhappy capital, how factiously power has usually been seized in it, how bloodily maintained, and with what violence wrested away, will recognise under British occupation of Lahore a public confidence and sense of security as new as it is complete'.

The time for the British troops to leave Lahore was fast approaching, and Lord Hardinge asked the Durbar formally what arrangements they had made for the future. This caused the greatest excitement. Previous warnings had been given that the British would withdraw by the end of the year. But this had not been believed. And the majority of the *sirdars* were now filled with alarm at the prospect before them. At first the Maharani expressed the most anxious desire for the British to remain, declaring to Henry even on the day when her lover was deposed that 'she would leave the Punjab when we did'. But on second thoughts she began to devote her whole energies to an attempt to win over 'the *sirdars* of high and low degree, and unite them altogether in a scheme of independent government, of which she herself was to be the head'. She won the wholehearted support of Rajah Dina Nath, one of the most successful survivors in Lahore politics, who reckoned that under the Rani's rule he could appropriate vast wealth from the treasury. But the other *sirdars* opposed the Rani with great steadfastness and perseverance. What follows is described in Henry's official report to the Government of India.

After a few days of fierce intrigue it was clear that the Governor-General was not getting what he desired, 'viz. an honest expression of the wants, wishes and opinions of the great body of the chiefs who, during the boyhood of the Maharajah, are the natural representatives of the state'. But the Government of India had made adequate contingency plans. So, on 15th December 1846, Currie held a Durbar, which was 'more fully attended than any state meeting I have yet seen at Lahore'. This great occasion was embellished by many picturesque figures from the countryside, as well as all the principal officers of state.

Currie, presiding, conveyed to the Durbar that the Governor-General:

> would be best pleased could they assure him of their ability to carry on the government alone, unsupported, except by the sincere friendship of the British; but if they thought this was impossible, and they called on the Governor-General to assist them, they must understand that his interference would be complete: He would occupy Lahore, or any other part of the Punjab with what forces he thought advisable; a stipulated sum being paid monthly into the British treasury for the expense of the same; and further that the whole civil and military administration of the Punjab would be subject to the supervision of a British Resident, though conducted by the Durbar and executive officers appointed by them. This arrangement was to hold good till the maturity of the young Maharajah, when the British troops would retire from the Punjab and the British Government recognise its perfect independence.

Dina Nath wanted an adjournment to consult the Maharani, but Currie told him that the Governor-General was not asking the opinion of the Queen Mother, but of the *sirdars* and pillars of the state. Henry Lawrence and Currie then withdrew into another tent, leaving the *sirdars* to themselves. Soon Henry and Currie received a message that everything was agreed except that, as a point of friendship, the Durbar asked for a reduction of the monthly sum they were to pay. After discussing this in the light of the country's resources, the British agreed to reduce the stipulated sum from twenty-four *lakhs* to twenty-two *lakhs* per annum. The two British then returned to the Durbar tent, where fifty-one of the *sirdars* were considered eligible to vote. 'Though there were not a few in that Durbar who were foremost among the war party at this time last year' every single voter on that day preferred 'British protection to a short lived, anarchical independence'.

The Maharani was very angry at first, abusing the chiefs roundly but by holding together and reasoning with her they seem to have brought her to some sort of reason. 'I hear that Tej Singh told her that if she would only keep quiet and not commit herself before the world, he would be her brother and friend; but that, if she persisted in violence and nonsense, he would have nothing to say to her.' At length she accepted the new situation with a good grace, saying repeatedly if not sincerely that the arrangements which had been made had saved her own and her son's life and secured her throne.

(ii) After the Treaty of Bhairowal

Finally the arrangements agreed at Lahore were enshrined in the Treaty of Bhairowal between the two governments which laid down that there was to be a Council of Regency consisting of eight *sirdars*, whose members were not to be 'changed without the consent of the British Resident, acting under the orders of the Governor-General. The power of the Resident extends over every department, and to every extent.' This arrangement was to last until the end of the Maharajah's minority on 4th September 1854. All the *sirdars*, fifty-two in number, assented to these conditions and Henry Lawrence, as British Resident at Lahore, became the uncrowned King of the Punjab.

This Treaty was concluded with proper solemnity and ended with ceremonial visits between the Governor-General and the infant Maharajah, which produced an excellent affect upon the *sirdars*. In reporting this Henry wrote:

It was scarcely more characteristic of the Punjab than of India in general, that the meeting was no sooner fixed than it gave rise to all sorts of reports. Some thought the Maharajah was to be made a prisoner; others that all the *sirdars* were to be seized at once and sent after Rajah Lal Singh to Hindustan (i.e. British India). Nobody was content to think that there was merely to be a meeting. When therefore the interview took place and not only were neither the Maharajah nor the *sirdars* treacherously seized, but both received with even more state and ceremony than was ever shown to Ranjit Singh in the height of his power, the reaction was in proportion and for some days nothing was talked of at Lahore but the auspicious meeting at Bhairowal and 'the escape of the Maharajah' . . . This feeling was confirmed by the subsequent meetings at Lahore and the marked kindness of the Governor-General's manner to the little Maharajah.

The Rani's slave girls, who were her confidential advisers, joined in the congratulations. They 'first praised the honesty of the British and then deduced from it the singular corollary that gratitude required that Her Highness should no longer mourn after Lal Singh whom the British had deposed, but plunge into new intrigues'.

After the Treaty of Bhairowal the intention was still to work through the existing machinery but now British intervention would be immediately and visibly decisive. One of the first results was 'the arrival at the British Residency of complainants from the farthest frontiers of the Punjab seeking redress.' The progress of the news 'that the country is now under our management was curiously marked,' Henry reported, 'by the different dialect, dress and whole appearance of each day's petitioners, as they flocked in from a more and more distant district of the N.W. border'. Meanwhile George Lawrence in Peshawar was reporting privately to his brother 'that on both banks of the Indus the cry of oppression is very loud'. In passing this on to the supreme government, Henry wrote: 'I have called the serious attention of the Durbar to the conduct of their provincial agents, whom they are ready enough to eject. But this I am far from thinking is the surest remedy. A few signal examples are useful, but I tell the Durbar it is better to hold inducements to good than to be making constant changes, for assuredly the shorter the tenure of office the greater will be the plunder and oppression.' Henry's rule was to urge that 'no man or seat could be interfered with on account of his opinions or position, as long as he or they give no offence by their conduct'. Henry had to restrain the zeal of his subordinates, discouraging 'all direct interference and indeed all interference that could be avoided'. By degrees the best of the *sirdars* began to give Henry their sincere cooperation. He singled out for special praise the 'clear head, cold heart, and business like habits of no less a person than Dina Nath, who generally visits me at my house by himself every two or three days, on which occasions he speaks out like a European'. This was all the more encouraging in that earlier, Henry had found Dina Nath to be a choice manipulator of accounts for his own benefit. Henry cared more for the regeneration of those who had been corrupted than anything else.

Sometimes he failed. Under Ranjit Singh there had been no judges in the Punjab. The *kardars* who collected the revenue, and were themselves the principal oppressors, dealt with crimes, if they had a mind to it, but in general things just took their course without either police or courts, unless someone in authority was bribed or an 'importunate widow' made herself such a nuisance that even an official 'which feared not God nor regarded man' found it less trouble to give her her right (Luke 18, v. 2-5). Henry instituted judges who were independent of the *kardars* and in the first instance Rungore Singh, a prominent *sirdar*, was appointed Chief Judge. He, however, wanted to appoint only his own creatures as subordinate judges and the new system seemed likely to be little better than the old. Rungore was 'a rather ill-tempered person of loose habits with little or no principle' but 'after long and anxious consideration I could not discover any man on whose account it would be worth while to displace him. I therefore made much of the *sirdar*, tried to win him to propriety and to make him see that his interest lay in honesty.' Henry helped effectively in a bitter quarrel with his brother over the family property and promised him a suitable *jaghir* if he gave satisfaction as a judge, but Rungore behaved with bad faith and dishonesty throughout. Finally 'his manner and even words were disrespectful to me' and threatening to others. In the end he was caught out concealing several cannon on land under his control and when he was found out said he had been dishonoured and would serve no longer. Henry suggested that the Durbar should take him at his word, they agreed with alacrity and in a few minutes flat appointed one General Khan Singh Man in his place. Henry agreed to this, as he did not know of anyone better, and it turned out that this was not a bad appointment.

Others were appointed to subordinate judgeships in various districts with authority over the troops in their areas. Sirdar Lena Singh was judge of the Sikh homeland, the Manjha. After two or three conversations with Henry he prepared instructions to his subordinates. These were prepared under the orders of the Durbar but Henry thought them to be entirely Lena Singh's 'own concoction' and 'very creditable to his good sense'. And in reporting this to the Governor-General he added: 'Thus it is that I wish as far as possible to allow the Durbar not only to work with their own tools but to prepare their own instructions.'

The most telling criticism made of Henry's regency is that he and his colleagues 'were over active in their humanity and too sudden in their reforms,' as Kaye puts it. Henry agreed. In a letter to Kaye written a few years later he said 'my chief regrets are that we did so much' but 'ill supported by a venial and selfish Durbar' we were 'gradually obliged . . . to act directly when I desired to do so only by advice'. And looking back on this time more than a year later, Henry wrote to the new Governor-General, Lord Dalhousie (on 14th November 1849), that his great difficulty with all his assistants

> was to restrain their impulses and check their hasty judgments, whether it was my brother George at Peshawar, Nicholson, Edwardes, Abbot or Agnew, I occasionally found one and all calculating and arguing as if native chiefs were Europeans, and as if soldiers only just emerged from a five years anarchy were sober and disciplined veterans. All this was gradually righting itself through the zeal and kindliness of these same officers, when the Multan misfortune occurred. The people, soldiers and chiefs were becoming accustomed to us and we to them.

So much so that, when a drunken European sergeant killed a *fakir* and then lay down to sleep beside the corpse, the people waited till he woke and quietly handed him over uninjured to the authorities.

After the Treaty of Bhairowal all was peace in the Punjab except for what Hardinge called 'the perilous passions of the Queen Mother'. But could the tottering Sikh Kingdom really continue to be independent after such blows as it had now received? Henry thought on the whole that it could, provided that the *sirdars* were treated sympathetically, fairly and firmly. However he was not always consistent in his views. In 1845 in an article on the Kingdom of Oudh in *The Calcutta Review*, he had written: 'If ever there was a device for ensuring malgovernment, it is that of a native ruler and minister both relying on foreign bayonets and directed by a British Resident . . . Each of the three may work incalculable mischief but no one of them *can* do good if thwarted by the others.'

During this time he continued to recruit his band of assistants, both civil and military. And now he was able to go ahead with raising that wonderful regiment, The Corps of Guides, which he had conceived in the first few days of the Afghan War. At its head he placed young Harry Lumsden. The Guides were to be active men, good fighters, but also men who could disappear and live unnoticed 'while they hunt secretly for information of all sorts'.[6] For practice they were sent out in ones and twos to bring back detailed descriptions of the places where they had been sent, and to hunt out 'gambling houses, coiners, runaway jailbirds and the like'.[7] They were to get a habit of doing things quietly. 'One ass of a chap', when sent out on a mission, let it be known that he was a servant of the Government. 'This worthy got turned out of the Guides at once.' The *sepoys* of the regular army had a fine record of fidelity and would fight well, but faced with any unaccustomed task, they became like trade unionists in a demarcation dispute. The Guides would turn their hand to everything and it was not long before the utility of this became apparent. They helped both the civil government and the military. 'For example James Abbott in Hazara had immense trouble and little success in tracking a party of hillmen who had in June 1847 murdered three *sepoy* women and some children in cold blood, or again George Lawrence time and again found it necessary to arrange sudden night marches and early morning attacks on recalcitrant villages.' The Guides soon discovered who had done what and the culprits would be suitably punished. Those re-cruited to the Guides were sure to be adventurous. Many of them had been marauders and bandits, but they showed perfect fidelity to their new role. The problem which then arose was how were they to go about their work in secrecy without the regular army shooting them or hanging them as spies, unless they had some sort of uniform? Henry had put them into cool, loose-fitting native clothes in place of the hot stiff European uniforms of the *sepoys*. Lumsden added to this by dressing them uniformly in khaki which 'though not a very flash looking colour on parade' would be very serviceable in the jungles and would escape notice when a red coat would be riddled with shot. For further identification he gave them black belts in place of the buff belts that had been issued, which 'can be seen a mile off'.

The central parts of the Sikh Kingdom were reduced to order with surprising ease. As soon as the people became satisfied that under the new order they would be free from lawlessness and extortion, they settled down to cultivate the land and paid their taxes regularly. But across the Indus and in the mountainous districts, such as Hazara on the borders of Kashmir, tribal anarchy prevailed. There had never been any settled government so there was no proper assessment of taxes, but every few years a Sikh army would come and take what it could get after a stiff fight, leaving a track of devastation behind it. The ravaged districts were then left to their own devices till the next Sikh visitation. In the Old Testament times the kings of Assyria and other potentates practised a not dissimilar rule in the districts that were not under their immediate control, and so it had been ever since. Henry Lawrence entrusted Hazara to the idiosyncratic paternalism of James Abbott. He rapidly imposed order by methods that proved eventually unassimilable to Anglo–Indian bureaucracy.

At the same time John Nicholson was rapidly making his reputation on the North-West Frontier, working happily with George Lawrence at Peshawar. While the beautiful and fertile valley of Bannu across the Indus on the borders of Afghanistan was the peculiar sphere of Herbert Edwardes, Bannu presented many problems, and their resolution is the subject of a classic account in Herbert Edwardes' *A Year on the Punjab Frontier*, from which the quotations in the following pages are taken. In this biography the subjugation of Bannu must stand for a number of very tricky situations which were brought to a happy conclusion by Henry Lawrence's Young Men, in the short time between the treaty of Bhairowal and Henry Lawrence's departure on leave in 1848.

He chose his assistants very carefully and gave each of them an assignment which suited his gifts and experience but would stretch him to the limit. Having done this he gave each one of them a broad general policy to carry out but then left him to implement it very much in his own way with the minimum of interference from Lahore. The instructions which George Lawrence received from Lahore are typical. As it happens these came from John but both brothers thought alike on this subject.

> A country in which the land tax is lightly or equally fixed is a country pacified. Without that, any other remedy will prove fruitless and with it almost any other will be endured. Check the returns of the *kardars* by the statements of these people, particularly as to what they have been in the habit of paying. Hear what they say of their own villages and those of each other. Observe their dress, appearance and bearing. You will quickly observe if they are over assessed and therefore ill fed, ill clothed, miserable creatures, or a stirring, comfortable population.[8]

Herbert Edwardes went to India a little older than his contemporaries, having been one of the first students at the newly founded King's College in the Strand. In addition to his gifts as a man of action, he was a good writer and artist. A deeply religious man, he has left his mark on the life of what is now Pakistan through the foundation of Edwardes College, Peshawar, where the elite of the North-West Frontier and the nearer parts of Afghanistan have been educated for more than a hundred years. With his vitality and his gift for a telling phrase he was an agreeable companion. But he took his own interpretation of the mysterious workings of Providence too much for granted, and socially he seems to have been a little too noisy, almost a *bounder*. But his great positive qualities outweighed his defects.

Towards the beginning of 1847 the Sikh Durbar thought it was time to send an army to Bannu once more to collect tribute, so they asked the Resident for permission to do so. On the last occasion an army of fifty thousand men with artillery had been sent. When a certain village resisted, its inhabitants were put to the sword and the houses burnt, so that the village was entirely destroyed. Henry Lawrence could not sanction a repetition of this. But 'he said it was his duty to maintain the boundaries of the Sikh Kingdom as he found them; and if the tribes of Bannu refused to pay a reasonable revenue the Durbar might send an army to compel them; but a British officer, chosen from the Resident's staff of assistants, must accompany them, to see that it resorted to arms only in extremity, and committed no excesses'. Henry advised the Durbar to conciliate the Bannuchis by reducing the nominal revenue, which was never paid, to a moderate tribute in acknowledgment of sovereignty. The Durbar consented and it was intended to send John Nicholson with the army but he could not be spared from Peshawar and it was eventually decided to send Herbert Edwardes. This was in the middle of February 1847. From Lahore to Bannu was a month's march and this left only a month before the hot weather would make active operations nearly impossible. So the first expedition could hardly be more than a reconnaissance in force. As a preliminary to that necessary first step Edwardes sent a spy before him to draw a rough map of Bannu. 'He returned with a sheet of paper completely covered over with little squares and lozenges and a name written in each with no space between. "Nizamooddeen," I said, "What is this?" "That," he replied triumphantly, "why that's Bannu!" "And what are all these squares?" "Oh, those are the forts." A village and a fort were the same thing and there were about four hundred of them. Out of a population of about sixty thousand, Bannu could muster fifteen thousand men.

As soon as possible Edwardes started for Bannu with a task force whose numbers were fully sufficient; but there was another difficulty. On previous occasions the whole population had fled to the mountains at the approach of a Sikh army. This time at least a third of the population waited for their arrival. Word had gone round that this time it would be different. India is a country where a salutary change can take place with amazing speed when the conditions are right and there is good leadership.

'Long indulged in military licence, the Sikh soldiers were unable to believe that they were no longer to be allowed to help themselves from every farmer's field, pull their firewood from every hedge, and drag a bed from under its slumbering owner, in order that they might take a nap on it themselves', or to pull the door off a house to get fuel to cook breakfast. But when a 'few severe examples before the whole force showed what all plunderers had to expect, the men gave it up at once'. During the six weeks that the force stayed in Bannu there were only two breaches of the new disciplines. One of them shows the nature of 'the few severe examples' which had produced this good result. A *mahout* in the service of a Sikh chief started to cut green corn belonging to a Bannu notable in order to feed his elephant. On complaint being made, Edwardes ordered a parade of the whole Sikh force, and in spite of the personal entreaties of his master, the offending *mahout* was 'tied up to the triangles and flogged – then passed with bare back down the ranks of his comrades. Assembling the officers, I then explained to them, and desired them to explain to their respective companies, that the people of the country, relying on my protection had treated us as friends; but would resort to their old system of night attacks and assassinations, if the Sikh soldiers plundered them as of old'. After this 'the Bannuchis flocked into our camp and bought and sold with our soldiers, and sat and talked in our assemblies, as friends instead of enemies'.

Thereupon 'almost all the chiefs took heart and returned from the mountains and joined the national council in my tent; whether inclined to yield or determined to resist – their different characters were discriminated; many were won over to our side, and friendships formed, which afterwards stood us in good stead'. Thus, in a few weeks this section of the Sikh army had been brought from lawlessness to a state of discipline that was better than that of the Bengal army.

It should be explained that at this time the British Indian forces were divided into three armies, 'Bengal', 'Bombay', and 'Madras'. In the Bengal army discipline had been deteriorating for a long time. In it there was 'nothing so difficult as to convict a native soldier of plundering or, if convicted by evidence, to get a sentence of punishment from the native officers who compose the court'. The European officers too, felt a mistaken obligation to protect their own men, even when they were clearly in the wrong. Moreover, the commanding officers of the Company's armies had long lost their power to inflict immediate punishment, having become involved in the tangle of red tape which was the curse of the British Raj. By contrast the British officers serving under the Lawrences during their rule of the Punjab had a very wide discretion. These differences greatly influenced the course of events when the test came ten years later in the Indian Mutiny.

The time was now approaching when heat would compel the Sikhs to withdraw until the next cold weather but Edwardes had had time to reconnoitre the whole valley and had made his plans for a return. The Sikhs in their day had approached Bannu by a circuitous route through difficult country. Having 'entered Bannu, as usual, by the old deceitful road', Edwardes found it so bad that he determined not to go back by it. So instead of retracing his steps he pushed right across the

valley from west to east, going where no Sikh army had ever gone
before

> and feasting our eyes on the richest portion of Bannu, lying *perdu* in
> a corner under the mountains, we emerged upon a fine natural high
> road for an army, which proved to be the real entrance and exit of
> Bannu, so long and so successfully concealed. It would be difficult
> to say who were first most chagrined at this discovery – the
> Bannuchis themselves, or the Sikh chiefs and grey beards of our
> camp.

But at last both sides laughed heartily at the joke.

Edwardes and his task force left Bannu on 4th May 1847. He put a
proposal to the Bannuchis: 'Your revenue is sixty-five thousand
rupees a year; and as you refuse to pay it, the Sikhs come and destroy
your harvests, burn your houses, plunder your flocks and herds, and
sell your wives and children as slaves . . . What for? . . . Only pay
. . . an annual tribute of forty thousand rupees . . . and no army shall
again enter your valley.' This offer had been refused.

So when the cold weather began in the late autumn of 1847 Herbert
Edwardes was back again with the Sikh army in Bannu to complete
the unfinished business. His aim was to induce the people to pay a
modest tribute peaceably and with regularity and to accept the rule of
a *kardar* or provincial agent appointed from Lahore, like other parts of
the Sikh Kingdom. A fort would be built and a garrison would remain
to back the central authority. Such terms were unheard of in Bannu
but it was hoped that the good reputations that the Lawrences and
their assistants were earning would make it possible for peaceable
diplomacy backed by the possible use of force as an ultimate deterrent
to induce the people of Bannu to accept the new situation without
recourse to arms. It was an essential element in the proposed terms
that by the treaty of Bhairowal there would be a British officer to
control the Sikh agents.

In the proclamation which Edwardes sent before him to prepare the
way, he said: 'You know very well that no *Sahib* ever fixes a heavy
revenue. *Sahibs* are at this moment settling the Punjab, and making all
the people happy.' This was believed, because Arthur Cocks, one of
Henry's principal assistants, was at that moment causing great satisfaction to the cultivators of the Punjab by substituting a light assessment for the land tax, which had risen to a most oppressive height
during the financial difficulties of the Lahore Government previous to
the First Sikh War. But in Bannu every village was fortified and
bristled with arms; and the one point on which the population of
Bannu were agreed was that they did not want to give up their

cherished, if anarchical, independence. The proclamation concluded: 'Let all good subjects therefore fear nothing, but pursue their labours of harvest and cultivation; and let every *malik*, who does not wish to be ejected from his chieftainship, come in to me. Above all keep in mind that the army which is now coming to Bannu, is not going away again after a month, but is coming to stay. Make your calculations therefore accordingly. (17th November 1847).'

This proclamation was conveyed by a trusty messenger, distributed and deliberated upon. It had a good effect. By 2nd December almost all the chiefs had come in, including those of the distant western '*tuppehs*, whom neither I nor anyone had ever seen before, and who still looked as wild as hawks, prepared at the least ill omen to . . . fly to their usual hiding places in the hills'. Not only these, but all the chiefs were utterly astonished at everything they saw in the British camp. Edwardes' watch was a bird and the tick was its 'song'. One chief wanted to know whether it was true that English people could not lie and appeared to attribute this to some cruel malformation of their mouths. A generation earlier Mountstuart Elphinstone encountered a similar belief in the same part of Asia.

The social structure and ethnic composition of these people was very intricate since the fertility and inaccessibility of their valley had over many generations attracted immigrants from a vast area of India and Central Asia. Each group had its own peculiarities. All were armed and most were formidable in arms. All were prepared to resist an invader though not to combine for this purpose; private feuds had a general priority over the public interest. Seldom has Tacitus' aphorism *ut sunt acerrima proximorum odia* (the keenest hates are the hates of neighbours) been more strikingly illustrated. But somehow Herbert Edwardes with his Sikh army succeeded before the cold weather was out in inducing the inhabitants to acquiesce in the construction of a strategically placed government fort, and then with their own hands to pull down all four hundred of their own forts, to cease fighting with each other or the Sikhs and to accept the payment of a moderate tribute.

All this was achieved without bloodshed. Much credit must go to Edwardes and the other British officers who served with the Lawrences, but they did not operate in a vacuum. Even today anyone who reads the news from India in the daily papers must sometimes be brought to despair of human nature, but anyone who gives close attention to Indian affairs is also likely to become aware that there is something in Indian society which rises to the need, when it is given the chance. At the beginning of 1847 Bannu enjoyed a *de facto* independence joined with a violence and degradation produced by an explosive combination of local vices and the vices of Ranjit Singh's kingdom at its moment of worst decay. By the spring of 1848 Bannu was prosperous and at peace both internally and with its suzerains at Lahore. Other but not dissimilar transformations had taken place throughout the Sikh Kingdom. These were the fruits of the treaty of Bhairowal, as administered by Henry Lawrence and his band of chosen assistants, working so far as they could through the existing Sikh Government.

Henry Lawrence could now concentrate on going home on furlough with a clear conscience. The Punjab was bound to remain explosive for a year or two more, but for the moment all was peace. On 2nd June 1847 Henry was able to write to Currie that the people had settled down in a manner that could never have been hoped or believed of them; but yet they had not lost their spirit. He added, however, that 'among the crowd who are loudest in our praise, there are many who cannot forgive our victory, or even our forbearance, and who chafe at their loss of power in exact proportion as they submit to ours'.

The continual riding about, exertion and excitement suited Henry's temperament. As Hardinge observed, 'knocking about seemed to do him good'. None the less he had suffered severely from the hot weather of 1846 in the Punjab. He went to the hills and recovered there but the heat of 1847 was too much for him. Henry – or was it Honoria? – described it in their novel:

> Such a sun! He only can understand its power who has been exposed to it in the hot winds. The burning rays showering down on a man's head, penetrating every defence, reflected in a thousand directions from the parched, arid ground; while the scorching wind catches the breath, the eyes are blinded with the glare and dust, and the brain feels absolutely boiling . . . Getting under a roof I felt as if an iron cap had been removed from my head.

At the end of the year he left for England on sick leave, travelling home with his devoted friend Lord Hardinge, with the Governor-General's staff on the *Mozuffer*. Hardinge's successor was Lord Dalhousie, a man of a very different stamp.

In Lahore Henry left John behind him as Acting Resident to carry out measures which he had organised, and especially the suppression of slave dealing, *suttee* and infanticide. If the chief credit for what had already been achieved goes to Henry, without John it would have been imperfect, as Henry was the first to recognise, though he was touchy about suggestions from his younger brother. In the two years of Henry's incumbency at Lahore he had been resident for ten months and John for fourteen months. Lewin Bowring, afterwards highly distinguished as Commissioner in Mysore before that state was returned successfully to native rule, was at this time an assistant at the Residency. He records that:

> John . . . had taken immense trouble in producing order out of chaos. He was a far abler man at details than his brother . . . He introduced a summary settlement of the land revenue, which was at that time in a most disorganised state, accomplished many judicial reforms and devised a system analogous to our penny postage, which was of great benefit. In his endeavours to reduce expenditure he insisted on all orders for disbursing money being brought to him for counter signature, a proceeding to which the Durbar greatly objected.

On taking over from his brother, John had summed up his feelings by saying, 'I can see how much has been done since last year . . . but I cannot fail also to observe that there are still no ordinary difficulties to be encountered and overcome.'

George Clerk, now Governor of Bombay, and friendly as ever, wrote to Henry, 'I quite agree with your *bundobust* across the Sutlej . . . during your absence you will require a vigilant man there – a rough and ready one – for, if not very vigilant for the next two years, we shall be tript up.' All the wisest heads saw that in Henry's absence there would be great opportunities, but also great dangers. The whole of the Punjab was at peace for the first time in living memory, the roads were relatively safe, and the British occupation was at present looked on with unmixed pleasure by the majority of the population. But the people expected too much and as they discovered this, Henry expected that 'their zeal in our favour will soon sink to that cold indifference so apparent among the inhabitants of the longest acquired British provinces'.

Henry saw some immediate dangers of unrest in the Punjab but did not expect a serious rising for the present. 'No, the time has not yet come for anything beyond private schemes of treachery.' He did, however, foresee great, if more distant, dangers both here and else-where. He wrote to Hardinge:

> I have more than once said to your Lordship that I consider our danger in India . . . to lie in our native troops. We need to guard much more against them than any foreign enemy or combination of native sovereigns or chiefs. I have been struck by the confidence always expressed by Sir John Littler whenever I have hinted at the necessity of looking after the *sepoys*. In this very confidence is danger. I am perfectly aware how often the *sepoys* have been tried and how *wonderfully* faithful they have been, but we have no right

always to expect wonders . . . I am satisfied that our *sepoys* do not like the idea of destroying the few remaining Hindu principalities . . . I well recollect the hearty cheers with which Rajah Gulab Singh and the young Maharajah were received (at the signing of the treaty of Bhairowal). I watched the countenances of the men. Many were glad to have hopes of peace but there were as many who rejoiced to save a dynasty.

(iii) Henry Lawrence's Young Men

It is not often that any country has been served by a group of men who combined in such a high degree devotion, ability and humanity, as those who served in the Punjab in the days of the Lawrences. The choice of the Company's servants was in the main the work of Henry Lawrence. It is true that all his Young Men were British, but if he could have had his own way there would have been Indians among them from the first. His unerring choice of men flowed from a combination of intuition with method. He chose them after careful thought and comparison but his method was checked and inspired by an artist's perception of character.

He had no routine way of dealing with his assistants, treating each man in accordance with his nature, and thereby drawing out the best in him. Henry expected his subordinates to speak their minds freely to him, and exposed his own thoughts with equal openness. Once he had chosen his assistants, he trusted them completely and was as loyal to them as they to him. His 'tragic sense of life' gave him a humility which engendered a feeling of brotherhood, equality and sympathy with his assistants and also with those he ruled. His hot temper and occasional lack of consideration were forgiven. Hesketh Pearson has some perceptive pages about Henry Lawrence in his life of John Nicholson (*Hero of Delhi*). He concludes that 'No leader in history has deserved or inspired the love and admiration of so many remarkable men.' Such a claim could only be substantiated or refuted by one who knew more than it is possible to know.

One day a great book will be written about Henry Lawrence's Young Men. Some of them appear all too briefly in these pages. Many others are left out. As individuals they are all remarkable but they also had a collective character about which something must be said. Their qualities of courage, integrity, enterprise and humanity speak for themselves. Such a combination of qualities in a fairly small group is not common, but it is hardly unique. It would however be hard to find a parallel for a group of people engaged on public work who loved both their chief, those they ruled and each other so much. One indication of this is the way in which Henry Lawrence's Young Men signed their letters to each other 'yours affectionately'. They had their full share of ambition and each wanted to be recognised, but there seems to have been no striving to surpass one another in their careers and little jealousy of the success of others. In the Viceroyalty of John Lawrence, it was commonly expected that Herbert Edwardes would succeed Robert Montgomery as Lieutenant-Governor of the Punjab. He wrote to John saying that this was the one unfulfilled ambition of his life, but he would willingly stand aside, if John would prefer to appoint Donald McLeod and proceeded to argue in favour of the saintly McLeod who was so unassuming that his claims might easily be passed over. Eventually McLeod was chosen and was an outstanding success.

The instructions which Henry's Young Men received were few, just make the people happy, make low assessments for land tax and see there are no rows. Easier said than done. But many of them had seen their chief in action with his flashing eyes and had learnt his methods from their source. The best description of Henry with his young men is by Herbert Edwardes, not in his biography of Henry, but in Charles Raikes' *Notes on the Revolt in the North-Western Provinces of India*.[9]

> Besides this (i.e. teaching by example) he was forever talking the new officers into his views; and influencing them to live among the people, to do as many cases under trees, and as few under the *punkah*, as possible; to ride about their districts and see and hear for themselves, instead of through the police and *Omlah*. And his cheery, earnest way of doing this, his glad praise of any rough and ready officer, and his indignant contempt for all skulks, idlers and *nimmuk huram*, drew *models* on young fellows' minds, which they went forth and copied in their administration. It sketched a *faith* and begat a *school* and they are both living things to this day (i.e. some years after Henry left the Punjab).

These young men were deeply religious, but their religion was of a kind that was not always understood by late twentieth-century man. Yet it formed them through and through. They were Protestant and Evangelical, and most of them were Anglican, but denominational differences were not considered important. Donald McLeod had indeed developed his own idiosyncratic version of the Christian faith which seems to have caused no difficulty. Indeed it was a common saying among the Punjabis that there were in the Punjab 'two *ferishtahs* [angels], Robert Montgomery Sahib and Donald McLeod Sahib'. Indians respect genuine faith, even when they do not share it.

Henry Lawrence's Young Men read the Bible faithfully and pondered upon it continually. For those who were Anglican the Bible was seen in the light of the Book of Common Prayer. I have Henry Lawrence's Prayer Book which he adapted in manuscript for use in house prayers. He crossed out the Athanasian Creed. He was not theologically minded; and no doubt he found the references to damnation repugnant. Though Henry's Young Men were Evangelicals, they were not much involved in the parties which rent Victorian Christianity, though after his return to England Herbert Edwardes was unduly and publicly involved in combating the Ritualists. He might have been surprised by the fact that the eventual acceptance of many of their practices has not entailed the evils which he anticipated.

It may puzzle readers to find Edwardes asking the question whether John Nicholson and Henry Lawrence himself were Christians. The answer to that question seems obvious and the question was over scrupulous, but it was not meaningless. The point at issue was whether in the last resort these two were trying to do right by their own strength or whether they knew that they needed the help of Christ, accepted as their 'personal Saviour', working in their hearts, strengthening them and guiding them in a sense that must be called mystical, even if they would have denied the word.

They were great supporters of Christian missions but this does not seemed to have caused any difficulty in their personal relations with people of other faiths, once the ice had been broken. Some of the early Victorian received opinions about heathens and idolaters were naive, but it is only fair to remember that four generations ago close contact with people of other faiths was a relatively new experience, and the problems which arise therefrom had not then, and still have not been thought through. The Lawrences and their circle criticised the Government of India, rightly in my view, for having circumscribed Christian missionary activity too tightly. It was, indeed, right to protect all religions impartially, but this need not have involved treating Christian teaching almost as a guilty secret, which must be kept from the natives for fear that they might regard its exposition as an attack on their own beliefs. The Government's critics claimed with some reason that danger arose rather from Indians being unaware of the nature of Christianity. One consequence of this was a belief current among the natives that one could become a Christian without intending it. The danger of this misconception was shown in the celebrated case of the cartridges which sparked off the Indian Mutiny.

No one who knew anything about Christianity could have supposed that the Government of India proposed to make Hindus or Moslems into Christians by making them bite a cartridge greased with the wrong kind of fat.

From the standpoint of posterity it is not difficult to criticise the religious opinions of the young men who set out to remake the Punjab nearly a hundred and fifty years ago. Their faith was only shared by a very few of those they ruled, but its genuine quality was perceived by all who got to know them and, as John Lawrence put it, 'a Christian thing done in a Christian way' will never do harm. The fact that these men believed with all their hearts that human destiny is in the hand of God gave their work a cosmic perspective.

It is interesting to compare the circle of the Lawrences with that of Henry and Annette Beveridge, the parents of Lord Beveridge. In his celebrated book *India Called Them*, Lord Beveridge describes the life of his father who went out to join the ICS in 1857, the year in which this book ends, and of his mother who went out a little later. This wonderful pair, who may be called the grandparents of the welfare state, were as agnostic as the Lawrences and their circle were Christian. The Beveridges were just as high minded, and they sympathised eagerly with Indian aspirations at a slightly later stage of development, and at the other end of India – in Bengal instead of the Punjab. But their horizon was much narrower and their Positivism for all its ethical purity was much farther removed from the feelings of India, the most religious country in the world, than was the Christianity of the Lawrences and their world.

Most of those who had been with Henry Lawrence as Resident remained after the annexation of the Punjab. An exception was Arthur Cocks, who had been Chief Assistant to the Resident. He left the Punjab soon after the annexation because he could not bear to see 'the fallen state of the old officials and *sirdars*'. Edwardes observes that 'He had been unfortunately made Deputy Commissioner of Lahore where he saw this only; had he got a country district he would have been happy, I believe, in the real good of the lower orders.'

It will be asked whether there were no misfits among those who ruled the Punjab under the Lawrences. There were, of course, human difficulties, but these seemed to have been well contained. Two exceptions stand out. Mackeson was an important official who had been inherited from an earlier period. He was very able and had great experience but Henry and he could not get on with each other, either in the Afghan War, when Mackeson was the superior, or under the Board of Administration which took its place after the annexation.

Hodson of 'Hodson's Horse', if not the black sheep of the flock, was, to vary the metaphor, a fly in the ointment. He was introduced to

Henry by Thomason. In writing to thank Thomason for this, Hodson says that he has received 'every sort of attention and kindness' from Major Lawrence and adds, 'I have been very much struck with his superiority and freedom from diplomatic solemnity and mystery'. Indeed the two men shared the same room night and day at Simla. Hodson made such recompense as he could, by making précis of letters and copying confidential papers. Henry, he says, in a letter home, 'is amazingly kind and tells me all that is going on, initiating me into the mysteries of political business and thus giving me more knowledge of things and persons Indian than I should learn in a year of ordinary life, aye or in three years either . . . He makes me work at Hindustani, and has given me a lesson or two in the use of the theodolite . . . to the end that I may get employed in the Surveying Department, after two years of which he says "I shall be fit for a political".'

All in all William Hodson (1821-58) was a man whom it was easier to admire than to like. He was arrogant and aggressive, with a slightly disagreeable wit. Yet his impetuous nature brought him much affection, if we may believe the testimony of a friend of his youth, G. E. L. Cotton who afterwards became Bishop of Calcutta. It is only fair to say that as one reads his letters home, he grows on one. Hodson liked animals more than people and women more than men. At any rate he preferred the company of educated and accomplished ladies to that of his companions of the mess table. But he was contemptuous of those who could only be known to be women because 'they were not men'. On the eve of his marriage to the love of his youth after a seven years' delay, he could write to his old tutor, 'I thirst not for the calm pleasures of a country life, the charms of society or a career of ease and comfort, but for the maddening excitement of war, the keen contest of wits involved in dealing with wilder men and the exercise of power over the many.'

Herbert Edwardes and John Lawrence's wife, Harriette, were among those who disliked Hodson. Henry could not understand why they did not like him and they could not understand why Henry did like him. John Lawrence evidently distrusted him. When Hodson was appointed to command the Guides, Edwardes paid a generous tribute to Hodson's soldierly qualities. But he quarrelled bitterly with his colleagues in the officers' mess, and he set his face against doing anything that bored him, so that the regimental accounts got into a tangle and Hodson's enemies suspected that money had stuck to his fingers. Nothing was proved, but a doubt remained. Unpopular as Hodson was with many of his British colleagues, the rank and file of the Guides thought the world of him. Many of them cried like children when he was killed. Hodson also played a key part in the building of Sanawar, the first of the hill schools established by Henry for the children of the other ranks in the British army. This is now one of India's leading 'public schools', using the phrase in its British sense, but its beginnings were humble. From the start it took both boys and girls, as it still does. Sanawar stands in a delectable position in the Simla hills 5,000 feet above sea level on one of the lower ridges of the Himalayan foothills where the 'hot weather' is never too hot. School life was strenuous, but not too strenuous, with plenty of physical activity, running up and downhill, and learning manual trades that would make the children independent when they grew up. There was also more book learning than those particular boys and girls would have got elsewhere, and a good grounding in a devout but tolerant brand of Christianity.

Sanawar became a happy place but in 1848 there was nothing but a bare hillside. Hodson had four hundred and fifty workmen under him and instructions to build a school. When he asked for guidance Henry only answered, 'Do what you think right'. The workmen appeared to know nothing, but Hodson taught them. 'You begin from the forest and the quarry,' he wrote to his sister, 'get the lime burnt, trees cut down, bricks made, planks sawn up, the ground got ready, and then watch the work foot by foot, showing each man exactly what to do.' In May he was joined by George Lawrence's wife Charlotte, whom he found 'a great acquisition to forest life'. Together they went through the floods of applications for places in the 'asylum', and by August the school was completed.

CHAPTER 11

While the Cat's Away

The ship, the *Mozuffer*, that bore Henry Hardinge and Henry Lawrence home reached England in March 1848. By this time the 'overland route' through Egypt had been developed. So they were able to call at Aden and from there Hardinge had written to Sir John Hobhouse, the President of the East India Company's Board of Control, requesting a K.C.B. for Henry Lawrence. He wrote: 'There is nothing which you can do for me which will give me more pleasure than to honour him as he deserves.' When they arrived the East India Company gave a great dinner in honour of the retiring Governor-General at which his old chief, the Duke of Wellington, gave a speech. Henry Lawrence was one of the guests and Lord Hardinge singled him out for special praise.

When Henry had left a still Georgian England, he was an unknown young man. Now he was returning for a brief space to Victorian London to be knighted and lionised. He had parted from Honoria and his sons three years before. Now the family was reunited but Henry was only to spend a bare six months in England and Ireland renewing severed friendships and basking in the love of Letitia, the rest of his family and their devoted circle of friends. His health soon began to mend but he needed two years' furlough.

Those who saw him for the first time on this visit to England 'were struck by the remarkable simplicity and unworldliness of his character'.[1] He was not unfriendly 'but his active mind, ever intent upon great realities, overleapt the social surroundings of the moment'. This could be disconcerting and he no longer fully belonged in England. Kaye describes how on Henry's first day in London they were walking along Regent Street and 'met the usual afternoon tide of well dressed people'. Henry was wearing an antiquated frock coat with an old grey shepherd's plaid crossed over his chest, and even he realised that his appearance at that time and place was startling. He turned to Kaye with an amused and puzzled look, asking whether there was somewhere near where he could buy something to hide the imperfections of his attire. In a few paces they were 'in front of Nicols great shop', where he exchanged his plaid for 'a fashionable *paletot*'. There was no

defiance of convention about him, no studied eccentricity, but he had
no taste for general society and was glad to escape from London to
Letitia at Bath and old friends in Ireland. Kaye observes: 'I do not
think that he cared much more for titles than he cared for dress.' 'As a
loyal and devoted subject' he rejoiced in his Knighthood as a sign of
the Queen's recognition of his work but continued to call himself
Colonel Lawrence.

He had left John temporarily in charge at Lahore and it was hoped
that he might remain there until Henry could return, but it was
judged invidious to show too much favour to one family. So John was
passed over, and Henry's old friend Currie, now Sir Frederick, was
appointed to Lahore while Henry was away. Until Currie arrived,
John was under instructions to take no initiative. So the cold weather
had ended before the new master took over. Unfortunately there was
one major question which required prompt action. Failure here led to
the insurrection known as the Second Sikh War.

Mulraj, the Hindu governor of the city of Multan, was immensely
rich but timid withal. He was piqued by the control of a British
Resident, and wanted to resign his post. But the terms on which he
was to go involved delicate negotiations about his accounts. John was
ready to conclude the matter in February but his instructions forbade
him to act before the new Resident arrived. John wrote afterwards,
and Henry agreed with him, that if his (John's) plan had been carried
out, there would probably have been no trouble, and in any case there
would have been more time to deal with Mulraj before the hot
weather.

When Currie arrived, John wrote to Henry that he, Currie, was 'a
regular Pecksniff', but promised to 'get on very well with him'. The
fact is that John felt that Currie had elbowed him aside for the benefit
of his own career, and done it to no purpose, since Currie was already
a member of the Governor-General's Council and gained nothing by
coming to Lahore. If John had not thus unburdened himself to his
brother, it would have been impossible to guess that his helpful
attitude to Currie's problems concealed a deep resentment. The Sikh
notables, for their part, viewed the change with apprehension, saying
to John: 'With you we contest and badger and dispute. You are one of
our own. But what can we do with Currie Sahib?'

Sir Frederick was an able man, who knew the Sikh Durbar well
from the outside but had not had the opportunity to observe them at
close quarters over a long period. He was not the 'rough and ready
man' that George Clerk wanted to see in Lahore, and did not make
himself readily available to the Sikh Durbar. And he had been too
long desk bound to act decisively in an emergency.

On his arrival Currie tactlessly gave junior staff notice to move out of the Residency, where under Henry each of them had lived in his own little corner. Reporting this to Henry, John wrote: 'In yours and my time there was neither privacy nor comfort. Now there will perhaps be too much of both.' The Lawrences and their staff had lived with a simplicity that contrasted with the usual ways of higher Anglo-Indian officials. John, his wife, three children and a European servant had only two rooms twelve feet by fifteen to divide between them. Henry shared a small room first with Herbert Edwardes and then with Robert Napier. The rest of the staff counted themselves lucky if they had half a room each.

Both the Sirdars and the junior European staff got to like Currie very much as they got to know him, but the common people complained that they had no access to him and that their affairs did not get a hearing under his rule.[2] It is not pleasant to record these criticisms of an honourable public servant who was a good friend to the hero of this biography, but the disasters of the Second Sikh War were largely due to Currie's inadequacy.

After much haggling, terms were eventually agreed with Mulraj by which he was to resign his governorship. To implement this change, Currie sent a detachment of the Sikh army under two British officers, Vans Agnew of the Bengal Civil Service and Lieutenant William Anderson of the First Bombay Fusiliers. Agnew was much liked and admired, but Henry described him as 'our most inflammable man'. If John had had his way, he would have sent Arthur Cocks, 'a fine resolute, good tempered fellow', as John called him and one of the best of Henry's Young Men.[3]

Agnew and Anderson travelled separately from their troops, so that they neither knew them nor were known to them. And when they reached Multan, Mulraj received them well, taking them round the fort and showing them the stores and ammunition. Then, as they were leaving, two or three *sepoys* suddenly attacked them, wounding them severely. In a few hours this incident grew into an insurrection. Agnew and Anderson were murdered in cold blood and Mulraj, willingly or reluctantly, put himself at the head of the rebellion. He does not seem to have been involved in any plans for rebellion, but since these events happened within his jurisdiction and no loyal government force was at hand, his life would have been in danger if he had refused to lead the rebels.

Currie was thunderstruck. He wrote plaintively to Henry: 'Who could have anticipated such a catastrophe?' John thought that what had happened was 'purely fortuituous' and no one was to blame;[4] but this was the kind of accident that could easily happen in a province that was only just emerging into ordered rule. And all the Lawrence brothers were clear that the rebellion must be put down quickly or it would spread and there would be more loss of life. John wrote to Currie suggesting that he should summon a brigade from Ferozepore and Jullundur in British India and march two European corps and six native corps on Multan, 'a place of no great strength', which could be shelled from a nearby height. Having in mind, no doubt, that the hot weather was now upon them, he added, 'I see great objections to this course but even greater ones in delay.'[5] What he meant by greater dangers is made clear in a letter to H. M. Elliot at the Governor-General's headquarters on 30th April 1848, when he wrote: 'If we do nothing the whole of the disbanded soldiery of the Manjha will flock down and make common cause with the mutineers.'

Yet the Commander in Chief, Lord Gough, absolutely refused to move European troops in the plains in the hot weather. John Lawrence thought there was an element of pique in this. At any rate he wrote to Henry on 4th November that Currie 'seems to have annoyed the C. in C. and those about him. And one would almost think they had delayed to make matters as bad as possible.' But the Governor-General, Lord Dalhousie, being new to India, was persuaded by Gough's arguments. So some men were spared a death from heat stroke but more suffered death in battle, when the weather was cooler, the rebellion had spread, and Lord Gough was ready to move. On 3rd October 1848 Henry wrote to the new Governor-General in strong terms:

> What I always urged on my brother John and on my assistants was never to allow rebellion one day to make head . . . No one could surely assert that Multan is half the strength of Kangra and yet, four months after Sobraon, I was allowed to take four native regiments without a single European against it in the month of May . . . Although the autumn in the Punjab is very hot, the months of April and May are seldom hotter than February and March in Hindustan.

Referring to sunstroke, he added: 'as if war is to be made without loss of life'. There was much more expressed in equally plain terms, but Dalhousie was not accustomed to such direct speaking from subordinates and did not take it well.

If these events had happened a year or two later, the imperious Dalhousie would have rejected Gough's advice, or at least made sure, as Gough did not, that when the campaign did begin adequate supplies, transport and all necessary intelligence were ready. But since Dalhousie had accepted Gough's advice, he was determined that he was right. He therefore jeered at Henry Lawrence for describing Multan as a contemptible place, when it took a full-scale siege to reduce it, forgetting that fortifications that might be 'contemptible' at the time of the revolt would become formidable if their defenders were given six months in which to strengthen them.

Currie first got the Durbar to send a Sikh force to reduce Multan but it had no British officer with it and, instead of fighting, it joined the rebels. In his letter written to Dalhousie from England on 3rd October 1848 Henry Lawrence observes that neither Currie nor any of his very able assistants had any personal acquaintance with any other native court. If they had, they would have learned that when Indians were acting in their own affairs they could often act energetically, but when they were acting on British instructions 'we must not only *order, we must lead*: [HML's italics] we must not tell them to work but work with them. Everything depends on this.' And he gives instances to show that Indian troops who are on the verge of mutiny when left to themselves, will cooperate enthusiastically with a British officer whom they have come to know and perhaps to like. If Agnew and Anderson had travelled to Multan with their troops and got to know them, there would probably have been no trouble.

After his initial failure Currie was nonplussed and kept changing his mind. The trouble did not spread at once. Lahore, where there was a British force, remained quiet. And throughout the Punjab the majority of the population avoided taking sides, as far as they could and for as long as they could. About five-sixths of them were not Sikhs. So they just waited to see which masters, the Sikhs or the British, would win. But the Sikh army were emotionally on the side of the rebels and in the end they nearly all joined them. 'It was almost impossible that it should be otherwise. We stood, looked on and did nothing,' John Lawrence wrote to Henry on 14th November 1848.

In this emergency much depended on the Young Men whom Henry Lawrence had put in charge of their various districts. Herbert Edwardes was in a particularly difficult position, across the Indus but still in the province of Multan. Yet he collected the taxes, improvised a small army out of nothing from among the wild and untrained fighters of that region, beat Mulraj in two pitched battles and captured most of his artillery, but was eventually forced to retreat.

At the beginning of the outbreak Edwardes was still in his twenties and was a lieutenant, though he was promoted to major and given a C.B. after his astounding success. How was it possible for a junior officer almost completely isolated among untamed tribes and out of reach of support, instructions or advice from Lahore to do all this? In the first place he was a man of exceptional ability who had been on the far side of the Indus just long enough to get to know his subjects and to gain their confidence. Even so he could not have succeeded if the population had been on the side of the rebellion. But the Sikhs were an unpopular minority, and even they were divided. Moreover the province of Multan bordered on Afghanistan and Baluchistan. A large part of the population were Pathans or Baluchis who had suffered grievously under Sikh rule and had correspondingly much to gain from a British victory. In particular the Pathans recruited by Edwardes were first-class fighting men and were movingly faithful to the side they had chosen and to their British chief, who on his side showed flawless judgment in his choice of allies.

Pre-eminent among these was a Baluchi chief, Kowrah Khan Khosah who with his clansmen, at the beginning of the campaign, captured on his own initiative the important fort of Derah Ghazi Khan in a most gallant action. Edwardes writes with warm affection of Kowrah Khan, 'so brave, so humble, so hot in fight, so cool in council, so sober and dignified in triumph, so smooth browed and firm amid disaster; a man at all times to be relied upon'. Even more important was a Pathan chief, Foujdar Khan Alizye, who knew every boat on his long stretch of the Indus and had reliable information about where it was at any given moment and the characteristics of the owner. He combined high courage and fidelity with a rare gift of organisation. Foujdar Khan continued in the British service, cooperating in 1854-5 with his friend Herbert Edwardes in negotiating a treaty of friendship with Afghanistan. This treaty wiped away the bitterness of the First Afghan War. It realised Dost Mahommed Khan's lifelong ambition of friendship with the British and it gave twenty years of peace to Afghan–British relations which stood the British in good stead during the Mutiny. John Lawrence, who signed the treaty under instructions from the Governor-General, was given a knighthood for doing so. Which was ironic since he had strong reservations against the treaty on the ground that it was impossible of attainment and even if attained would be useless. Most of the credit should go to Edwardes and Foujdar Khan. For the former it was the high point of his career; the latter received for his services the high title of Nawab from the Government of India.

The Sikh troops in the Trans-Indus were under the command of General van Cortlandt, an officer of mixed blood who had taken service under Ranjit Singh. He was a first-class and experienced soldier but by the treaty of Bhairowal he was under the command of the young English lieutenant. It speaks well for both men that they cooperated cordially and without friction.

In form the revolt was a rising against the infant Maharajah Dhulip Singh, and the Sikh Durbar continued to function formally throughout the war under Currie's advice. But in reality the revolt was more directed against the Maharajah's British protectors than against the Durbar. The rank and file of the Sikh standing army and the disbanded troops sympathised with the rebellion but had no special liking for Mulraj, the Hindu whom chance had placed at its head. It would have surprised no one if his troops had murdered him. Cortlandt and Edwardes, however, had every reason for thinking that the Sikh regiments under their command would have joined Mulraj if a good opportunity had presented itself. With unshakable nerve and great skill they kept some of these troops true to their salt throughout but others eventually went over. The Sikh *sirdars* were in two minds. They had done quite well out of British protection and were safer than they had ever been before but they naturally hankered after a restoration of Sikh independence with all its risks. Some stayed loyal to the treaty of Bhairowal while others joined the revolt, long after its prospects had begun to wane.

The Sikh subordinate officials were generally cautious. They did not openly join Mulraj but they did not stop recruits joining him. And they obstructed the transmission of official messages in a way that added greatly to the British difficulties without laying themselves open to a charge of treachery.

Edwardes was not the only hero of the Second Sikh War. Unfortunately his independent success aroused the jealousy of Dalhousie, who maintained that Edwardes had been 'over praised at home', that his operations were unwise in that he could not have taken Multan without artillery, and that the fact of one European officer keeping the field in hot weather with native troops did not prove that European troops could have kept the field with equal impunity. However Dalhousie was too just not to defend Edwardes from what he called 'the whole Gough set' who 'hate Edwardes and run him down', even suggesting that he had disobeyed orders.

The Sikh army did not all defect at once but, as the British did nothing they gradually plucked up courage to join the rebellion. 'Our best friends said, "Why do you delay?"' Henry Lawrence's Young Men did more than would seem possible to keep their districts quiet and to postpone the evil day, but in John Lawrence's phrase, 'like the waves of the sea, step by step the rebellion spread'.[6] John Lawrence did even more than his colleagues. 'With a skill, energy and ruthless power, which no soldier could have surpassed'[7] he kept the hills and the Jullundur Doab quiet until the war was over.

The Corps of Guides had scarcely been raised but they took a prominent part in the Second Sikh War and some of them were sent secretly to Multan to take service under Mulraj and supply intelligence to the British. The *sepoys* of the regular army fought well and not one of them deserted to the side of the insurgents, but Herbert Edwardes observes that 'hardened by caste' they could do nothing but their regular drill. 'To the Guides on the contrary, it was a perfect game, a lark, to disguise themselves and take service with Mulraj and come out of the fort with Mulraj's army to fight against their own masters, and have to run away when Mulraj ran away; and then towards the close of the siege to come out and join their own side, and help to take the place.'

Nearly ten years later during the Indian Mutiny the Bengal Army of 'pipe clayed Hindustani *sepoys*' (Edwardes' phrase), had melted away and the nucleus of the new Indian army which grew upon the ruins of the old was the army of volunteers from the Punjab, a hundred thousand of them first and last, raised and equipped and dressed in khaki on the model of the Guides.

George Lawrence, ably aided by the Sikh Governor, General Gulab Singh Povindea (not the same man as the Maharajah of Kashmir) kept the frontier tribes and the Sikh garrison at Peshawar quiet for some time. Dost Mahommed Khan in Kabul at first resisted the temptation to invade this former Afghan province, but eventually moved into Peshawar and gave half-hearted support to the Sikh rebels in exchange for the prospect of keeping Peshawar. George Lawrence left that city at the last possible moment, being warned by General Gulab Singh Povindea that there was only just time for him to escape. He had already sent his family on under the protection of a friendly Pathan chief but on his arrival it turned out that he and all his family, though treated with kindness, were in fact prisoners. Thus George Lawrence for a second time became a prisoner of the Afghans. He remained in the hands of captors, first Pathan and then Sikh, till the end of the war, when he was sent on parole to discuss terms with the British authorities. In his memoirs he makes no claim about his share in these negotiations but Colin Campbell thought that George's influence with the Sikh generals, Sher Singh and his father Chatar Singh, 'frightened them into a far more speedy surrender' than they would otherwise have thought of.[8] George kept his parole, returning to the beaten Sikh army just as they were on the point of surrender. They were surprised to see him and greeted him with a cheer.

Twenty-six-year-old John Nicholson was at this time assistant to his close friend George Lawrence in Peshawar. The greatest of Henry's Young Men, he remains the hardest to describe. He made an impression on Europeans and Indians of almost superhuman strength and he was gifted with mental, physical and moral powers of a very high order. His achievement before his heroic death in 1857 at the siege of Delhi at the age of thirty-four was extraordinary, even among that chosen band to which he belonged.

He was taciturn to the verge of moroseness and would sit through a meal at mess without opening his mouth except to put food in it. His letters were few and brief. Robert Montgomery once had an official communication from him which read: 'Sir, I have the honour to inform you that I have just shot a man who came to kill me. Yours obediently, J. Nicholson.' On that occasion he did write a longer description of what happened to Herbert Edwardes. Montgomery was lucky to have any report at all from 'old Nick'. He would sometimes carry out the most high-handed actions without bothering to report them. And brief and few as his letters were, many of them were destroyed in a fire. The evidence that remains is sparse but it is impressive.

John Nicholson was another Protestant Irishman. He was brought up by a very religious widowed mother and it was from her that he inherited 'that grand lifting of the head which all who knew John Nicholson can remember in him'. He was deeply imbued with Christianity and used to read a chapter of the New Testament every day, but his enquiring and rebellious spirit could not easily accept orthodoxy. Sometimes it seems that in him the fiercer parts of the Old Testament were not tamed by the spirit of Christ. One would like to know what he made of the tenderer passages in the Psalms and the Prophets, but the inner recesses of his spirit remained secret, except perhaps to his closest friends, Herbert Edwardes and Honoria Lawrence. On her deathbed Honoria sent him a message through Henry. 'Tell him I love him dearly, as if he were my son – but tell him that he is a sinner, that one day he will be as weak and near death as I am now.' I have a New Testament with Honoria's name on the title page and these words in Henry's writing: 'John Nicholson – in memory of his friend and warm well wisher, who was this day laid in her grave.'

John Nicholson was well over six foot, broad in proportion and very strong. A contemporary quoted by Kaye[9] describes him as he was at the siege of Delhi: 'There was something of immense strength, talent and resolution in his whole gait and manner, and a power of ruling men on high occasions that no one could escape noticing at once.' He was remarkably dextrous with a sword. In those days tigers were a pest, and it was considered a good deed to kill them. Nicholson's method of doing this was to ride round and round the tiger in ever diminishing circles, never giving it time to leap and reducing the animal to a bewildered state until he got near enough to kill it with one stroke of his sword; a second stroke would have been too late. He had no training in military science, and his methods of warfare were equally bold and original. Sizing up a situation in a flash, he would see what had to be done and do it himself, ignoring dangers and inspiring his followers of both races to emulate him.

John Nicholson could be insubordinate almost to the point of mutiny. Nelson could put his blind eye to the telescope; Nicholson seemed to have two blind eyes. On the North-West Frontier in those years there were many emergencies that called for quick decision. And Nicholson was nearly always right when his superiors were wrong.

Little as he said, Nicholson was outspoken when he thought anything was wrong, which made him unpopular with his fellow officers. After the Second Sikh War he was furious both at the looting by the native troops and by the way that their European officers protected them. If he had had his way he would have put the looting down in two days. The gradual decline of discipline in the Bengal Army was one of the chief factors that led to the Indian Mutiny.

As a magistrate John Nicholson combined an unfailing memory for faces and what sometimes seemed to be an almost supernatural power for reading motives. He was thorough and energetic in investigating a crime and severe in his punishments, flogging the guilty freely in preference to sending them to prison where they would only be further corrupted. He was greatly feared but his justice was never questioned, and lawlessness was replaced by peace almost at once wherever his writ ran. The Punjabis of all communities revered him with an awe that had a strong tincture of love. Many brave men with brown skins were in tears at his funeral.

During the siege of Delhi a European lady who had survived the Delhi massacre was brought into camp by two Afghans after a number of bloodcurdling adventures and narrow escapes. The two Afghans had concealed her with great difficulty and at considerable risk to themselves for three or four months. Nicholson received them sitting on his horse in the full glare of the Indian sun and gazed at them. Then he said to one of the Afghans, 'You were tried at Peshawar three years ago, convicted of felony and sentenced to fourteen years imprisonment.' The man fell flat and exclaimed, 'My Lord and my God.' Nicholson then addressed the other, giving him details of his crimes, also. He too prostrated himself but they were told to get up. Nicholson pardoned them on condition that they continued to act faithfully. They were to be spies, and he gave a warning: 'Do you believe that if you are faithless to my trust my arm is long enough to reach you, wherever you are?' The two men confirmed with trembling that they did so believe.

During the advance on Delhi of the famous movable column commanded by John Nicholson in the Mutiny it was a common sight in the evenings for a number of Sikhs to appear and to seek admittance to the General's tent in bodies of about a dozen by turns. They sat on the ground, fixing their adoring eyes on Nicholson for a while and then made way for another group. John Nicholson just got on with his work, taking no notice of his visitors, unless they prostrated themselves before the object of their worship, when they were soundly whipped and ejected.

These men were presumably Orthodox Sikhs by faith. Indian religion can be very elastic. There was also a small sect of devotees known as Nikalseinis who worshipped Nikal Sein as an incarnation of Brahma. He always had them flogged and sent away when they came to worship him, but they only came back the more. Eventually he dismissed them on condition that they transferred their devotion to John Becher, one of the gentlest, best and most charming of Lawrence's Young Men. When the news of Nicholson's death came through one of his *gurus* committed suicide saying that there was no gain in living any longer. But another reminded them that Nikal Sein had worshipped an invisible God. If they hoped to please Nikal Sein while they lived and to see him again in another life, they must worship his God. Accordingly they sought instruction in Christianity and after a year sought baptism.

So far John Nicholson appears an awe-inspiring figure, but those who knew him best always said that he could be as 'tender as a woman' and had a loving heart behind his ferocity. There are many stories about his ways with children. He succeeded Herbert Edwardes in Bannu, and writing from there to Edwardes in Peshawar he asked for a supply of toys to give to the Waziri children and told the following story:

Fancy a wretched little Waziri child who had been put up to poison food, on my asking him if he knew it was wrong to kill people, saying he knew it was wrong to kill with a knife or a sword. I asked him why and he said 'because the blood left marks'. It ended in my ordering him to be taken away from his own relatives, who ill used him as much as they ill taught him, and made him over to some respectable man, who would engage to treat him and bring him up well. The little chap heard the order given and called out 'Oh, there's such a good man in the Miri Tuppeh please send me to him'. I asked how he knew the man he named was good, and he said 'He never gives anyone bread without *ghee* on it.' I found on enquiry that the man in question was a good man in other respects, and he agreeing, I made the little fellow over to him, and I have seldom seen anything more touching than their mutual adoption of each other as father and son, the child clasping the man's beard, and the man with his hands on the child's head.

Most of all John Nicholson loved his mother and next to her Herbert Edwardes. After them his brother, Charles, and Henry and Honoria Lawrence were nearest to his heart. Henry understood him and gave him wise advice in April 1848 when at the age of twenty-six he was settling down to rule the Sind Sagur Doab, a province the size of

Wales between the Indus and the Jhelum, much of which turns into an ocean – as its name indicates – when the melting snow in the high mountains causes the Indus to overflow. At this time Henry wrote to him: 'Bear and forebear with natives and Europeans and you will be as distinguished as a civilian as you are as a soldier. Don't think it is necessary to say all you think to everyone. The world would be a mass of tumult if we all gave *candid* opinions of each other. I admire your sincerity as much as any man can do, but say this much as a general warning.' Nicholson took this well and tried hard to follow in this path but without much success. When John Lawrence succeeded Henry as Nicholson's chief, he suffered much from Nicholson's neglect of all rules but tolerated it gladly, for he too saw John Nicholson's worth.

When the Second Sikh War began to smoulder John Nicholson was in Peshawar as George Lawrence's assistant, but the chances of war brought him to many parts of the North-West Frontier. 'What corner of the Punjab is not witness to your gallantry?' So Henry wrote to him, when the fighting was over. During the war the energetic Nicholson had been characteristically scathing in his criticism of Currie, whom he called the 'Rosy One'. Writing to Abbott on 1st July he said: 'It is impossible ever to fathom the Rosy One's intentions . . . We are without further news of Multan or Lahore, save that the Resident talks to *his* "Muhammadan combinations" and of the way in which he "humbugged the Khalsa". This is remotely verging upon the extreme confines of coolness. I imagine he will make a favourable report on Edwardes for so well carrying out *his* plans.'

It was important to prevent the rebel forces concentrating in any one place. In particular, the Sikh General, Chatar Singh, whose intentions were suspect, had a large force in Hazara, where James Abbott was in charge. Abbott with the help of the local population slowed down the movement of the far more numerous and better armed Sikhs as much as he could. Nicholson had raised an irregular force of 380 horse and 700 foot from tribesmen who were glad to take service in any war and would often be particularly glad to fight the Sikhs. On 27th September, when the war was moving towards its climax, Nicholson wrote to his mother that 'Chatar Singh and his son, who are in rebellion, have eight regiments and sixteen guns so that I am unable to meet them openly in the field. I received a slight hurt from a stone in a skirmish in the hills a week or two ago.' He had often had 'a worse one when a boy at school'. What had happened was as follows: The Margalla or Cut Throat Pass runs through the limestone ridge on the road from Hazara through Hassan Abdal to Rawalpindi. This pass was commanded by a *burj* or tower built of huge stones without mortar. From this tower a few marksmen might greatly hinder the march of the whole brigade which Atar Singh was leading to the support of his father Chatar Singh in Hazara. Nicholson hoped by a timely rush to seize this tower and keep the two forces apart for some time longer. He quietly brought his men up to within easy reach of the tower and gave the orders for a charge. He led the way himself followed by about a dozen of the most trusted chiefs. On reaching the tower he found that the rest of the force were nowhere in sight. When he went ahead with his back to the men, they stayed behind, reckoning in Abbott's words that 'he being ahead could not possibly see who misbehaved'. Worse still, it was then discovered that the *burj*, like an Irish round tower, had only one entrance so far above the ground that it could only be reached by scaling ladders. And Nicholson's force had no ladders. If his men had followed him, they might have forced the garrison to surrender by piling burning brushwood round the tower, but this was no longer possible. Anyone else would have retreated but Nicholson took shelter right under the walls of the tower. The garrison were too timid to lean over far enough to hit them and John Nicholson began to demolish the tower with his own hands by tearing blocks of stone out of the mortarless wall. The defenders retaliated by hurling large stones on to their attackers and one of these struck John Nicholson severely in the face. By that time a body of Atar Singh's troops were seen approaching the tower and Nicholson reluctantly withdrew. An impressive memorial to John Nicholson now stands on the site of the Margalla Tower.

His fame was neither transient nor confined to his own countrymen. Within ten years of his death a Punjabi ballad about the death of Nikal Sein was being sung in the streets of Delhi by those who earned their livelihood by singing for the pleasure of the lower ranks of society. In this ballad there is no suggestion that Nicholson was a foreign conqueror. He had become a Punjabi folk hero, about whom many tales, some true and some apocryphal, were told. The ballad is written from a Sikh point of view, reflecting both hatred of the mutineers and high praise for the British and particularly for Nikal Sein and Jan Larens. It ends:

> We ceaseless pray the warrior's God with all a soldier's love
> That he would make brave Nikal Sein a prince in heaven above.
> O Godlike chieftain Nikal Sein our children lisp thy name
> Thou'lt not forget the *Khalsas'* prayers, their babies prate thy name.

It was accidentally overheard by a passing British officer, Captain Newbury, who translated it as best he could.

Nearly a century later the time came when an independent Indian Government decided to take down the statue of John Nicholson in Delhi. A British officer who was passing by at the time found a number of police and workmen gathered round the statue. Why, he asked, did they need armed men? The superintendent of police said, rather sheepishly, that Nikal Sein was very *zubberdast* and they could not be sure that his spirit would not return to punish those who disturbed his rest.[10]

During the Second Sikh War Nicholson cooperated closely with James Abbott whose bailiwick adjoined his own. On the upper Indus by the border of Kashmir lies the mountainous district of Hazara, the land of a thousand warring chieftains. Originally allocated to Gulab Singh, Hazara was part of his Kingdom of Kashmir but it was so unruly that he was unable to take possession. So it was reunited with the rest of the Punjab in return for frontier rectifications elsewhere. Hazara had been conquered by Ranjit Singh but never administered by the Sikhs. The best they could do was to exact occasional tribute in proportion to the strength of the army sent to collect it. By nature Hazara is a charming country, well watered with a profusion of orchards with limes, peaches, apricots, vines twining from tree to tree and wild roses and clematis in the hedges. But in 1847 it was desolate and denuded of timber: the Sikhs destroyed trees wherever they went.

Henry Lawrence had placed his old friend James Abbott in charge of this difficult, fertile frontier fief of the Sikh Kingdom and under him peace had succeeded anarchy with astonishing rapidity. Henry Lawrence describes him: 'Major James Abbott is of the stuff of the true Knight errant; gentle as a girl in thought and word and deed, overflowing with warm affections and ready at all times to sacrifice himself for his friend or his country; he is at the same time a scientific, courageous and energetic soldier with peculiar power of attaching others, especially Asiatics to his person.' Abbott was of the same generation as Henry, rather older than most of the Young Men. Before coming to the Punjab he had made a journey to Khiva in Central Asia, which was at that time an independent Khanate, practising an Islamic way of life, and living by slave raids into Persia on the south and the Russian Empire on the north. Abbott's object, which Honoria called 'a work of simple benevolence', was to negotiate the deliverance of some Persian slaves. He suffered the loss of the first finger of his right hand and was imprisoned on the shores of the Caspian before liberating Russian as well as Persian slaves and making his way through Russia to St Petersburg. He remained as Deputy Commissioner of Hazara from 1847 to 1853.

Honoria Lawrence describes him in the journal she kept for her children in England. Among the people of Hazara

> Major Abbott lives as a patriarch. It is delightful to see a British officer loved and respected, as he is. I do not mean that he is

perfect, for he has some failings that make it difficult to deal with him officially, and he gives papa more trouble than many a man of not a tenth part the merit. The more so because papa has so high a regard for him. Abbott is morbidly sensitive, and he has lived so long without coming in contact with other educated minds that he cannot apprehend any view but his own. He is aged about forty, small make with eager black eyes and well marked features. I suppose it is many years since shears or razor approached him, and his hair and beard are silver white. A broad brimmed white hat, coat and trousers made after the taste of a Hazara tailor, a spiked staff about seven foot long, and the whole man alive with energy, a remarkably sweet and gentle voice.

In Hazara Honoria found a general prosperity with 'no absolute poverty in the whole place', and she noted that tens of thousands of trees had been planted but had not yet had time to grow.

Herbert Edwardes, who succeeded Abbott in Hazara, wrote that after Abbott's six-years rule 'the district of Hazara which was notorious for its long continued struggles with the Sikhs, is now about the quietest, happiest and most loyal in the Punjab . . . During his rule exiles driven out by the Sikhs, ten, twenty, thirty, forty years before had flocked back again from behind the border and resettled on their paternal lands; Hazara had passed from a desolation to a smiling prosperity.' And all this was the work of James Abbott who

had literally lived among them as their patriarch – an out of door, under tree life. Every man woman and child in the country knew him personally, and hastened from their occupations to salute him as he came their way. The children especially were his favourites. They used to go to 'Kaka Abbott', whenever their mouths watered for fruit or sugar plums. He spent all his substance on the people.

His last act was to invite the country – not the neighbours, but all Hazara – to a farewell feast on the Nara Hill; and there for three days and nights he might be seen walking about among the groups of guests and hecatombs of pots and cauldrons – the kind and courteous host of a whole people.

And Hazara is about the size of Wales, though at that time much less populous.

Almost at once Abbott's touch produced such a degree of peace and good order that it was possible to place a large contingent of the Sikh army in this hitherto inaccessible province but, as the rising in the Second Sikh War spread slowly, the Sikh regiments in Hazara caught the contagion and joined the rebels. With the help of the local people

Abbott contained the Sikh regiments for longer than might have been considered possible and it has already been described how John Nicholson, in close collaboration with James Abbott, tried to prevent them joining with the main force of the Sikh army. But the odds were too heavy and in the end the Sikhs in Hazara were able to join up with their comrades further south. The city of Abbottabad perpetuates the name of James Abbott and his memory remains green. A recent traveller was told with admiration how Abbott once stayed the night with one of his subjects and came back specially to pay the full cost of his board and lodging.

As the news reaching England worsened, the home Government sent Sir Charles Napier out to replace Gough as Commander in Chief, but after the terrible drawn battle of Chilianwala, while Napier was still on his way, Gough had on 21st February won a decisive victory at Gujerat. After a brilliant pursuit by General Gilbert, the best rider in India, the whole Sikh army had surrendered on 14th March 1849. Bosworth Smith describes the scene:

> With noble self restraint . . . thirty-five chiefs laid down their swords at Gilbert's feet, while the Sikh soldiers, advancing one by one to the file of English drawn across the road, flung down *tulwar*, matchlock and shield upon the growing heap of arms, *salaamed* to them as to the 'spirit of the steel', and passed through the open line, no longer soldiers. But it must have been a more touching sight still when – as it has been described to me by eye witnesses – each horseman among them had to part for the last time from the animal, which he regarded as part of himself . . . He caressed and patted his faithful companion on every part of his body and then turned resolutely away. But his resolution failed him. He turned back again and again to give one caress more, and then as he tore himself away for the last time, brushed a tear drop from his eyes, and exclaimed . . . 'Runjit Singh is dead today'.

The officials appointed by the Sikh Government suddenly 'evinced amazing energy in collecting supplies and sending them up from districts where to that date (21st February 1849) not an article of carriage was to be had for love, fear or money'.[11] And in some more distant parts of the Kingdom the inhabitants seemed 'to have completely dismissed the *Khalsa* from their memories, or if it is ever called to mind it is with a feeling of heartfelt congratulation at the fact of its power having passed away.'[12]

When the news of the rebellion reached England, Henry Lawrence was in Ireland. He had gained ten pounds in weight, but his health was still precarious. Nevertheless, he wrote to Sir John Hobhouse, the

Left: miniature portrait of Henry Lawrence, by an Indian artist *c.* 1850. *Below Left:* John Lawrence and *Below Right:* Lord Hardinge, Governor-General of India 1844-48.

A battle during the First Sikh War, 1845-6, by a Sikh artist.

Left: Herbert Edwardes in Indian dress. *Below Left:* Henry Lawrence dictating to the Rajah Dina Nath *(see pages 132, 138, 140, and 200)*, and *Below Right:* Henry Lawrence in England, looking at miniatures of his children *c.*1847.

Above: Lahore 1849.

Below: The Sikh sirdars, 1850.

Left: George Lawrence, Herbert Edwardes and Henry Lawrence. *Below:* The Marquis of Dalhousie, Governor-General of India 1848-56.

The Durbar at Udaipur, February 1855. Centre is the Maharana of
Udaipur, Sarap Singh. On his right are Henry Lawrence, his brother
George, Captain Brooke and Dr Ebden, the Residency Surgeon. On his
left are the Thakurs of Udaipur. Painted by F. C. Lewis, 1855.

Above: Mount Abu, 1854. *Left:* Silhouettes of Henry, Honoria, and Harry, drawn by Mrs Kate Hill in 1852.

Right: Henry Lawrence at Lucknow in 1857. *Below:* Lucknow after the siege, from inside the billiard room of the Residency.

President of the Board of Control, volunteering to return to India. Hobhouse summoned him back from Ireland, and Henry assured him that the resources available in the Punjab were fully adequate to contain the 'political disturbance' at Multan, as indeed they should have been. But Hobhouse remained uneasy and arranged for Henry to see the Duke of Wellington who told him, in the light of increasingly bad news, that he ought to go back to India at once.

He sailed with Honoria, his second son Harry, and his sister Charlotte, now aged thirty-four, reaching Bombay early in December 1848. Henry went on by himself by steamer to Karachi and then, as fast as only he could go, up the Indus, reaching the Punjab in time to take part in the closing scenes of the Second Sikh War, and to bring Dalhousie the first news of victory at Multan.

Arriving in Lahore, he not unnaturally supposed he could pick up the threads where he left off and that he could count on the new Governor-General to give him much of the room for manoeuvre that he had enjoyed under Hardinge. He prepared a Proclamation saying that 'he was anxious that it should be generally known that he had returned to Lahore desirous of bringing peace to the Punjab.' When, however, the draft of this Proclamation was submitted to Dalhousie, his hackles were aroused. He describes his reaction in a letter to his intimate friend, Sir George Couper: 'I told him this sort of thing would not do at all . . . I could not permit him to substitute himself for the Government, whose servant he was, or permit a word to be said or an act to be done which should raise the notion that the policy of the Government depended in any degree on the Agent who represented it; or that any measure and intention would be the least affected by the fact of his being the Resident or Sir F. Currie in his stead.'

This was overkill. But there was a reason. The Home Government was in perplexity about what to do with the Punjab and had decided not to take any decision for or against annexation until Henry had seen the situation himself and had conferred with the new Governor-General.[13] Dalhousie must have got wind of this and was determined to show that he was master. For this purpose he was prepared, if he judged it necessary, to address senior men with harshness and rudeness. Two years later Henry complained to John that 'he vents his imperativeness on us in a way that would be unbecoming if we were his servants.'

Yet James Ramsay (1812-60), tenth Earl and First Marquis of Dalhousie, was a remarkable man. His superior ability, energy and devotion to duty made him one of the greatest administrators, but of the opposite school to Henry Lawrence. Dalhousie's *forte* was paper work and he looked with a disapproving eye on Henry's absences from Lahore, to see the country for himself. Dalhousie was a little man but he had a great sense of his own importance, not only as Governor-General of India but also as the head of all Ramsays. Sir Charles Napier, the new Commander in Chief, was soon to make himself a pest equally to the Lawrences and to Dalhousie whom he used to call 'the laird of Cockpen'. Dalhousie was still in his thirties when he was appointed Governor-General but already, as President of the Board of Trade, he had done much to give Britain the network of railways on which it still depends. In India his services were enormous on the utilitarian level, but he was deaf to all overtones. He was very touchy about any suggestions or criticisms that came from his masters in London, but not always sensitive to the feeling of those who served him in India. Yet he had the devoted admiration of those who were closest to him in his work. He surrounded himself with able men but his judgment of character was fallible: he thought that Colin Campbell was not capable of high command.

Henry Lawrence and Dalhousie were temperamentally incompatible. Henry was too sensitive. Dalhousie was overbearing and he started with prejudices. He thought that 'Lawrence has been greatly praised and rewarded and petted, and no doubt naturally supposes himself a king of the Punjab, but . . . I don't take the Brentford dynasty as a pattern . . . it will soon be settled'.[14] Dalhousie did not mince his words and, if he required submission from his own subordinates, he equally expected them to require a like submission from their own subordinates. His style of correspondence is illustrated by a letter he wrote to Henry towards the end of the Second Sikh War:

I observe what you say regarding General Campbell (Sir Colin) having told you that there was 'no thought of crossing the Jhelum this season.' Your brother will have ere this reassured you on that point, which he incidentally mentioned to me. What 'thought' the camp of the Commander in Chief has signifies very little. The camp's business is to find fighting; I find thought; and such thought as the camp has hitherto found is of such damned bad quality, that it does not induce me to forego the exercise of my proper functions. It is too late to enter tonight into the details of your letter. I will only say now generally, that the camp will cross the Jhelum this season, and, please God, the Indus also; that the Commander in Chief and General Thackwell, or the Departments, will not cross it; that General Gilbert will command, and I hope the job will be well done. All this I communicated to the Commander in Chief some time ago, authorising him, and requiring him, in the event of the opportunity presenting itself, to make the arrangements himself, and expedite matters as much as possible.

I am greatly surprised with what you write to me about Major

Edwardes, or rather I should say I am greatly vexed, but not surprised at all. [Edwardes, it should be explained here, had without prior authorisation disbanded a Pathan regiment, whose fidelity he had every reason to suspect.] From the tone of your letter I perceive it is not necessary to say that you should pull up Major Edwardes for this at once. But I further wish to repeat what I said before, that there are more than Major Edwardes in the Residency who appear to consider themselves nowadays as Governor-General at least. The sooner you set about disenchanting their minds of this illusion the better for your comfort and their own. I don't doubt you will find bit and martingale for them speedily. For my part, I will not stand it in quieter times for half an hour, and will come down unmistakably upon any one of them who may 'try it on' from Major Edwardes, C.B., down to the latest enlisted general, ensign, plenipotentiary on the establishment. Tomorrow I will write again.

Believe me, Yours sincerely, Dalhousie.

Dalhousie was not disposed to wait for instructions from London before deciding how to dispose of the Punjab. It was urgent to get the country settled and, as he pointed out, London could always change his arrangements, if it did not like them. Henry still hoped that the Punjab would not be annexed but John, after a good deal of hesitation, had come down on the side of annexation, which was what Dalhousie wanted. So the Punjab was annexed to British India and placed under a Board of Administration consisting in the first instance of Henry Lawrence, John Lawrence and C. G. Mansell. Writing to Sir George Couper in 1857, after he had returned from India, Dalhousie described the circumstances with the benefit, no doubt, of some hindsight. 'I found him [Sir Henry Lawrence] Resident and could not help making him the head of the new government. But I would not make him sole head. Well aware as I was of the innate evils of a Board, I created a Board rather than have what I considered the greater evil of a sole authority vested in Sir Henry Lawrence.' Henry was for a time so depressed that he would have been glad to cut his connection with the Punjab, if he 'could do so with credit'.

On 9th June 1849 Dalhousie wrote to Sir George Couper from Simla describing how he handled his relations with Henry. 'Sir Henry Lawrence is disgusted, of course, with being a Board, and that Board being under strict control. He has tried restiveness once or twice. Lately, here, where he has come sick, he began to try the stormy tone. Upon this I tipped him a little of the 'grand seigneur', which I had not given him before, and the storm sank into a whisper in a second.' When Lord Dalhousie gave a reproof, he knew how to turn the knife in the wound.

CHAPTER 12

Remaking the Punjab

(i) *The Board of Administration*

The Board of Administration which was to rule the Punjab from 1849 to 1853 received its instructions on 31st March 1849 in a detailed minute from 'H. M. Elliot, Secretary to the Government of India with the Governor-General'.

Henry had accepted the Presidency of the Board not without misgivings. He wrote to Lord Hardinge:

> I am, as I was, of opinion that circumstances and our gross military misconduct have brought things to the present pass and that elsewhere in India, a shorter period of military misconduct would have effected a similar crisis. Still as so many of all ranks have deserted, and as so few of those with us have been actively loyal, the Government have it in their own hands to do as they choose, if I were sure that Mackeson or someone like him would not get my berth, if I vacated, I would resign if annexation is decided on.

If the making of the decision to set up this Board brought out the petty side of Dalhousie, the document by which it was established showed him at his best. Much of the detail is only of interest to specialists but the vigour and clarity of Dalhousie's mind shine through the bureaucratic minutiae. And the broad sweep of his instructions show that in a very short time the new Governor-General had absorbed many of the lessons of Anglo–Indian history. It was also clear that he intended to take a close personal interest in the Punjab, a fact which may account for a glaring gap in the instructions. It was not laid down what was to happen if members of the Board disagreed.

This point could hardly escape a man with Dalhousie's experience and his practical turn of mind, but from his summer eyrie at Simla, he intended to keep a close grip on Punjab affairs and he may well have supposed that his personal decision would be more than sufficient to compose any differences. Yet he does not seem to have realised that there might be endless important but relatively minor matters which were not worth bringing to the Governor-General, but could still be the subject of acute friction and that the cumulative effect of such friction could place an intolerable strain on the personal relations of the members of the Board. Although Henry was its President he could not overrule his colleagues. Dalhousie's study of Indian history might have led him to remember that his greatest predecessor, Warren Hastings, had been in the same position and had found it intolerable. Dalhousie owed his own unfettered powers to the fact that Hastings' successor, Cornwallis, had refused to serve as Governor-General unless he had power to overrule his Council. It was right that all members of the Board should have direct access to the Governor-General who had the ultimate power to overrule any of their decisions. But it was a mistake to leave the Board with no internal procedure for settling differences.

Mansell was a quiet man who could see two sides to every question. But both Henry and John were strong willed, and disagreed strongly on certain subjects. While John was acting for Henry as President, at Lahore, he always deferred conscientiously to his brother's known opinions, but, when the two were placed roughly on the same level as members of the Board of Administration, John pressed his views with all the force of his character. Henry did the same. And the resulting clashes placed an appalling strain on both, all the more so because of their love for each other. Neither was entirely right but each had his strong points, and it was thought at the time that the Punjab benefited more from their uneasy partnership than it would have from the rule of either alone. Dalhousie, able as he was, lacked the subtlety to foresee the likely interaction of complex characters.

The instructions to the Board begin by laying down the establishment, with names and salaries, which were to govern the Punjab. They were a *corps d'élite*, and these instructions observe in their restrained official language that 'as they have all been selected for their known or presumed qualifications, the Governor-General has no doubt that you will find them as efficient a body of public servants as have ever been employed in a single province in India'.

Then Dalhousie came to the nub of the matter. 'The Governor-General would wish to uphold native institutions and practices, as far as they are consistent with the distribution of justice to all classes.' He then modifies it by saying that 'except for some of the wild districts, Trans-Indus or the Afghan country of the Sindh Sagur Doab, there is no portion of the country which will not be benefited by the gradual introduction of the British system at the earliest possible period'. I conclude that Dalhousie had received conflicting advice and that for once he failed to think clearly on a vital matter.

The Board's hierarchy in order of ranks consisted of Commissioners, Deputy Commissioners, Assistant Commissioners and Extra Assistants. These last could be natives of India and would also be designated as *Adalutees* and *Kardars*, 'being terms familiar to our new subjects'. The new administration had been strengthened by the transfer of some of the best officials who had been trained in the North-West Provinces where Thomason was now Lieutenant-Governor. They had generally been specially selected by Henry. With characteristic generosity Thomason sent his best man at Henry's request. The Governor-General did not expect a corps of qualified Punjabi civil servants to spring instantly from the ground. Therefore 'the chief Civil Officers called from the North-West Provinces have been invited to bring a few trustworthy and experienced men with them to form the nucleus of their establishments . . . ' but 'every means should be taken to employ the natives of the country (i.e. the Punjab), who before long, and in some cases immediately, will be found able to conduct the duties which in our Regulation Provinces devolve upon the highest class of native functionaries'.

Little distinction was made between executive, judicial, and fiscal functions. All the servants of the Board of Administration were maids of all work.

The law to be applied was a simplified form of the law current in British India, 'calculated to ensure substantial justice without the observance of unnecessary forms, and the technicalities which fetter our regular courts of law. The Governor-General has no wish that our voluminous laws should be introduced into this new country.' The British system of law eventually became better accepted in India and is carefully maintained by independent India and the other succession states, but in the first half of the nineteenth century there were continual complaints, both from British and from Indians, about the bad effects of an alien system of law, which in Indian conditions seemed to encourage litigation and perjury. Henry Lawrence thought that traditional village justice was very good in its own sphere and that, for cases that could not be settled in a village, something simpler than the voluminous laws and technicalities of British India was needed in the Punjab. It is not known whether their instructions were discussed in draft with the members of the Board. On this point their instructions would have had the enthusiastic approval of both the Lawrences.

In the report on their first three years of administration the Board show themselves sensitive to the danger that experience of the inconvenience and delays of British justice 'to which witnesses and prosecutors are too often exposed in attendance on our courts' may discourage cooperation with the police. 'But this result the Board will strive to avert. They know that the remedy's in their own hands; and that if our officers are accessible and assiduous, if oversize districts are reduced' and lastly 'if the native local authorities are rendered competent to exercise judicial process', then the population may be expected to work with the police for law and order.

Much the longest section of these instructions concerned the rent-free feudal grants known as *jaghirs*. This was to be 'the very first object to which the Board should direct their attention'. Under the Indian form of feudalism the grant of *jaghirs* was one of the chief means by which Indian governments maintained their civil, military and religious establishments. These grants were freely resumed when the native rulers saw good. They had multiplied inordinately in the Punjab and were a heavy burden on the treasury. Some had to be resumed, others regranted on modified terms and others commuted to pensions. 'In our older provinces . . . the investigations were delayed to so late a period as to give our proceedings a character of injustice and severity.' That mistake must not be made again. Adjustments made quickly would often be accepted with a good grace, but 'the longer the investigation is delayed, so much the more do these tenures acquire the force of prescriptions'. This proved to be the most difficult and contentious branch of the Board's work.

'It will be advisable that the members of the Board should occasionally proceed on a tour of inspection.' Henry was to make these grand tours, when he ruled almost from the saddle, into a leading feature of his personal approach to all the problems and opportunities presented by the Punjab. These helped him to get to know every corner of those vast domains and the leading personality in every place. But Dalhousie made it clear that he did not like the President of the Board being away so much from Lahore.

Finally, it is clear that through weekly abstracts of correspondence and through its fiscal control, the Government of India could exercise a close control, if it so wished. But Dalhousie was determined to make a success of the annexation of the Punjab and it is fair to say that he encouraged more than he restrained.

(ii) The Punjab Described

The Punjab, the land of the five rivers, which the Lawrences now received into their care was a rough triangle filling up the north-west corner of the Indian subcontinent. It measured about three hundred miles north to south and a little more from east to west. Its base lay in the foothills of the western Himalayas and its apex was just beyond Multan on the Indus. South of this point lay Sind. To the east across the Indus, the political boundary was formed by the Suleiman range, which was joined to the Punjab by a narrow strip of cultivation along the Indus. To the south and south-west the Punjab is bordered by the great Indian desert, except for a broad opening of fertile land between the Himalayas and the desert; this was the gate by which all previous invaders had come; just beyond it lay Delhi, as if beckoning them on. The strict boundary of the Punjab was the river Sutlej but in a loose sense the left bank of that river to the gates of Delhi was part of the Punjab with all the land up to the gates.

The five rivers of the Punjab, tributaries of the mighty Indus, all rise in the mountains and enter the plain at a considerable distance from each other, converging gradually until they are all lost in the Indus. Thus the country was made up of triangular slices with their apex to the south. Each of these was called a *doab* or mesopotamia, and each had its special character. Moslems, Hindus and Sikhs were found throughout but the Sikhs and Hindus preponderated in the east and Moslems in the west.

The Punjab is well described in the opening pages of the Board of Administration's Report for the years 1849-50 and 1850-51. It was drafted by Sir Richard Temple, at that time a young man learning the trade of an Indian Civil Servant under the tutelage of the Lawrences. He writes:

> The face of the country presents every variety from the most luxuriant cultivation to the most sandy deserts, and the wildest prairies of grass and brushwood. A traveller passing through these lines of communication, which traverse the northern tracts, would imagine the Punjab to be the garden of India; again returning by the road which intersects the central tracts, he would suppose it to be a country not worth annexing. The culture manifestly depends on two causes, the lower Himalayan range, and the rivers. From the base of the hills southward, there stretches a strip of country from fifty to eighty miles broad, watered by mountain rivulets, and for

fertility unsurpassed in Northern India. In their downard course the rivers spread wealth and fruitfulness on either side and their banks are enriched with alluvial deposits and fringed with the finest cultivation. These tracts though unadorned with trees, and un-relieved by any picturesque features, are studded with well peopled villages, are covered with two waving harvests in the year, and are the homes of a sturdy, industrious and skilful peasantry . . .

Far different is the sad and strange scene which meets the eye in the centre of all the *doabs*. These are interminable wastes, over-grown with grass and bushes, scantily threaded by sheep walks and the footprints of cattle. The chief tenants of these parts are pastoral tribes, who, knowing neither law nor prosperity, collect herds of cattle stolen from the agricultural districts. Here and there a hamlet stands alone in the wilderness . . . Around the homesteads there will be patches of good cultivation, for the soil is rich and repays irrigation though the water be deep below the surface. But there are constantly recurring tokens to show that once this region was not inferior to the most favoured districts. Everywhere are seen ruined cities . . .

This region also had a practical importance. It was the only source of fire wood for the towns and 'the great British cantonments . . . It yields an abundant supply of grass for all equestrian establishments. It sustains with its inexhaustible pasturage a noble breed of cattle, buffaloes, sheep and goats. Its boundless grazing supports the camels' which carried most of the trade with Central Asia. 'And portions of it will become the scene of gigantic undertakings, which will tax the skill and resources of the State, but which will ultimately yield an ample return for the outlay of capital. Indeed the Punjab could ill spare its wastes: they are almost as important as the cultivated tracts.' The 'gigantic undertakings' referred to are, of course, the canals and roads which the Board constructed at an almost incredible speed. The deserts in the centre of the *doabs* have passed away long since, to be replaced by closely peopled, well irrigated land. Which has produced its own difficulties, for after four generations of irrigation the salt has been working to the surface, thereby posing problems that are both urgent and complicated.

Finally it should be added that the western *doabs* are cut in two by the great Salt Range, running east and west from the river Jhelum to the Suleiman mountains. Temple adds: 'The fiscal and commercial importance of the range with its inexhaustible veins of rock salt will occasion its frequent mention hereafter.'

The left bank of the Sutlej had been under British influence for forty years, sometimes as a part of India and sometimes in the form of

Native States such as Patiala and Jhind which accepted Britain as the Paramount Power, but ordered their own internal affairs, subject to the advice of a British Resident – advice which was sometimes pressed to the point where it would have been unwise to disregard it. The easternmost of the *doabs*, the Jullundur Doab, which was the most prosperous part of the Punjab, had been a part of British India for three years, and John Lawrence had already made progress in giving it peaceful and efficient rule. After 1849, the Native States of the Punjab continued as before. So there was less to be done in the eastern parts of the Board's territory, i.e. the Cis-Sutlej districts and the Jullundur Doab. West of that there was everything to do and it was the four western *doabs* and the new North-West Frontier which took up most of the Board's energies.

(iii) *What the Board Did*

In the account of the Board's achievements, I have generally followed the two Punjab Reports for 1849-51 and 1852-3, written for the Board by the future Sir Richard Temple. These were continued in the third Punjab Report still written by Temple after the Board had been abolished at a time when John Lawrence was Chief Commissioner of the Punjab. Unless otherwise indicated, all quotations in this section of this chapter are from the first two Punjab Reports. The general tenor of this account is borne out by many other sources; and the Board were candid in making corrections, when experience showed that first estimates were too optimistic. At the end of Temple's life, Bosworth Smith asked him whether he now thought that any part of the Punjab Reports was too highly coloured. Temple, who had held high office in nearly every part of India, answered emphatically: 'There is not a word in the Punjab Reports which I would wish unwritten. On the contrary, I should feel justified in speaking now even more highly of the achievements of the Board than I did then.'

Eighteen forty-nine and eighteen fifty were, in Temple's words, 'years of originating'. Eighteen fifty-one and eighteen fifty-two were rather years of 'perfecting' what had begun. The first task was to secure peace in a turbulent land with hardy, courageous and lawless tribes to the north and west, tribes who were accustomed from time immemorial to raiding their neighbours in order to supplement the meagre livelihood afforded by their barren hills. According to the census taken just after the Board of Administration had been abolished the population of the Punjab was thirteen million with a further seven million in the Native States that were politically dependent on it. It was further calculated that two-thirds of the population of the Punjab proper were Moslems, mainly the descendants of converts from Hinduism; the remaining third of the population were Hindus or Sikhs. Temple observed that

with the single exception of the Sikhs it is remarkable that the Hindu races, whether converts to a foreign creed or professors of their ancestral faith, consider themselves as subjects by nature and born to obedience. They are disposed to regard each successive dynasty with equal favour or equal indifference, whereas the pure Mussulman races, descendants of the Arab conquerors of Asia, retain much of the ferocity, bigotry and independence of ancient days. They look upon empire as their heritage, and consider themselves as foreigners settled in the land for the purpose of ruling it. They hate every dynasty except their own and regard the British as the worst because the most powerful of usurpers . . . Beyond the Indus it is these pure bred Moslems who predominate . . . up to the Indus, then, the vast majority of the population are our natural subjects; beyond the river they are our natural antagonists.

The historical ethnography of this statement is open to question as are some geographical details, but the characterisation of the races in question as they were at the time is realistic. Peace in the Punjab had both an internal and an external aspect.

Regiments of the Company's Bengal army and also of the British army were stationed in the Punjab for use in the event of major hostilities and were under the control of the Commander in Chief and ultimately of the Governor-General. But a force under such a distant command was not suited to deal with the continual incursions and minor insurrections which had always broken out in the wild borderlands, whatever government was nominally in power. The Guides were admirably suited for such tasks. And their Corps was tailor-made to operate in the wild hills in the North-West Frontier, where the plain-dwelling *sepoys* were at a disadvantage against the taller Pathan tribesmen, who could move like goats on their native rocks and were armed with long-barrelled *jezails* that had a longer range and greater accuracy than the smooth-bore muskets of the Indian army. So the Corps was enlarged from just under three hundred men to eight hundred and forty and the Board were empowered to raise ten new regiments, five of cavalry and five of infantry which, it was later decided, would be under the Board's immediate control and instantly available in those sudden emergencies which were continually occurring. These regiments, with the Guides, formed the celebrated Punjab Irregular Frontier Force, the *Piffers*. The word 'irregular' suggests that there was something slipshod about them, but they were only irregular in that they were not bound by all the regulations of the Bengal army. Their discipline and efficiency were as good and sometimes better. The chief differences were that, first, instead of the stiff and constricting British uniforms of the day, they, like the Guides, wore a more comfortable uniform. The Board would have liked to dress them all in khaki, like the Guides, but higher authority insisted for the time being that eight of the ten regiments should be dressed in red. Secondly, they had only a sprinkling of British officers so that positions of real authority could be occupied by Indians. The *Piffers* are now a *corps d'élite* of the Pakistani army, preserving with deep affection and sometimes improving on the traditions implanted by the British.

Henry did not rely on force alone to bring order to the frontier. He established dispensaries under picked doctors. 'The consequence of this was many a strange scene of war and confidence; men wounded on the hillside fighting against us were brought to our pickets and shouts came across the rocks for permission to bring their wounded to our hospitals – even while the fight was going on.'[1]

In the old Indian army a regiment would often contain units of different faiths and races, but each unit would consist of men from the same community and often from the same village, and the same families in that village, generation after generation. In this way variety and cohesion were skilfully combined, and the combination produced and still produces in the armies of the Raj's succession states, a truly remarkable cohesion and loyalty. The honour of all is involved in the honour of each and honour not infrequently rises to heroism. These qualities were conspicuously exhibited in the Corps of Guides, concerning whom Temple wrote,

This interesting and remarkable corps are formed, so that in the same body of men shall be united all the requisites of regular troops with the best qualities of guides and spies, thus combining intelligence and sagacity with courage, and endurance and soldierly bearing and a presence of mind, which rarely fails . . . To ensure the combination of so many diverse qualities, the corps has been composed of the most varied elements; there is scarcely a wild or warlike tribe in Upper India which is not represented in its ranks. In raising this corps, although soldierly qualities were chiefly regarded the other qualifications were not overlooked. Men, habituated from childhood to war and the chase and immune to all the dangers of a wild and mountainous border, were freely admitted to its ranks. To whatever part of Upper India the Corps may be marched, it can furnish men conversant with the features of the country and the dialect of the people.

Through the efforts of the *Piffers* combined with those of the other regular regiments of the Indian and British armies and backed by a sound and imaginative Civil Administration, the wild tribes of the North-West Frontier soon found themselves moving towards a peaceful coexistence with their neighbours such as had never been known before.

The first Punjab Report sums up the progress towards peace made in the first three years.

On the whole the Board cannot but feel satisfied with the degree of internal and external peace which has been maintained on the Trans-Indus Frontier. That not a single *émeute* from within should have occurred is a matter of congratulation, that occasional attacks from without should have been made, only proves the propriety of the preventive measures which had been adopted and it is hoped that the presence of the force now collected, the enlisting of the sympathies of our own subjects, the overawing and ultimately the conciliation of our warlike neighbours may lead to the establishment of comparative quiet.

The Board further observed that the mountaineers can both attack and fly with the most utmost rapidity and 'they seem to hope that they may make themselves troublesome enough to be bought off', an aim in which they were not successful.

The North-West Frontier is never completely quiet. Its peculiarities are of absorbing interest, illustrating as they do the heights and depths of human nature in a highly romantic setting. Elsewhere there has been and is nothing like it except to some extent the experience of the Russians in the Caucasus. I observe that the policy initiated by the Lawrences was maintained for a hundred years by the British Raj and has since been continued virtually unchanged by the Government of Pakistan, operating largely through the same agencies among which the Piffers remain conspicuous.

If there was always some fighting on the Frontier, internal peace reigned throughout the Punjab from the time of the Board's first establishment. As soon as peace was restored after the Second Sikh War a Disarming Proclamation was issued and placarded everywhere.

It was carefully administered and completely successful. The former Sikh army was summoned to Lahore and other centres, where they were given their long arrears of pay before being disbanded.

The most promising among them were taken into the British service. All those we could not admit received gratuities and pensions. The infirm and the superannuated were also pensioned . . . That large bodies of brave men, once so turbulent and formidable as to overcome their Government and wield the destinies of their country should lay down their arms, receive their arrears and retire from an exciting profession to till the ground, without in any place creating a disturbance is indicative of the effect which had been produced by the British power, of the manly forbearance which characterises the Sikh and of the satisfaction felt of the justice of the British Government.

Hazara and the Trans-Indus districts were exempted from the Disarming Proclamation. In these regions which were open to sudden attacks from across the Frontier, the keeping of arms was 'not only licensed but enjoined. The villagers must be taught the art of self-defence, and with this view they are ordered to fortify the plain villages.' In the rest of the Punjab the civilian population handed in just under 20,000 arms of all kinds. Violent crime did not cease altogether but 'the robbers and murderers subsequently captured, have never been found with effective weapons. Their arms were either rudely manufactured, or worn out and rusty with age.' The Punjab police were under Richard Lawrence, the youngest of the brothers, 'Dick the star that would not shine'. If indeed by comparison with his brothers, he did not shine, none the less he had a distinguished career, following Henry as Resident in Nepal and ending up as a Lieutenant-General.

At the outset the Punjab police had a task that was more medieval than modern. They had two branches, military and civil. The task of the military police was prevention, that of the civil police was detection. The military police, known in the family as 'Dick's invincibles', were divided into infantry and cavalry. In regions adjacent to the Frontier they had the task of backing up the military and their best units were esteemed nearly as good as the best irregular regiments.

Their first task was to put down *dakoiti* or banditry on the high roads. This was rapidly accomplished but corpses were still discovered in shallow graves in the clumps of trees that grew by walls or in the jungle near to roads. This led to the surmise that *Thugs* were at work. *Thuggi* had been discovered and suppressed only a few years before in the rest of India, but was not known to have spread to the Punjab. The

Thugs were secret associations of men who robbed and murdered rich travellers with exquisite skill and on the grand scale, for the glory of the goddess Kali and the profit of themselves. They appear to have carried on their work for several centuries without being detected over a vast area of India. But the *Thugs* of the Punjab were of recent origin. They were low caste and they lacked the skill of other *Thugs*. So their bungling led to their detection and then to their rapid suppression at the hands of the civil police who soon became expert detectives.

In the extensive desert tracts between the rivers, cattle thieving was a hereditary occupation, resisted by the victims so far as they could, but not regarded as a crime by the beneficiaries. This custom was first brought under control by the construction of roads, which made the robbers' lairs more accessible and then by the use of professional trackers among the police. John Lawrence before he came to the Punjab had already had experience of the outstanding skills of the members of this remarkable profession. They could pick up marks in the soil that might be invisible to any other eye and interpret them with sureness. If cattle had passed that way they could tell how many and what kind, accompanied by what guard or how many horses. If one was lame they could interpret that. If horses were shod with horse shoes put on back to front, so as to conceal the direction in which they were going, the trackers were not deceived. They could trace stolen cattle to a village where they had been taken and could pick up the tracks (or lack of them) on the other side, so as to discover whether they had gone further.

The progress in the prevention and detection of crime is summed up in the Third Punjab Report: 'The proportion of stolen property subsequently recovered by the police, ranges at about one-third' which was about the same as in London at that time. The second Punjab Report observes modestly that 'The character of the police can rarely in India furnish matter for congratulation – with all diffidence, however . . . the Punjab police are rather above than below the average.'

The killing of female babies was a deeply ingrained custom in some communities of the Punjab, but not in others. Its cause was the difficulty of obtaining suitable husbands for the girls and the great expense of their marriages. 'Female infanticide is so secret and domestic a crime that its prevalence or otherwise is hard to be predicted.' The First Report stated optimistically that infanticide

if not extinguished, is verging upon extinction. We have the concurrent testimony both of Local Officers and of the Native Tribes not themselves concerned in this matter and therefore quite impartial to the effect that the daughter-killing tribes have ceased from

infanticide or nearly ceased. Police measures without being inquisi-
torial have been quite effective and many female children have been
preserved in families where, a few years ago their existence would
have been considered a bane and a stigma. The two incentives to
this secret crime, namely pride of birth and pride of purse have
been nearly removed, facilities for inter-marriage with other tribes
have mitigated the difficulty which some families felt in disposing of
their daughters. The sumptuary rules regulating marriage expenses,
which are now generally obeyed with fidelity, save the father of the
bride being beggared on this account.

The Second Punjab Report shows that this claim was too optimistic. It
was possible to verify that many girl babies were kept alive but it was
not possible to be sure that others had not been done away with.
Infanticide was not the only case where something that would hitherto
have been treated almost as a matter of course was considered by the
new rulers to be a serious crime. Forgery and perjury were others, as
was torture.

The practice of torture had its place in Roman Law and in some
continental systems of Law, but had never formed part of the English
Common Law. The Third Punjab Report had this to say:

The attention of the Punjab Authorities has been earnestly directed
to the prevention of torture by the police. It was rash to assert,
perhaps vain to hope that the practice may not be occasionally
resorted to in a mitigated form, it is to be borne in mind that this
practice has been resorted to for ages and having actually become an
integral part of native institutions, is now difficult to extirpate, but
every police officer has to enter into the most stringent engagements
not to countenance the practice. The magistrates consider themselves solemnly responsible to prevent and prosecute the evil.
Whenever this guilt is brought home to the police, the offenders are
sentenced to long terms of imprisonment, ranging from two to
seven years.

Henry Lawrence hated having to inflict imprisonment as a punishment on anyone, because he felt it degraded a man and injured his
self-respect. Imprisonment therefore was only inflicted for specially
heinous crimes such as torture, or for crimes such as cattle stealing,
which experience proved could only be deterred by imprisonment.
The other punishments, apart from capital punishment, were fines
and flogging. Where there had to be punishment this was inflicted
in preference to imprisonment. The twentieth century has become

more squeamish in its treatment of criminals but hardly less cruel or more effective.

Henry's hatred of imprisonment made him all the more solicitous for the welfare of prisoners. It was a matter of principle to him 'to take immense pains with the prisoners, considering that we were responsible for their lives and health and morals, if we put them into durance'.[2] After entertaining guests to dinner he would often say 'let us go to the gaol'. In this way he could often discover whether the prisoners were being made more unhappy than the mere fact of imprisonment made inevitable and could form a shrewd opinion whether the circumstances of their confinement subjected them to any unnecessary health risks. Improvement in such a matter is, as the Board pointed out, necessarily a work of time, depending as it does on measures such as the replacement of the old forts and other buildings used as prisons by the previous Government. At first there were some epidemics in prisons but by the time that the First Punjab Report was written, the Board could report that according to the findings of an independent Committee the previous year's mortality in Lahore jail 'resulted from local and incidental causes and not from mismanagement. The general ventilation and the cubic space allowed to each prisoner were found to exceed the allowance prescribed by the highest European Authority at that time. The general arrangements of the jail were pronounced to be excellent. The buildings were better even than the accommodation ordinarily provided at Lahore for the troops.' While glad to have achieved this much progress, the Board pointed out a number of faults which it would take time to remedy. Finally, they attributed the improvement 'to the zealous exertions of Dr Hathaway', Henry Lawrence's own doctor, who excelled both as a doctor and as a jail reformer, as well as having many other duties, including those of Henry's secretary.

Turning to civil justice

the Board desires that substantial justice should be plainly dealt with to a simple people, unused to the intricacies of legal proceedings. Their aim is to avoid all technicality, circumlocution and obscurity – to simplify and abridge every rule, procedure and process. They would endeavour to form tribunals, which shall not be hedged in with forms, unintelligible to the vulgar, and only to be interpreted by professional lawyers, but which shall be open and accessible to Courts of Justice, where every man may plead his own claim or . . . conduct his own defence.

It was, perhaps, naive to suppose that in real life these desirable aims can ever be realised except to a very limited extent. A concerted effort to simplify could only do good, even if it could not do all that might be hoped from it.

Where possible the Board built on Indian foundations and notably on the *Panchayat*, an ancestral system of arbitration and conciliation which was used to settle among other things the disputes of neighbours by neighbours. It was thought that neighbours are more likely to know the merits of a quarrel and in any case have to live with their decision. The Board praises the *Panchayats* as 'that rude tribunal, whose voice is all powerful in the regulation of private affairs where individuals are most vitally concerned, and of those social and family interests which are dearest to mankind'. *Panchayats* were found especially valuable in ascertaining truth; but none the less they had their own abuses. The Board therefore laid eminently sensible rules for the conduct of their proceedings. These rules are set out in the First Punjab Report,[3] but 'with good officers they are almost superfluous and with bad officers they are ineffective'. The Board therefore exercised great care in the appointment of officers with judicial powers and supervised them with vigilance. While justice was impartial, its execution was tempered to the means of the loser. Immediate payment was forced from 'moneyed defendants, while an opportunity is given to poor defendants to pay by instalments and care is taken that landed property shall not unnecessarily be brought to the hammer'. In their First Report the Board said that 'on the whole the Board can hardly consider that civil justice has advanced as satisfactorily as the other branches of the administration. Indeed they are not sure that it will ever be very successful. There is no part of the British system so difficult to popularise.' In the Third Punjab Report it was already possible to say 'Our civil system may appear rough and ready; whether it would be suited to other provinces in a different stage of civilisation and with a different machinery at command, may be a question. But in the Punjab it attains the broad and plain object aimed at, and without doubt gives satisfaction to the people.'

As regards material improvements Henry's policy was 'to go ahead at a tremendous pace and cover the country with the means of communication – roads, bridges etc.'[4] This, however, required money. It was said that Ranjit Singh, like Peter the Great before him, taxed everything that was taxable. But the land tax was of necessity the staple of the revenue in a country at the Punjab stage of economic development. Henry Lawrence as Resident after the First Sikh War, had made a beginning in abolishing many vexatious taxes and in reducing the onerous land tax. This process was carried to culmination by the Board of Administration. There was now free trade throughout the Punjab and commerce flourished. The Revenue Survey begun between the two Sikh Wars was now completed. The land tax was greatly reduced and regularly collected, even in what had been the wildest regions. Moreover it was remitted in full to the treasury without any profit to tax farmers or 'squeeze' by tax collectors. The burden on the people decreased and agriculture flourished, with the help of a succession of good seasons, to such an extent that the price of food dropped so low that the farmers had difficulty in meeting their cash obligations until adjustments were made. Few however, went hungry. It is sufficient to say that while the burden of taxation was reduced, the revenue received by the treasury increased, till there was a surplus available for capital development.

Roads and canals were constructed under the skilled and inspired leadership of Robert Napier, a brilliant general purposes soldier who could construct public works to the standard of Brunel one day and the next day lead a military expedition in difficult country against a brave and resourceful enemy. Broad tracts of desert and semi-desert were traversed by roads and watered by irrigation canals, till the Punjab began to take on its present closely cultivated appearance. In times past there had been great irrigation works in the Punjab but in most of the country these had fallen into decay. Only in the province of Multan, during the long and benevolent Governorship of Sawan Mall, the father of Mulraj, had irrigation been extended and kept up, to the great profit of the inhabitants. In mountainous districts such as Kangra, where it was hardly practicable to make regular roads, numerous mountain tracks were constructed for local traffic – a process which at the time of writing is still going on in Nepal: 'Talk of the "development of resources" so prevalent at the end of World War II was also current among our ancestors 100 years earlier and was constantly translated into action by the Board of the Punjab. New varieties of crops were introduced on an extensive scale.'[5]

The Punjab was at this time proverbially treeless; the Sikhs had destroyed trees thoughtlessly on an enormous scale. But under the Board, trees were planted everywhere, by roads and canals and round public buildings, and the foundations were laid of a first-class government forestry service. This continues to do excellent work at the end of the twentieth century. In 1856 it was calculated that the Punjab only had one-tenth of its proper complement of trees, but the planting of trees by private individuals was encouraged with some success.

It is not without a thrill that one can step on the original cobbles of the grand trunk road, as it was constructed by Napier, after overcoming many unforeseen difficulties, at the Margalla pass just below the spot where the Nicholson monument was to stand.

A start was made with care for public health and popular education. In many of these things, the Board set themselves a rough standard of comparison with what Thomason had already done with such great effect from his provincial capital in Agra. And the newly settled and lately turbulent Punjab was rapidly catching up the long-settled and peaceable North-West Frontier, as that part of the future United Provinces was then called.

In concluding their Report, the Board invite the Governor-General, who had seen the Punjab and inspected its government, to judge for himself 'whether the country is richer, whether the people are happier and better'. Dalhousie indicated his hearty approval when he forwarded this Report to the Directors of the East India Company, who were known as 'good masters but very chary of gracious words', as Kaye expressed it. But they rose to unwonted eloquence in their reply to the Board, finally signing themselves 'Your affectionate friends'.

Nevertheless the Board ended their Report with a caution: 'When a state falls, its nobility and its supporters must to some extent suffer with it, a dominant sect and party, ever moved by political and religious enthusiasm, cannot return to the ordinary level of society and the common occupations of life without feeling some discontent and some enmity.' In their next Report, however, the Board felt that society was already settling down and that there was 'among all classes a greater regard for vested rights, for ancestral property, for established principle'. It must be remembered that Sikh rule had risen and fallen in the space of one lifetime and that for many it had represented both a minority tyranny and an upheaval almost as great as the British rule which had succeeded it. The Board summed up the social change which began under their rule by saying that 'while the remnants of a bygone aristocracy are passing from the scene, not with precipitate ruin but in a gradual and mitigated decline, on the other hand the hardy yeoman, the thrifty trader, the enterprising capitalist are rising up in robust prosperity'. To handle the difficulties connected with the decline of the former ruling class gave rise, however, to delicate human problems concerning which Henry and John were not at one.

(iv) The Quarrel

The Board's achievements were remarkable, but the men who accomplished them were flesh and blood, and there was a hidden agenda, which is not self-evident. In particular the condition of their service placed a severe emotional strain on the Lawrence brothers, a strain that in the end became more than either of them could bear.

Both Henry and John were born to command but neither were solitary autocrats. Their decisions were firm but they were reached in consultation with colleagues whom they trusted, whom indeed they had chosen. Both could work together *in* a team. They could obey as well as command, if they knew where they stood. But the two could not work *as* a team. Many years later when John was Viceroy of India, he had by the nature of his office to work with a Council, which was appointed by others and took collective decisions. He adapted himself to this without repining but it did not bring out his best abilities. Henry was scrupulous in obedience to lawful authority and he attracted devoted obedience from his subordinates but he was not fitted to be joined in any team in which no one was supreme. To be so joined with a brother, to whom he was devoted, made his task doubly difficult. Sir Henry Daly, a great friend of both brothers, summed it up by saying: 'The Lawrences were not like other men, nor were they like each other, their powers were very different. If I were dealing with a new country, I should take Henry through it first and he should say what was to be done, and then I would leave John to carry it out and to modify it.'

John Lawrence was more complex than has sometimes been understood. John Lawrence at work and John Lawrence at play seemed to be two different people. The figure of a just but unsmiling John has gone down to history. He could certainly be grim. When my parents got married towards the beginning of this century, the bride-to-be was introduced to the survivors of the great period of the Lawrences. Among those was George Ricketts, who had served with distinction in the Punjab. After many years her brief account of her conversation with him remains. 'Have you read *Uncle Tom's Cabin?*' 'Yes.' 'Do you remember Simon Legree, the slave driver?' 'Yes.' 'That was your Uncle John.' This was one side of the truth. John asked nothing of others that he did not require of himself, but he expected those under him to drive themselves to the limit and beyond. Being very strong himself he did not seem to realise that other people might be weaker. He went without a proper holiday for fourteen years, and he did not apparently realise that others might not have the same endurance. So there were casualties of health, and 'The Punjab Head' became a byword.

John seemed pitiless to those who knew him from a distance. But there was another side. He had a boundless bubbling vitality and must have been very good company, with his rough good-humoured, never-failing sense of fun. And those who were close to him knew that he was not heartless. Sir Richard Temple who saw John Lawrence continually from 1851 to 1859 writes:

> It was one day in the first half of June 1851 that I was introduced by George Barnes to John Lawrence, who was then living in a picturesquely situated house on the spur of Mount Jacko in the centre of Simla. You can imagine the interest and curiosity with which I went to this, my first interview with a man whose repute had left so deep an impression on the public mind . . . I had in my imagination pictured Lawrence as an iron looking man, somewhat severe in tone and aspect, with a massive brow, straight features and compressed lips, uttering few words and those only of a dry and practical import . . . Great was my surprise then, on finding that he had an open countenance, an expressive forehead, a frank genial bearing, and a vivacious manner of conversation. His lips so far from being closely set, were constantly parted by smiles and laughter. The conversation turned on the state of the country between Simla and the Punjab, on the rainy season which was just setting in favourably for agriculture and on the incidents of travel from the valley of the Sutlej to the heights of the Himalayas, as illustrative of the character of the country and the ways of the people. He was full of animation and seemed anxious to make me feel at ease. It was only when his features occasionally relaxed, after the play of light and fancy during conversation that I could perceive the full strength and solidity of his head, and the lines which anxious thought and energetic resolve had marked on his face.

John took to Temple and a few days later he took him to dine alone with the Governor-General. 'Lord Dalhousie had the staid yet bland demeanour ordinarily associated with the statesman. Lawrence, though also self-possessed, was full of animation and vivacity, urging with much earnestness some view which Lord Dalhousie did not seem wholly to accept', views on the feudal system in the Cis-Sutlej states. 'After dinner they sat conversing on a sofa. Lawrence was telling some of his own experiences and Lord Dalhousie was listening with amused attention.'

John would have been a first-class farmer and had 'a discriminating insight for all that related to animal life', being a very good judge of horses. He had little feeling 'for the more delicate points in landscape or the tamer beauties of nature' but 'stern and wild' scenes touched a poetic streak in his makeup.

I have heard him describe the crossing of the Indus, the valley of Peshawar, the mouth of the Khyber Pass, the rocks of the Kohat defile, the floods of the Sutlej, the thunderstorms of the Himalayas,

in brief, graphic, pithy, though perhaps rugged sentences . . .
Nobody could ride with him across the fields in the busy season
without deriving instructions as to what should be observed. It was
a branch of his great profession to perceive at a glance the material
condition of the natives of all ranks and callings. He was benevol-
ently keen to note the signs of poverty or distress in the humblest
classes.

And 'the play of wit, the flight of fancy, the originality of illustration,
the raciness of expression, the unpremeditated eloquence imparted a
fragrance and flavour to Lawrence's intimate conversation with those
who were constantly about him'. These qualities were unfailing when
he was off duty. Temple had 'seen men and cities'; he knew John
intimately, and his evidence does not stand alone. John, like Henry,
thought everything out for himself; they did not think alike but both
were original. This is the meaning of Sir Henry Daly's aphorism: 'The
Lawrences were not as other men are and John was not like Henry'.

The outside world little guessed at the secret garden behind the
alarming exterior of a man who might have stepped out of one of the
more awe-inspiring episodes in Roman history. Even to those on the
inside he could be frightening enough. When he was in England after
the Mutiny and before he went back again to India as Viceroy,
Henry's daughter Norah, a little girl of ten or twelve, was living with
her Uncle John. There is a story that is characteristic of them both.
One day Norah had been very naughty. So John held her over the top
of the stairs in the large mansion where he was living, and said he
would drop her if she went on being naughty. 'No you won't, Uncle
John,' said Norah, 'because that would be murder and then you would
be hanged.'

'Though not at all satirical or cynical', he was acutely aware of the
funny side of everything. 'When on horseback, before the public or in
his office chair, he kept his humour quiet, but at mealtimes or after
dinner, or in walks or when talking with his secretary alone, he hardly
touched upon anything without investing it with an air of pleasantry.'
When talking with Indians high and low, he teased them unmerci-
fully, often quite contrary to protocol, but his rough good humour
made them laugh aloud in spite of their habitual abstinence from even
smiling on public occasions or in the presence of superiors. He had an
unconventional eloquence in Persian or Hindustani and was the only
Viceroy who could address gatherings of Indians in their own
language, but he had scant respect for ornate oriental imagery and by
applying it to current events, or by free renderings from Persian into
English, he could be very funny. But he always felt awkward when he
had to make speeches in English. He had spent so much time with

Indians when he was young that he had learnt how to use their most commonly used languages for all purposes in his highly idiosyncratic way but he never mastered the art of public speaking in his own tongue, not even when he was Viceroy and later a member of the House of Lords.

Unlike Henry, he did not read widely. Shakespeare, the Bible, and Plutarch's *Lives* gave him what he wanted for most purposes. When the chapters on Ireland in Macaulay's *History of England* came out, John Lawrence read them with close attention. He kept his religion private but studied the Bible with ever-increasing zeal, so much so that latterly, when he spoke of serious subjects his language became tinged with scriptural phraseology.

He was immensely strong, as Henry was before he got Arracan fever, but he worked so hard that he got increasingly severe headaches. In the summer of 1854, after Henry left the Punjab, John had terrible headaches, during the paroxysms of which he gasped out to Temple, 'I feel as if *rakshas* [Hindu mythological giants] were driving prongs into my brain.' 'Afterwards from time to time he assured me that he had an affection of the head which seemed like a current of air rushing through his brain.' But he went on working. This was the sometimes contradictory character of the brother who was yoked uneasily with Henry. The awesome figure with the skin of a bear, inspiring respect but not affection, was the same man as the delightful companion with a heart of gold.

Both Henry and John had a basic nobility but their quarrel showed neither of them to the best. John kept his vanity in an iron subordination to his duty but he had his share of obstinacy. Henry had a strain of humility which in the last resort was stronger than vanity, but one of his greatest faults was a tendency to mistake honest disagreement for hostility. The brothers agreed on most things, but when they did disagree and yet had to take action together it was not easy for them to compose their difference. While Henry was Resident, John had often taken his place when his brother was absent or ill. While this lasted John was scrupulous never to do anything which Henry would not approve of, even if his own judgment would have led him to act differently. But both brothers were equally members of the Board of Administration, even if Henry was President and John was at first the junior member. Each member of the Board had a right to his own opinion and could push it as hard as he liked. When John disagreed with Henry he said so and argued the case as forcibly as he could.

John always recognised generously that Henry had transcendent gifts and a power over men which for all his ability and strength of character, he, John, lacked. And in the records of John's life I can find nothing to suggest that he was jealous of his elder brother though he was often resentful of him. Both were quick tempered, but John had his temper more under control. Both were in their different ways supremely good administrators and both were good if rather fierce arguers. Henry would reach his conclusions with great speed, leaving a good many details to be worked out afterwards. John was one of the most thorough civil servants of the nineteenth century, and a master at setting out a case. His arguments were far more likely to appeal to Dalhousie, when any matter had to go up to the Governor-General.

Dalhousie, though deaf to overtones, was a very able administrator. So John had the sympathy of the Governor-General, and generally prevailed on appeal to the Supreme Government. Henry's fault was to be too easily hurt by disagreement and when the disagreement came from a loved brother, the hurt went very deep. Mansell, the third member of the Board, could see both sides of any argument, but had a deep dislike for reaching a conclusion. Both Henry and John liked and respected him. After about a year he was succeeded by Robert Montgomery who had been a friend of the Lawrence family since his earliest boyhood and was, I suspect, a blood relation. Montgomery was a neighbour of the Knoxes and Marshalls from Inishowen and he had known the wives of both Henry and John from their girlhoods. He had also been a fellow pupil with John at Foyle College and at the boarding school not far from Bristol.

When John and Henry could hardly bear to meet each other, so acrimonious had their exchanges become, both poured out their hearts in letters to Robert Montgomery. Most of these letters are now lost and do not seem to have been read *in extenso* by anyone except Robert Montgomery himself and his son, Bishop Montgomery, the father of the Field Marshal. But earlier biographers evidently had access to more details of the difficulties between the brothers, than are now extant. Both Bosworth-Smith and Merivale wrote able and sympathetic accounts of these sad exchanges. Other contemporaries, such as Sir Richard Temple, have also left enlightening descriptions of this quarrel. It is no longer possible to reconstruct the cut and thrust but the general course of the quarrel is clear.

The main subject on which they fell out was the treatment of the aristocracy of the Sikh Kingdom. There are only two ways of governing a state, the feudal system and bureaucracy. Under feudalism those who perform the functions of government are assigned land or the right to collect and keep the revenue assessed on particular holdings of land. This was the native Indian system as it had been the European system in the Middle Ages. Indian and European feudalism were very different, and it would be misleading to press the analogy, but the basic resemblance remains. The grants of land through which the Indian form of feudalism operated were called *jaghirs*. By Indian custom the grant of a *jaghir* was freely revocable at the will of the sovereign, but in practice there was a degree of stability. The British on the other hand governed through civil servants paid out of the central revenue. The Punjab could obviously not afford to pay two governments, and the feudal aristocracy had now lost their function. Henry thought that their influence and help were still important to the British Government, but John had his doubts. What was to be done?

The *jaghirs* of the Sikh *sirdars* could not be maintained in full in perpetuity. This was not even expected. By Indian custom any new government would make extensive changes in the *jaghirs* which it inherited. On the other hand all *jaghirs* could not be resumed instantaneously. That would not have been practical or just. There had to be a compromise and this involved examining about ten thousand cases, each with meticulous care, or else great injustices would have been inflicted and potential friends alienated. On the other hand the state would be bankrupt if too many or too generous grants were made. Those who had supported the British in the Second Sikh War must be rewarded and defeated enemies would expect to suffer, but if their punishment was too severe the wounds would fester. Moreover the dispossessed *sirdars* would be surrounded by hordes of former hangers on and other sympathisers, who could become a danger to the new order. The *jaghirs* were of many different kinds. Some were new, some were old, some were given to recompense the holders of office of state, some were for religious purposes, some were for Ranjit Singh's numerous wives and concubines. If a settlement were delayed too long there would be great resentment, as had already happened in other parts of British India. But if there was undue haste in settling any cases, difficulties and injustices of another kind would arise. So the task of the Board was not easy but they tackled it with great vigour and the end result was generally agreed to have been as good as it could have been in the circumstances. Many of the *sirdars* realised that the new rulers had treated them better than Ranjit Singh would have done. But this result was not reached without serious friction between Henry and John.

Edwardes has left a record of a famous conversation between himself and Temple which took place after Henry's death, with all passion spent:

> Temple said that it was best that the two brothers were associated together, though it proved so unhappy for themselves. Neither was perfect, each had lessons to learn. Sir Henry would soon have had to close the treasury with his ideas of *jaghir* improvements, light revenue, etc., and John would have had a full revenue but a mutinous country. Both were so naturally truthful and candid, that

when they had done the mischief, they would have owned it and retraced their steps, but by both being together the mischief was prevented. One checked the other. At the same time they confirmed each other's faults. Sir Henry was more lavish in his proposals because he thought that John would cut down any proposals which he made, and John was more hard and stingy upon parallel reasoning. We both agreed that John had begun to adopt Sir Henry's view in many things from the moment that Sir Henry left the Punjab and that the crisis of 1857 had very much more softened, and modified John's former principles.

The views of both brothers flowed from a concern for principles. John felt that *jaghirs* in effect took money from the poor to give it to worthless landlords, while Henry was not at all sure that a European power had the right to interfere with Indian social structures as they had evolved. Thucydides says that wars arise from trifles but that wars are not about trifles. Likewise the quarrel between the Lawrence brothers was about serious matters of principle but it arose from a succession of minor disagreements whose cumulative effect destroyed both Henry's and John's peace of mind and posed a grave threat to the health of both of them.

Both were magnanimous by nature but their disputes would be petty; quarrels between siblings generally bring both back to the nursery and it is in this context that sometimes petty exchanges should be understood. One could always tell when both of them were at Lahore because one could hear their wrangling all over the house. Lawrence voices can be penetrating. John accused Henry of not doing his proper share of work, leaving impossibly too much to his younger brother. Everyone else was astonished at the amount of work that Henry got through in spite of recurrent bouts of violent fever, though his ways of doing it were unusual. Henry felt insulted; and wrote a furious reply. In both cases Robert Montgomery, with his cherubic face, was the tactful but helpless intermediary. He described himself as like a tame elephant between two wild bullocks.

Henry complained to Montgomery:

I have seldom or ever made a proposal that he has not opposed it [with an implication that] I am either dishonest in my view of patronage or that I am incompetent to judge . . . . I might say a good deal of *jaghirdars* and pensions and how sorely I am daily vexed about them, mainly owing to John's own line of conduct and the spirit that he has engendered against the whole class. Independent of feelings of humanity, I look on the manner in which these people are treated as most impolitic. The country is not yet settled,

[199]

troubles may arise at any hour almost in any direction, when the good or ill will of such men as Dina Nath, Tej Singh, Sheikh Nizammudin, Lena Singh and others would be of consequence. [And finally:] It is not my fault.

Montgomery showed this to John, as he was meant to, and John replied with equal petulance, again through Montgomery, 'At annexation Henry was ill, apparently in mind and body, he was not well apparently when he came out and was sorely chafed at annexation. He did consequently comparatively little work. All details were thrown upon me, everybody was referred to me for explanation.' John went on to say that while Henry's long and frequent absences from Lahore might be good for the political superintendence of the country, as well as for Henry's shattered health, they rendered it extremely difficult to work the machine of a Board composed of three members. Moreover the effect of Henry's long absences was to place John in a more direct relation with the Governor-General, which increased Henry's own dissatisfaction at finding himself sometimes thwarted. More specifically as regards pensioners and *jaghirs*, John said:

> I give way as much as I can. I could point out many cases where my consent has been violently opposed to my own personal views – but I found it did little good. So long as I opposed any of Henry's recommendations, he was no better satisfied than if I had gone on my own views. He thinks we treat these classes badly. I think we have been very kind to them. I cannot see the political value of such allies as Tej Singh and Dina Nath and others!

John changed his mind about that after the Mutiny, when the support of members of the former ruling class was very important. Here he continued: 'However I have always treated them with the greatest consideration.'

John ended saying that 'with our utterly different views of civil administration it is not possible that we can work together pleasantly to ourselves.' Here he was forgetting the nine-tenths of questions on which they agreed. But sensible as nearly always, he concluded with a practical suggestion:

> I would wish that we discussed public questions together as little as possible, that when we differ we record our views in writing, when the one or the other will be supported by yourself, Robert Montgomery, when the party in the minority will either give way or in special cases go before the Government. If we are scrupulously careful to record no expression which we are not prepared shall

stand and eventually, if necessary, go to Government, neither will probably give reasonable cause for offence.

Henry was cut to the quick by John's picture of him 'which would make me a clever diseased malingerer utterly unadapted for business', a man who got in his, John's way 'while he was doing the work of the Board'. Henry points out that John made no complaint at the time when this was supposed to be happening. Each seems to have construed the other's accusations in the worst light and then sharpened up his own complaints. They were angry with each other because the other was angry, and each accuses the other of being more angry than he himself. Henry had promised to try and make his letter short but it grew under the influence of emotion. He ends, however, on a more reasonable tone. John's

> great error is excess of reliance on his own judgment and denial or doubt of the labours of others, especially when they are not exactly akin to his own. Indeed, it would sometimes appear as if he thought that two or three are the only men in the Punjab, who work at all, all others being idlers and drones. I fully grant that he has hit on my defects, though I think he has caricatured them. I hope and will try to benefit by the lesson. I will be glad if he will think over what I have said to him.

Robert Montgomery loved and understood both brothers. He gave soothing advice which was duly neglected, and his final comment was: 'Hereafter when the daily strife of conflicting opinions is at an end, when we shall all have run our courses, how wretched will appear all the bickerings and heart burnings which occupied so much of our time.'

(v) Diversions

The Board's time was not entirely divided between working and bickering. There was the day when they almost lost the Kohinoor, the 'mountain of light' which now adorns the Queen's state crown. The history of this famous diamond is lost in legend. Nearly five hundred years ago the Mogul Emperor, Babur, reported that his son Humayun had won from some Rajah a jewel 'which was valued at half the expenses of the whole world'. In the mid eighteenth century Nadir Shah, the Persian conqueror of the Moguls, saw the Kohinoor in the turban of the then Emperor whom he had just defeated and proposed in an offer of friendship, which could not be refused, that they should exchange turbans. The Afghans took the gem from the Persians and it was in the hands of the exiled King of Afghanistan, Shah Shujah, when he took refuge at the court of Lahore before the First Afghan War. Ranjit Singh extorted this diamond from his guest, and it was in the crown jewels of the Punjab, when the Board of Administration took charge. Dalhousie told them to be careful with it. It was given to John who wrapped it up and put it in his waistcoat pocket. John never wore a jewel in his life until he had to wear the clasps and orders that he was given. And then 'he used to put them so remorselessly in the wrong place that court costumiers exclaimed in despair that they would lose reputation by him'.[6] True to character, when John changed for dinner after being given the Kohinoor, he threw his waistcoat aside forgetting what he had put in his pocket. About six weeks later a message came from the Governor-General saying that Queen Victoria had ordered the Kohinoor to be sent to her immediately. 'Send for it at once,' said John. 'Why *you* have got it,' said Henry. John gave no outward sign of trepidation, merely saying, 'Yes, of course, I forgot about it.' But he thought to himself, 'Well this is the worst trouble I have ever got into.' And when he could he slipped out of the room, sent for his old bearer and asked him, 'Have you got a small box, which was in my waistcoat pocket some time ago?' 'Yes, *Sahib*, I found it and put it in one of your boxes.' 'Bring it here.' The aged bearer fetched it from a rusty tin box. 'Open it and see what is inside.' Fold after fold, layer after layer of rags was taken off, and when the gem appeared the bearer said with astonishment, 'There is nothing here but a piece of glass.' John went back to the meeting, presented the Kohinoor to the Board, and caused great amusement when he told them what had happened.

On Christmas day 1851 the three Commissioners, Henry, John, and Robert Montgomery were having Christmas dinner with their wives and Dr Hathaway. He was Henry's secretary and was to be John's secretary, when he went back to India as Viceroy. The ladies had retired, as the custom was, and Henry's thoughts went back to the days when the three of them had been boys together at Foyle College. After a short silence he turned abruptly to his brother and said, 'I wonder what the two poor old Simpsons are doing at this moment and whether they have had any better dinner than usual today.' The

Simpsons were twin brothers, who were much respected but lived in very humble circumstances. They had been ushers, i.e. junior masters, at Foyle College. An usher in those days was not much regarded and often bore a galling yoke. The old pupils, now so strangely reassembled, realised that when they were boys they had not been as kind to the Simpsons as they might have been, then Henry said, 'I'll tell you what we will do. The Simpsons must be old and I should think, nearly blind. They cannot be well off. Let us all put down £50' – quite a large sum in those days – 'and send it off to them tomorrow as a Christmas box from a far off land with the good wishes of three of their old pupils, now members of the Punjab Board of Administration at Lahore.' 'All right,' said John, 'I'll give £50.' 'All right,' said Montgomery, 'I'll give another.' And when George heard what his brothers had done, he added a fourth £50. Many weeks later a letter of thanks came, written in a tremulous hand and barely legible from the tears which had been shed on it. The Simpsons could not find either the Punjab or Lahore on the antiquated school atlas and did not know what a Board of Administration might be. The gift would go far to keep them from want during the short time that might be left to them, but far more precious was the thought that they had not been forgotten by four old pupils in what 'seemed to be the very high position to which they had risen.' 'Oh,' said Henry to Dr Hathaway, as he opened the letter, 'if you could only see as I can see it now, that grimy old atlas grown still more grimy by its use during the thirty years which have passed since I knew it, and the poor old fellow trying to find in it what it does not contain.' The writer of this letter lived on to a time when everyone knew where the Punjab was and all the members of its Board of Administration were national heroes. The citizens of Derry gave a banquet in honour of Sir Robert Montgomery when he visited his home after the Mutiny and the half blind old school master was given a ticket for it. He died very soon afterwards – happy, as Bosworth-Smith observes, like Odysseus' dog at the sight of his returned master.

As bad news came in at the beginning of the Second Sikh War, it was decided to replace Gough as Commander in Chief in India. At that time some of the heroes of the Peninsular War were active and pre-eminent, among them General Sir Charles James Napier, whose life-like statue stands in Trafalgar Square, 'erected by public subscription, most of it from private soldiers'. When he was reluctant to go, the aged Duke of Wellington said to him, 'If you don't go, I shall have to go.' Napier had been in India before as the conqueror and first Administrator of Sind. The story that he announced his conquest in the words '*Peccavi*, I have Sindh' is apocryphal, but Napier was a ripe British eccentric. It is impossible not to like him, but in his old age eccentricity began to verge on madness, and he carried on a bitter

contest against everything that was done by any civilians and particularly the Governor-General and the Punjab's Board of Administration.
His biography written by his admiring brother William, still more his
own posthumous work on *Indian Misgovernment*, contain in Bosworth-
Smith's words 'a strange medley of petulances, egotisms, and
vagaries, which overlie and overshadow the flashes of insight and even
of genius embedded within them'.

Napier set sail expecting war. He looked forward to crowning his
career with magnificent schemes of Eastern conquest and reform. He
arrived to find that the fighting was all over and the reforms were in
the hands of others. He wrote to his brother William that he 'would
rather be Governor of the Punjab than Commander in Chief'. That
post was not open to him, so he used his position as Commander in
Chief in a way that made it doubly difficult for anyone else to govern
the Punjab. He declared a war of obstruction on the Lawrences and
Dalhousie, which had the result of bringing Henry Lawrence and
Dalhousie closer together. Napier became celebrated for 'believing
without a reason and hating without a cause'. He used to call
Dalhousie 'the laird of Cockpen', that place happening to be very
near his estate. Napier refused to see the Lawrences for any serious
discussion yet abused them up hill and down dale. But he made an
exception for George, whom he called 'a right good soldier and a right
good fellow'. And curiously George's grandson, Sir Henry Stavely
Lawrence, married a Napier, and when she died, married her sister
Rosamund, who wrote a very successful book about her Indian years,
Indian Embers. Moreover, Henry Staveley Lawrence made his career
in Sind, which was Napier's stamping ground, becoming Chief
Commissioner of Sind and Acting Governor of Bombay. Napier had
been high-handed in the annexation of Sindh, but he had governed it
well. Writing to the Governor-General on 31st March 1850 John
Lawrence summed up Napier's administration fairly. 'I believe he did
in Sindh wonderfully well . . . But to suppose that a man ignorant of
the manners, customs, habit and language of a people, with untrained
men under him, could really have governed a country as he thinks he
did Sindh, seems to me an impossibility . . . A man may make a good
many mistakes, and still be a better ruler than an Amir of Sindh.'

Rivalry between Sind and the Punjab is almost a law of nature. It
did not cease with the death of Napier, nor with the independence of
Pakistan. Napier made it a cult. And he carried his hostility to such a
point that he refused to say where the Lahore cantonments should be
located. And until the Commander in Chief had made that decision,
the planning of the defence of the Punjab was held up.

One day when Napier was in Lahore, the three members of the
Board of Administration together with Montgomery who was then

Commissioner of Lahore, were out taking their early morning ride together, when they saw Napier and his staff in the distance. Henry said to John, 'Let us go straight up to him and see if we cannot manage to get an answer out of him at last where the cantonments are to be.' When they did so, Sir Charles said, 'You want to know where the cantonments are to be, do you? Follow me then.' And forthwith he dug his spurs into his horse and rode off hell for leather across country for three or four miles. His staff followed him as best they could and the civilians followed behind them, no doubt not having such good horses as the army chiefs. At last he stopped apparently at haphazard. And when the last pursuers came up, he cried out amid the smoking steeds and breathless riders, 'You asked me where the cantonments are to be. They are to be here.' Such is the origin of the famous cantonment of Mian Mir. It was a particularly marshy and pestilential piece of ground but by stretching their authority the engineers succeeded in drawing back from a rather more to a rather less unhealthy spot.

Eventually Napier behaved with such insubordination to the Governor-General that he had to resign. His attacks on the government of the Punjab received devastating answers and have not been taken seriously for a very long time, but they were a major nuisance while they lasted.

Dalhousie was a great administrator but one who did his work by sitting long hours at his desk. Henry thought it best to do as much as he could sitting under a tree with the people gathered round him. And even when he was at home in this own *Kutchery*, his children ran in and out all the time. He thought it essential to see with his own eyes as much as he could of the country that was in his charge. He would ride enormous distances with a very small retinue, a striking contrast to the armies of hangers-on who traditionally followed Indian or Anglo-Indian grandees, devouring everything in their path. Merivale describes Henry's travels: 'Endowed with a restless activity of body as well as of mind, which seemed to defy the climate, notwithstanding the fever tribute which he had been compelled to pay ever since his Burmese campaign, he was never so happy as on horseback, escorted by his "tail" of British and native followers, threading the wild gorges of the lower Himalaya in summer, or spurring across the green expanse of each Doab champagne in the flush of spring.' 'I have been twice all round the Punjab,' he writes to his friend Mr Kaye, as he then was,

> visiting every station and staying at each a few days. I have not missed one and though I have not travelled in the usual style of Indian Governors or, indeed, in the style of most collectors, I have

managed to see everything from the bottom of the salt mines at Pindadun Khan and Kohat to Ladakh and Iskardo on Gulab Singh's Northern Frontier. Each year I have travelled three or four months; each day riding thirty or forty miles with light tents and sometimes for days with none at all . . . At stations or where anything was going on, we halted one, two or three days visiting the public offices, gaols, bazaars, etc., receiving visitors of all ranks and inspecting the Punjab regiments and police and receiving petitions which later were a daily occurrence, sometimes a couple of hundred coming in.[7]

Merivale then quotes an anonymous 'colleague' writing in March 1850 to the effect that 'The President of the Board has lately gone a circuit of not less than 1,000 miles . . . often for days with a single soldier and only for one march in the Kohat Pass with half a company and half a troop, so complete was internal security and so lacking ostentation the President of the Board.'

John's complaint that Henry's long absence from Lahore made it difficult to work the machinery of a Board was justified but the other advantages of Henry's unconventional methods more than made up for that. Dalhousie, however, saw the disadvantages much more clearly than the advantages. In April 1850 Henry had applied to the Governor-General for leave to make an extended tour of Kashmir and to be absent from the plains for the whole of the rainy season for the purpose of re-establishing his health. Dalhousie gave a very reluctant consent, observing that 'whether for your health or otherwise, I am bound frankly to tell you that I did not think absence habitually for half the year nearly was compatible with your office or fair to your colleagues. Gulab Singh's territories cannot be said to be within your charge.' Henry travelled on this occasion with Hodson and his small son Henry, my grandfather. Hodson, he describes in writing to George as

one who makes a good travelling companion, energetic, clever and well informed . . . he has his faults . . . but it is useful to us to have companions who contradict and remind us that we are not Solomons. I believe that if Sir Charles Napier stood on his head and cut capers with his heels . . . Hodson would consider it quite right that all Commanders in Chief should do so . . . He insists that all Indian editors are blackguards and that, comparatively, all English editors and newspapers are gentlemen and dealers in truth and propriety. Toryism and Absolutism are right, Liberty only another name for Red Republicanism. So you see we have enough to differ upon.

Henry did not like his Young Men to overdo their respect for him and he loved an argument.

This lively party joined up with Honoria and her last baby, little Honoria, who were accompanied by Dr Hathaway, before entering the famous Vale of Kashmir, where no European woman had been before. Here they lived out of doors by the lake in one of those magical gardens laid out by the Mogul Emperors for their enjoyment. Honoria describes in a letter to her eldest son in England how one morning

> after an early breakfast we got into our boat, such a fairy-like skiff, long, narrow, sharp at either end. In the centre a cabin open all round with lattice work to close at pleasure. Thirty or forty boat-men with green shovel-shaped oars pull us along, an oarsman at either end steering. No necessity for turning the boat, as either end is bow and stern. I was called to look at the fun in the large pond, just below bordered with green sward and there was papa, the doctor and Harry tumbling about like porpoises. He had on a swimming belt with which he floated merrily about in water about four feet deep, making off however, when Dr Hathaway turned the gush from a great fountain right against him.

After about a month of this idyllic happiness, Henry went on with Hodson to explore the higher valleys of the Himalayas which Gulab Singh had succeeded in annexing to his kingdom of Jammu and Kashmir. They went right to the Chinese frontier, including on their journey, Ladakh, Skardu and Gilgit, places that were then practically unknown to Europeans. Henry wrote nearly every day to Honoria and this diary was greatly enjoyed by all who read it. It was unfortunately among the papers which were lost or destroyed before the beginning of this century. He wrote, however, in a letter to Colin Campbell, 'I have had a very nice trip and am all the better for it. Five times I have been above 14,000 ft high. I am now moving from the commercial to the warlike side of the frontier. Three weeks ago I gave a dinner to three hundred traders from and to Yarkand, last week to a rather more numerous party of merchants and soldiers at Iskardo.' And Honoria adds, 'Dear Papa has gone on a tour of the Chinese frontier . . . He is greatly enjoying the strange land he is in and gathers strength daily. He is moreover, doing all he can to heal enmities and to relieve oppression among the tribes.' From Ladakh he brought back a horse, Ladakhi, which became famous throughout India and went through the siege of Lucknow.

On another of his tours Henry was accompanied by Lord Stanley, the future Fifteenth Earl of Derby, who was the first Secretary of State for India, after the abolition of the East India Company. He sent

John Lawrence to India as Viceroy, in spite of precedent that it had to be a nobleman. He impressed the Lawrences with the speed and intelligence with which he drank in information about India. But he blotted his copy book by laming Henry's favourite horse and Honoria records that he 'was sadly annoyed; indeed I suspect frightened, when Nicholson or Lumsden or any of the young men with papa proposed a scamper'. The moral, so far as Honoria was concerned, was that her own sons must learn to ride properly.

History and biography tend to concentrate on the high points in their story but this can become like chronicling the course of a river in terms of its waterfalls, leaving out both the long stretches of quiet flow and all the eddies and currents which distinguish flowing water from stagnant. Henry's friends testify that never did a man struggle harder day by day with his own weaknesses. Yet it is not often that these struggles break surface in the record of his life. At the height of his quarrel with John at the beginning of October 1852, he was floating down the Ravi in a small boat whose tossing made his writing even harder to read than usual. Here he committed to paper a prayer, part of which has been adapted for daily use at Sanawar. After a short meditation on the Incarnation of Jesus Christ, Henry wrote: 'Restrain my tongue and my thoughts. May I not fear man or man's opinion, but remember that thou knowest my motives and my thoughts and that thou will be my judge. It is not in me to be regular; let me be so as much as I can. Let me do today's work today not postponing, clear up and finish daily.'

In this and many other things he depended on Honoria, in spite of her increasing ill health. 'A perusal of her husband's letter-books shows how much in mere routine she did for him; how now and then she restrained or trimmed his more characteristic replies, or helped him in the innumerable cases of charity which ever constituted the undercurrent in the life of both, or gave shrewd advice to struggling mortals who came for counsel to them.'[8]

(vi) The Break

As the year 1852 wore on, it became ever clearer not merely that Henry and John could not work together in the Punjab, but that their estrangement was beginning to affect the public interest. The post of Resident at Hyderabad at the other end of India became vacant at this time. It was a post of 'equal honour and emolument . . . though not entailing duties of equal importance' with the Punjab. The Nizam of Hyderabad was the premier ruler of all the native states by now subordinate to the British Raj. Hyderabad is a pleasant place and the climate of the Deccan is healthy. John wrote to Dalhousie offering to go to Hyderabad if that would solve the difference in the Punjab. And Henry wrote almost simultaneously making the same offer. Dalhousie quite naturally wanted to keep John in the Punjab. It was Henry he wanted to send to Hyderabad. That particular appointment fell through but at the same time the similar post of Agent to the Governor-General in Rajputana fell vacant and Henry was appointed to it just before Christmas in 1852. In communicating his decision to Henry, Dalhousie did not simply say what he had decided and express regret if it caused pain, he wrote a long letter, beating about the bush and trying to soften the blow. It had the opposite result. 'It has for some time,' he wrote, 'been the recorded opinion of the Supreme Government that, whenever an opportunity occurred for effecting a change, the administration of the Punjab would best be conducted by a Chief Commissioner, having a Judicial and a Revenue Commissioner under him.' This was sense but he added after some fulsome praise, 'We nevertheless do not consider it expedient to commit the sole executive charge of the administration of a kingdom to any other than to a thoroughly trained and experienced civil officer.' Henry was maddened by what he took to be an implied insult. He had held one of the highest civilian positions in India for several years and now he was told that he was not 'thoroughly trained'.

On 20th January 1853, his last day at Lahore, Henry wrote to John a gentle letter venturing to offer a few words of advice on the subject of *jaghirdars*.

They should not be considered as nuisances and enemies. I think we are doubly bound to treat them kindly because they are down and because they and their hangers on have still some influence as affecting the public peace and contentment. I would simply do to them as I would be done by, I by no means say much in favour of most of their characters. I merely advocate their cases on the above grounds . . . I will not trouble you on the other subjects. On most of them you are more at home than I am. I strongly recommend you to hold weekly durbars – an hour or two thus spent will save much time and cause much contentment. Wishing you health and all success, Yours affectionately.'

In his last moment before leaving Lahore, Henry knelt down with Honoria and asked God's blessing on the Punjab and its prosperity and on John's rule there.

Sir Richard Temple in his excellent biography of John insists that the quarrel never affected the personal relations of the two brothers, but Henry's character being what it was the wound never entirely healed. It is always easier for the victor to be magnanimous. And henceforth John seems to have shown no jealousy of Henry or resentment at their past quarrels. In later life the phrase 'as my brother Henry used to say' was continually on his lips. And as soon as Henry was gone, John became more like Henry, adopted measures that Henry would have approved and did everything that he could to conciliate Henry's friends. Some of them indeed were very awkward customers, but John took infinite pains to meet their wishes. Most of them came to appreciate John's 'heroic simplicity'. They worked happily under him, although he could never replace Henry in their hearts. Yet there were those, including Robert Napier, who refused to work in the Punjab so long as John was there. Sir Henry Daly thought, that two such masterful spirits as John Lawrence and Robert Napier 'could not get on in the same sphere'. The two brothers corresponded occasionally and the tone of their letters was friendly and helpful but they lacked the old expression of affection. For Henry reconciliation was much harder and it was only on his deathbed at Lucknow that he could say, 'I forgive everyone. I forgive John.'

Later that day Henry and Honoria with Harry and little Norah and his sister Charlotte left Lahore accompanied by a great concourse of Punjabis and British who had come to see the last of a man from whom they had no longer anything to hope.

The Governor-General's decision in favour of John was fully expected and fully justified in the result; but it was widely resented and condemned, when it was made known in Lahore.

It was well said that Henry Lawrence's hold on the peasants of the Punjab was because he loved them and they knew it. Bosworth-Smith, who had taken pains to talk to very many of those who were there at the time, tells us that 'grief was depicted on every face. Old and young, rich and poor, civilians and soldiers, Englishmen and natives, each and all felt that they were about to lose a friend. Strong men . . . might be seen weeping like little children. Those who accompanied him on this last journey constituted a long living funeral procession from Lahore nearly to Amritsar.' Robert Napier, afterwards Lord Napier of Magdala, 'was the last to tear himself away . . . Kiss him,' said Henry Lawrence to his sister, 'kiss him, he is my best and dearest friend.' When he reached Amritsar a new group of mourners and a fresh outburst of grief awaited him. And then he passed on into

Rajputana wounded and 'dented all over' as Edwardes put it, 'with defeats and disapprovals, honourable scars in the eyes of the by-standers, honourable because all of them were received in defence of those who were down'.

PART SEVEN

RAJPUTANA INTERLUDE

1853–56

CHAPTER 13
Rajputana

A change had taken place in Henry Lawrence's character and by the time he reached Rajputana, or Rajasthan, as it is now called, his manners were very courtly. It had not always been thus. At an earlier stage of his career Thomason had given him the nickname 'gunpowder'. And about this time he is described by Kavanagh, who won the V.C. at Lucknow in the Indian Mutiny, in his book *How I won the Victoria Cross:*

> I knew Sir Henry Lawrence first in 1841 in which year he was assistant to Sir George Clerk . . . I was a clerk in his office and daily saw him. He was then an impetuous and indefatigable officer, and so wholly absorbed by public duties that he neglected his person and left himself scarcely any time for recreation. He had little of that gentleness of temper which afterwards grew upon him, and although very accessible was not always agreeable to natives. He was rather impatient and not so practical or philanthropic as he afterwards became. A good, straightforward native gentleman was sure to be treated with courtesy and with a cordiality that filled him with pleasure, but woe to the intriguer or deceiver! These, Captain Lawrence met with a stern aspect and sent sneaking away in fear and trembling. His brusque manner, grotesque appearance and shrewd sharp look attracted the notice of strangers at once, who always left him with a feeling that he was no ordinary man. His mind and body were always in a state of tension, and both alike were denied proper rest.

By 1853 he had become tolerant, always looking for the good points in any character and making excuses for deficiencies especially in native Indians. Merivale observes that 'his temper was naturally hot and impetuous; it was by self-discipline and constant watchfulness that he kept it in subjection; and the original man occasionally came to the surface to the last.'[1] It is not often that Victorian biographies give an instance of their heroes' failings, but Robert Young gives a story of how, even at the end, Henry could lose his temper. This was the only time I ever saw him angry . . . Owing to the stupidity of a *munshi* who mis-sent an order, much confusion and inconvenience was caused, putting Sir Henry out greatly . . . I was just entering the room, when I saw him storming up and down . . . at the wretched *munshi* . . . At once I withdrew until all was over, when I passed through to my room, Sir Henry having gone on to his. To get to my bedroom I had to pass his door and could not help seeing . . . a sight I shall never forget. There was Sir Henry kneeling by his bedside, his hands covering his face.

Robert Young continues:

on Sunday, in the absence of the chaplain, Sir Henry would conduct the service and read a good sermon which he always did in a very reverent spirit, but in the vigorous way so usual to him. He was always punctual to the moment and we had to look sharp if one wanted to accompany him. Sometimes he was off before he had even got on his collar or necktie right, when his sister would run after him calling for him to stop and let her adjust it properly, on which he would usually reply, 'Oh! Charlotte it's all right, there now, don't bother, let me go.'

Henry Lawrence to the end of his days set before himself as an ideal, Wordsworth's Happy Warrior. Kaye tells us that he read it often, he thought of it continually, he quoted it in his writings. Kaye continues: 'If I were asked what it was that more than perfected the picture of his character, I should say it was the glow of romance . . . He used to say, "It is the due admixture of romance and reality that best carries a man through life."'

In an article on 'Romance and Reality of Indian Life', published in *The Calcutta Review* in 1844 Henry wrote:

The quality variously designated romance or enthusiasm, poetry or ideality is not to be despised as the mere delusion of a heated brain, but it is to be valued as an energy imparted to the humble mind to prompt and sustain its noblest efforts . . . Where the two faculties are duly blended reality pursues a straight path to a desirable objective, while romance beguiles the road by pointing out its beauties, by bestowing a deep and practical conviction.

Henry's brother, George, was already appointed to the important position of political Agent to the Maywar States in Rajputana where he was stationed at Neemuch. George was to succeed Henry as Agent to the Governor-General. The work in Rajputana consisted mainly in guiding and overseeing the work of eighteen nominally independent states, the largest of which, Maywar, was the size of Ireland. Henry began it characteristically seeing for himself. 'On my way from Lahore,' he wrote to Sir John Kaye, 'I went out right and left paying flying visits to the chief cities of Rajputana, as Jaipore, Jodpore, Alwar, Bhurtpore etc. and have thereby been able to sit down quietly here [at Mount Abu] ever since.' And he adds, 'On my rapid tour I visited to the surprise of the Rajah and political agents, all the gaols or those called gaols, and by describing them since, I have got some hundreds of wretches released, and obtained better quarters and treatment. In the matter of gaol discipline the North-West Provinces are behind the Punjab, and even there every step taken by me was in direct opposition to almost every other authority.'

The Rajput aristocracy had been until the coming of the British a brave, chivalrous and noble race of men but the Pax Britannica had given them complete security and, lacking any incentive to defend themselves, they had within a generation become a race of debauchees. Sunk in sloth and and addicted to opium, they were not to be roused to exertion of any kind. Henry's previous experience was little help. He wrote to Kaye:

> Here I have to deal with twenty sovereign states as old as the sun and moon, but with none of the freshness of either orb. My Sikh experience gives me very little help, and my residence in Nepal scarcely any, in dealing with the petty intrigues and foolish pride of these effete Rajputs . . . The princes encroach, or try to encroach, on the Thakoors [the next rank below the princes] and the latter on the sovereign. We alone keep the peace. The feudal system, as it is called, is rotten at the core.

The temptation to annex these states outright was ever present and only prevented because it was doubtful whether it would be worth the trouble. Henry thought annexation would pay 'if we could persuade ourselves to manage them by common sense rules'. But he strongly opposed annexation on other grounds:

> I hope they will be dealt with honestly and that we will do our best to keep them straight. We have no right, as *The Friend of India* newspaper constantly now desires, to break our treaties. Some of them were not wise, but most were at the time they were made, thought very advantageous to us; it would be outrageous, now that we are stronger, to break them. Our remedy for gross mismanagement was given in my article on Oudh in *The Calcutta Review* nine

years ago, to take the management temporarily or even permanently. We have no right to rob a man because he speaks his mind,
and even because he ill treats his peasantry. We may protect and
help the latter without putting the money in our own pockets.

Henry was not very successful in rousing the Rajputs from their
opium smoking and debauches, but he did succeed in putting down
suttee, saying to Kaye again that

> Twenty years ago the case might have been different but we are now
> quite strong enough to officially denounce murder throughout
> Hindustan. I have acted much on this principle. Without a word on
> the subject in the treaty with Ghulab Singh, I got him in 1846 to
> forbid infanticide, *suttee* and child selling. He issued a somewhat
> qualified order without much hesitation, telling me truly that he
> was not strong to do more. We were, however, strong enough to see
> that his orders were acted on . . . I do not remember above two
> cases since 1846 and in both the estates of the offenders were
> resumed.

He describes the difficulties of getting the order against *suttee* observed in Rajputana: 'Banswara has been under our direct management for the last five or six years owing to a minority. The people
pretended they did not know *suttee* had been prohibited. The offenders have been confined, and I have proclaimed that henceforth
suttee will be considered murder.'

'Jaipore is my most troublesome state. The Durbar is full of insol-
ence. We have hitherto interfered too much and too little . . . The
present agent although a well educated man of good ability is, in my
opinion rather a hindrance than a help. He seems not to have a shadow
of influence and lets the country go to ruin without an effort at
amendment. And yet it is very easy, without offence, to give hints and
help.' Such cases as this show how much the Punjab Government had
been able to draw on the best of the British in India.

Henry's treatment of gaols was characteristic. He wrote a circular to
all rulers

> remarking that in different gaols (without mentioning names) I had
> seen strange sights that must, if known to beneficent rulers, revolt
> their feelings etc., etc. I therefore suggested that all princes who
> kept gaols should give orders to the following effect. Classification,
> so as to keep men and women apart; also great offenders from minor
> ones, tried prisoners from the untried; ventilation and places to
> wash etc., etc. Well, in the course of two or three months I got

favourable answers from almost all, and heard that in several places, including Jaipore, they intended to build new gaols. At Udaipore my brother [George] told me that they released two hundred prisoners on receipt of my circular, and certainly they kept none that ought to have been released, for when I went to Udaipore, last February I found not a man in gaol but murderers, every individual of whom acknowledged to me his offence as I walked round and questioned them. The Durbars do not like these visits – but they are worth paying at all risks, for a few questions to every tenth or twentieth prisoner give opportunities for innocent persons to come forward and petition. No officer appears ever before to have been in one of these dens.

The Lawrences lived at Mount Abu but alas! only enjoyed their life together for a short time. Honoria's health took a rapid turn for the worse. Before she died she left in a letter to her eldest son, Alexander, a description of their home in this lovely spot about four thousand feet above sea level. The famous Jain temples of Mount Abu were very close. She writes:

Our house here stands on a high granite rock round the edge of which are some flower beds of artificial soil not much bigger than cheese cakes. With diligent watering those produce roses, geraniums, passion flowers, cape heath, petunia and a few others, one thriving honeysuckle. From our bedroom is a door leading to a little thatched verandah, and out upon the tiny garden, which is in shade until 8 a.m. Here I greatly enjoy sitting, looking down over our rock down into the lake, surrounded by rock and wood. There is a delightful variety of birds, all very tame. I like to watch the kites sailing in circles high up and the busy little swallows swimming zig zag among them unmolested. There is a sweet little bird, just the size of a robin and as tame; but our bird is of a shining purple black, with scarlet under the tail and white bars on the wings, seen when he flies. Then we have a lovely little humming bird, not so tiny, not so brilliant as the West Indian, but the same form. I love to see it hovering like a butterfly over a flower, then plunging its long slender beak and sucking the honey. Altogether there is a great enjoyment here, of which the greatest to me is the tranquility and the quiet enjoyment of your father's society; such as we have never known since we left Nepal.

Honoria's feelings at being parted from her husband are given in a letter to her friend Emma Edwardes. 'You are one who wants another to turn to when you droop under sickness or anxiety; a more amiable nature than mine, for if I cannot have my husband and children, I would fain go like a wild beast to a den and there howl it out alone.'

The 'society' of Mount Abu consisted of about a dozen families belonging to the Governor-General's Agency for Rajputana and about twenty of the officers stationed nearby. With this Henry and Honoria were well contented. Honoria was pregnant again. Concerning her confinement she wrote as early as October 1853, 'My reasonable conviction is that I am likely to die then.'

She had had rheumatic fever, her health was weakened by previous illnesses and she died, as she expected, on 15th June 1854. The widowed Henry was broken-hearted and went through a phase of self-reproach. His love for her, he felt, had been a half love but to those who saw him, it seemed that more and more he was living in the next world near to her. In her last days, a friend, Mrs Hill, came to live with Honoria and nursed her tenderly through her last illness. This most dear and engaging person is enshrined in silhouettes that she made of Henry, Honoria and Harry while they were still at Lahore. Henry made Mrs Hill a sort of spiritual director to whom he unfolded his religious difficulties. These were many, but they made no difference to his underlying faith. They are summarised by Herman Merivale as follows:

'He hardly knew what he believed, what he disbelieved. He would believe all if he knew how. He believed that Christ was God yet cannot understand how, being so, he suffered. He wondered, as all men do, why we are allowed to sin and so often why some are born to bliss and others to misery and he thought God's dealing with the Jews very mysterious. And above all he wanted to be assured that he and his departed wife must dwell together hereafter.' To judge from the course of his spiritual life from then on, Mrs Hill must have comforted and consoled him and strengthened his faith.

Shortly after Honoria's death Robert Young, the son of James Young of Culdaff failed in his first attempts at a career and enlisted unknown to his family as a gunner in the East Indian Company's army, under an assumed name. He was too ashamed of his early failures in life to let his family know. He eventually plucked up his courage and wrote to his guardian aunt saying where he was. She wrote at once to Honoria who was an old friend from Ireland and also to Captain Pears commanding his battery, who happened to be her cousin. He was sent for by Captain Pears and wondered what was coming, when the Captain informed him that 'Sir Henry Lawrence has arranged to purchase your discharge, and wishes you to go up to him at Mount Abu, which you can do as soon as you like'. In the meantime he was to stay with George and Charlotte Lawrence at Neemuch. After a first meeting at which he was almost too confused to speak, Henry cut it short by saying 'It's all right', and went on to ask about his old acquaintances at Culdaff. He then wrote to Robert Young saying he fully trusted him and was sure he would not disappoint him.

Sometimes his faith in others was quixotic. He lent 4,000 rupees to a young subaltern in Rajputana who had no apparent claim on him apart from being in distress. He replied in such cases, 'I trust a man until I find he really deceives me, but I don't repeat the experiment when he does, and I find I am scarcely ever wrong in doing so.'

The Residency where Henry lived, so Robert Young tells us, was at that time 'a small, straggling building, indeed, much too small for its purpose' but in a very romantic situation. Charlotte Lawrence, in her brother's absence, did the honours of the house with 'a graceful homeliness and kindliness of manner that made all feel at ease, in the last matter too she was very well assisted by dear wee Honey [Henry's daughter] a child of seven or eight, so far as it was possible for a little thing like her to do so'. 'Honey' or Honoria must have been an enchanting child to judge from her letters to her brothers and she became in due time a dear, lively bright-eyed old lady. She was the only person of that generation whom I knew personally.

The duties of the household were divided between Charlotte and Dr Ebden, Henry's doctor and factotum who was a personal friend. Robert Young records that 'A more pleasant, kind and true friend than the doctor one could scarcely meet with, nor a more original one.' Henry never touched more than half his pay. The rest was for charity and Dr Ebden told him how much was left. The only drawback was the doctor's voice which was a shrill falsetto, or as Henry put it 'E's screech'. He would hold his hands up in mock horror at the first sound of Ebden's voice 'but especially when he got excited in argument, or in expostulating with Sir Henry for not taking care of his health'. Henry's return to Mount Abu 'was the signal for dinner parties . . . not that he ever cared for such things.' But when he did drop in on them 'he was the soul of the party'. On one occasion he had his famous pony Ladakhi with him and they visited the famous Jain temples, one of which stood on a very high and steep flight of steps. Henry caused general alarm when he took Ladakhi up these steps which 'was a very breakneck piece of daring, but he knew well what he was about and the capabilities of his pony, which could climb like a goat'. Henry alone could hold Ladakhi in. He 'had a capital seat if not a graceful one and a firm light hand'.

Robert Young liked the evening time best when they were by themselves. When tea was over 'Sir Henry set to work again at his papers, whilst Miss Lawrence and the rest chatted or read, enlivened now and then by a bit of humour or a droll remark from Sir Henry regarding the work he happened to be engaged on, which set us all laughing . . . I never saw such a rapid thinker and writer as he was, throwing down sheet after sheet, almost littering the floor, not altogether to Miss Lawrence's entire satisfaction.' But his writing was, as always, a scrawl. Once with a complete lack of self-knowledge he put up a large card in the drawing room, where everyone could see it, a notice saying in a large round hand, 'All persons writing for me are requested to write legibly thus: Henry Lawrence.' This caused much merriment among his army of clerks and part-time helpers. Everyone including the ladies had to help him.

The invalids of the nearby garrison were

also well looked after by Sir Henry and teas with games and athletics were of frequent occurrence, which they heartily enjoyed. Sir Henry, when time permitted, would come down among them to see that all was right. One evening I remember, two soldiers had been wrestling and came to loggerheads, and went in for a regular set to. In an instant, however, Sir Henry was between then, asking them what they meant. Looking very foolish they at once separated, when the whole body set up three cheers for Sir Henry and all went on as happy as before.

Robert Young thought they might all have joined in the quarrel, if Sir Henry had not intervened. Henry established another Lawrence 'Asylum' or school at Mount Abu, which after Independence was taken over by the Central Police College of India. And he was much concerned to get a third Asylum for the soldiers' children established in the Nilgiri hills in Southern India. After some early struggles this was taken over after Henry's death at Lucknow by the Government of India and a fourth Lawrence College was established at Ghora Gali in the foothills of Kashmir and on the Pakistan side of the border with India as a memorial to him.

About a month after Robert Young's arrival at Mount Abu two other young men joined the party, both recipients of Henry's boundless generosity and hospitality. Henry set them to learn Hindustani and surveying and was himself their chief instructor in both subjects. For Robert Young this was the foundation of a career in the Indian Land Survey. One of their text books was the *Prem Sagar*, in which book Henry's hero was the Persian King Hatim Tai. The story is that when his country was being invaded, in order to spare his people all the horrors of war, Hatim Tai gave himself up as a prisoner to his enemy, who was so struck by this, that he at once withdrew his army and declared Hatim Tai to be the greatest and best of men. 'Often did Sir Henry expatiate on the generosity and nobility of his hero . . .

accompanied with a touch of sly humour.' One wonders how such a busy man found time to give lessons.

Major Oldfield who served under him had the impression that he was 'restless, abrupt and unsatisfied,' but he came 'to feel towards him, the same strong affection and devotion which all his Punjab colleagues felt'.[2] He was, in the words of Major Oldfield 'a tall thin, wiry-looking man, with hollow cheeks and a long beard which extended nearly to his waist. The lines of care and hard Indian service were deeply stamped upon his brow and face, and he looked at least ten years older than he really was.'

At the end of Henry Lawrence's time in Rajputana, in 1856, India was on the verge of the Indian Mutiny. He gave continual warnings that the British were courting disaster. In writing to his friend Lord Hardinge in 1853, he said, 'How nearly we have more than once been extinguished, your Lordship knows.' And in writing to Lord Stanley: 'We act contrary to common sense and in neglect of the lessons of history, in considering that the present system can end in anything but a convulsion. We are lucky in its having lasted so long.' Ten years before he had published an article in *The Calcutta Review* in which he put forward his view on Indian army reform. There was little that he wished to retract, but it fell upon deaf ears.

The Charter of the East India Company was coming up for renewal and in the letter just quoted to Lord Hardinge he thanks him for sending a copy of his evidence before the Committee, which was considering this matter. He adds:

I hope we shall have a good deal of reform without materially altering the present constitution . . . But the native army, I think, wants reform even more than the civil branch. Is it not too much to expect from human nature that a man should under all circumstances be faithful in an army of more than 300,000 men wherein the highest rank is that of *soubadar* major or *ressaldar*. No doubt the service is an excellent one for ninety-nine out of every hundred, but we sadly want an outlet for the one bolder and more ambitious spirit which must exist in every hundred; and for want of this legitimate outlet we may some day meet a great catastrophe or be content to go on with a system that does not get out of a native army half of what might be got. I cannot perceive the danger of making *soubadars* and *jemadars* of irregular corps captains and lieutenants. They virtually are such but without the pay. Double their present rates and make these posts prizes from the line as well as from the Irregular Service and you will at once put the Irregular Corps on at least a footing with average corps of the line, commanded as these are by worn out colonels, aided by discontented captains and subalterns.

Rome survived for centuries by liberality to the soldiers of her provinces. So did the Mahommedan power in India. And nearer home, does not Austria at this moment hold Italy with Hungarian bayonets? And Hungary with Italians? And can many of the officers or men of the Russian army be considered more loyal than are the soldiers of India? At this moment we have six battalions in the Punjab under the name of Police Corps, all commanded by natives and doing excellent service, three of them on the frontier . . . If such men are good for the Punjab, why not for Bengal or elsewhere?

And in the letter already quoted to Lord Stanley he writes: 'France has its Arab generals, and Russia had many Asiatic generals but liberal England restricts its best native officers to posts subordinate to sergeant-major, obtainable to only by some thirty to fifty years servitude.'

In a further article in *The Calcutta Review* of March 1856 he says:

Ninety in a hundred *sepoys* have every reason to be delighted with the service. Several of the remaining ten are satisfied. One, two or three are dangerously discontented. The reason is plain. They feel that they have in them that which would elsewhere raise them to distinction. Our system presses them down . . . We must not wait until the 'excellent drills' and the 'tight pantalooned' continue to assert their claims. We shall be unwise to wait for such an occasion. Come it will unless anticipated. A Clive may not be then at hand.

In the meantime his thoughts turned more and more to home. As Merivale puts it, 'Failing in health, weary in spirit, his Indian dwelling vacant from the companionship which had been the delight and support of his existence in it, very solicitous about the future of his children in England, and left alone by the departure of his young daughter, who had outgrown the safe limit of stay in India, he longed more and more for that relief which he had so amply earned.' Finally on 9th November 1856 he wrote to Lord Canning, the new Viceroy, 'On account of my family I have long been anxious to get home even for a few months, and will be much obliged if you can permit me to go next month for nine or even for six months, making over charge of the Agency to my brother George . . . Had I not the fullest intention of returning to India, I should not thus intrude on your Lordship, but my present intention is to hold to my work as long as health and strength last.' And on 26th December he wrote again to say, 'My health has for some months been so indifferent that three doctors have given me medical certificates . . . On the army question generally as your Lordship did me the honour to ask my opinion when in Calcutta,

I beg to say that I am the author of the two articles in *The Calcutta Review* of March and September last – the first on the Indian army and the other on army reform. The question is one I have long had at heart and look on it as the vital one of our Indian Empire.'

PART EIGHT

OUDH

1857

CHAPTER 14

Lucknow

(i) A Precarious Peace

Henry Lawrence longed for home and rest but there was one more act before his Indian career was complete. On 19th January 1857 Lord Canning summoned him to Oudh to be Chief Commissioner at Lucknow. He answered by telegraph and post. 'I am honoured and gratified by your kind letter of the 9th, this day received. I am quite at your Lordship's service and will cancel my leave and move to Lucknow at a day's notice.' So Charlotte and little Honoria went to Bombay, never to see their brother and father again, and Henry started for Lucknow.

He wrote to Charlotte on the way to Lucknow: 'I have nearly given way more than once, but I hold to stay (in India) because I so much want to go, but the very offer of the Governor-General is a sufficient salve for my Punjab sores. I therefore stay simply because I think it is my duty, and that I can do good, but at utmost it would be for two years.' He had a presentiment of what was going to happen.

He spent three weeks with his old friend E. A. Reade at Agra where 'his forebodings of evil and troubled times were constant and repeated . . . He was worn and depressed. The mutual misgiving was shown by his last expressed wish that we might both be spared in 1858 to go home together, he to rest, and I to retire from the public service.' Neither of them could believe that they would meet again. While at Agra he surprised everyone by telling them, at least half in earnest, but disguised as a jest, that they would be besieged by their own army. He repeated this so often that it became engraved on the hearer's memory.

Henry arrived at Lucknow on 20th March 1857. Lucknow was the capital of Oudh and was the second city of the Indian Empire with a population of between six and seven hundred thousand. Blessed with good soil, it could have been the garden of India. Lucknow is an

[229]

extraordinary city, built in the eighteenth century, after the golden age of Mogul architecture. Honoria had described it on her journey to Nepal:

Parks and villas adorn the neighbourhood up to the very walls of the city . . . Lucknow, with its white stucco, gilding and red paint, has a very upstart look after the melancholy and gentlemanlike marble and desolation of Agra. Nevertheless this is a curious and even splendid city. There is a curious dash of European architecture among the oriental buildings. Travellers have likened the place to Moscow or Constantinople. Gilded domes surmounted by the crescent, tall slender pillars, lofty colonnades, half Grecian looking houses of several stories high with pillars, verandahs and windows, iron railings and balustrades entirely foreign in this country. Cages of wild beasts and brilliant birds, gardens, fountains and cypress trees, the winding river Goomtee, with its bridges and boats, elephants, camels, horses, *palkees* and *dhoolies* all make a confused and very dazzling picture. And to these are added a very strange accompaniment for a Mussulman city, to wit, innumerable statues of every imaginable design, from a gigantic soldier, painted to the life and presenting arms with a most valiant air, to Jupiter, Venus and all other personages entitled by prescriptive right to stand up in every material from Parian marble to plaster of Paris. On one side Hercules flourishes a club at you, and on the other stands a shepherd in a tie wig and three-cornered hat making love to a shepherdess in hoop and ruffles . . .

The suburbs of Lucknow are unlike any I have seen in India, for here there are buildings and gardens and a look of habitation, instead of the black desolate barren waste or wilderness, of tombs around Delhi and Agra. Here too all the principal thoroughfares are watered and the absence of dust is quite marvellous to those who have been used to other towns of the East. We went out one morning to drive through the city. Our road led first through a fine wide street with clean looking shops. In a native bazaar of the better sort the shops occupy the open front of the lower storey, generally raised a step from the street and screened by an awning of cloth or a mat supported by slanting poles . . .

One of the prettiest sights in Lucknow is the royal gardens . . . In the midst is a summer house gorgeously fitted up in an Indo-European style . . . In front of this building is a canal of exquisitely pure water with gold and silver fishes and a fairy ship with crimson cushions, into which I sat with Alick. We glided between hedges of roses, throwing parched rice to the fish, which assembled for it in troops.

The population of Oudh was reckoned by Henry to be about three million. It had once been a province of the Mogul Empire but in the decay of that once great empire the local rulers had appropriated their independence. As Delhi decayed, poets and musicians had migrated to the court of Lucknow. The city became the last refuge of Urdu culture and a wonderful refinement of manners was practised by all classes. One meets the remains of it even today.

The Wazirs of Oudh had been recognised as Kings by the East India Company, on condition that they accepted subordination in their foreign policy as the price of the Company's protection from danger, both external and internal. Being secure on their thrones and having nothing else to do, most of the Kings of Oudh had embarked on a life of debauchery. Sir William Sleeman, who was Resident at Lucknow, called Wajid Ali, the last King of Oudh, 'an imbecile in the hands of a few fiddlers, eunuchs and poetasters'.

Wajid Ali Shah was a strange person. He had long ceased to hold Durbars or to see his own family or any of the aristocracy of Oudh. His ambition was to be a good drummer, a good dancer and a good poet in Urdu. By all accounts he had some talent as a verse writer. He took a passionate interest in all kinds of animals, his collection of snakes was remarkable, and he was a gifted designer of architecture. A comparison with Nero springs to mind, but Nero was cruel whereas Wajid Ali Shah seems to have had no cruelty in his nature. He was rather indifferent to the fate of his subjects and had become completely incapable of serious business of any kind. Cut off, as he was, from all intercourse with his subjects, he spent his time entirely in the company of eunuchs, 'fiddlers' and women. His ministers were chosen from the 'fiddlers' or were at their mercy, and they were utterly corrupt. Knowing that their tenure of office was precarious they sold every subordinate office to the highest bidder. The *taluqdars* or great landlords had grabbed their neighbours' lands with impunity, though some of them had been settled in Oudh for centuries. Every *taluqdar* kept his own robber bands, who seized upon land by means of murder when necessary and, failing that, by torture. A favourite torture, though not the worst, was to smear a man's head with wet gunpowder and when it was dry to set it alight. The great landholders surrounded their lairs with two or three miles of thorny jungle and protected them by a matted wall of live bamboo. They were almost impregnable in their hideouts, and paid only a portion of what was demanded of them by the Government. Much land lay waste and there were no thatched roofs or any other sign of affluence in the rest. Oudh was in a miserable state and the Government was universally despised. Moreover, Oudh was the chief recruiting ground of the Company's *sepoys* and the Resident alone was often able to uphold their rights. This was indeed the only means of redress open to the people of Oudh and the reputation of the British Government was universally respected.

The British Government had powers, reserved under treaty, to take what steps might be required to restore good government, and it is hard to see what excuse there can have been to let things drift so long. The situation required strong measures, but Sleeman thought annexation a false solution.

> Were we to take advantage of the occasion to annex or confiscate Oudh, or any part of it, our good name in India would inevitably have suffered, and that good name is more valuable to us than a dozen of Oudhs. Annexation or confiscation is not compatible with our relations with this little dependent state. We must show ourselves to be high-minded by appropriating its revenues exclusively to the benefit of the people and royal family of Oudh.

Sleeman had his own well thought out solution in the appointment of a Board drawn from the best members of the royal family and the more respected members of the aristocracy of Oudh, aided by 'a few of the ablest of the native judicial and revenue officials of our own districts'. This was what everyone wanted and he was convinced that it would soon make Oudh 'the garden of India'. Nothing was done. It now seems obvious that this was the right solution, but Dalhousie was bent on annexation.

Henry Lawrence had quoted 'that honestest of Governors-General, Lord William Bentinck' (Morison's phrase) with approval. Bentinck, like Sleeman, thought that we should frame an administration for Oudh, entirely native,

> so composed as to individuals and so established on the best principles, revenue and judicial, as should best serve for immediate improvement and as a model for future imitation. The only European part of it should be the functionary by whom it should be superintended and it should only be retained until a complete reform might be brought about and a guarantee for its continuance obtained, either in the improved character of the reigning princes, or, if incorrigible, in the substitution of his immediate heirs, or in default of such a substitute from nonage or incapacity, the nomination of one of the family as regent, the whole of the revenue being paid into the Oudh treasury.

Henry's own remedies for the prevailing misgovernment were similar.

Wiser counsels were not lacking, but Dalhousie was honestly convinced that British government was better than native government. He wrote: 'It seems impossible that the home authority can any longer hesitate to overthrow this fortress of corruption and infamous misgovernment. I should not mind doing it as a parting coup, but I doubt the people at home having the pluck to sanction it, and I cannot find a pretext for doing it without sanction.' The 'people at home' did have 'the pluck' to sanction the extinction of a native state that had always kept its obligations to the British.

In February 1856 Lord Dalhousie was succeeded by Lord Canning. The two men were very different. Dalhousie was an autocrat. He did not welcome advice from subordinates, as all previous Governors-General had done. They were expected to wait for orders. Canning neither could nor would fulfil this role. At first junior officials could not get accustomed to the changes and began to take too much on themselves. Dalhousie had never fully trusted Henry, but Canning took to him at once and trusted his judgment implicitly. It was like the old relation with Lord Hardinge. Nothing shows this better than his willingness to trust the vast territories of Rajputana, the Punjab and Oudh to three brothers, George, John and Henry. He welcomed unlimited advice from both Henry and John.

Dalhousie had, in his proclamation of the annexation of Oudh, made certain promises which protected the interests of the royal family, the *taluqdars* and the dependants of the deposed King. Dalhousie had just time to preside over the first stages of the transition, and the man entrusted with this task was, of all people, Sir James Outram. He had succeeded Sir William Sleeman as Resident at Lucknow, but his views on the treatment of the Amirs of Sindh, in a very similar situation, were well known. However, his health broke down almost at once and he was obliged to go to Europe to recuperate. At first contentment reigned, but soon after Outram's departure some of the officials took it on themselves to violate the terms of the Proclamation. This brought much loss and misery on precisely those classes who were most influential in Oudh.

If Dalhousie took infinite pains to get the cream of the Indian Civil Service in the Punjab, he made run of the mill appointments in Oudh. The Chief Commissioner was Coverley Jackson, who showed himself as insensitive to the crowds of courtiers, who had suddenly found themselves without the means of subsistence, and to the landed aristocracy of Oudh, as Henry Lawrence had been sensitive to the Sikh *sirdars* who had earlier been in the same situation. Next to Jackson were Martin Gubbins, the Revenue Commissioner, who was able and intrepid but totally lacking in judgment, and Ommaney the Judicial Commissioner, who was not up to a very difficult task. The mutual ill will, reckless ill temper, and failure in cooperation combined with failure in discretion marked the reign of this unhappy triumvirate. Many of the leading families were reduced to selling their jewels after dark in the bazaars. Brigandage and disorder became even worse than before the annexation. Henry, as a first step, began at once to pay the stipends of the old nobility. In order to get to know the young men under him he started to play racquets with them. In spite of all, reforms had been introduced which, in quieter times, might have borne their fruit. Police posts had been established, transit duties had been abolished, law courts set up after the Non-Regulation system of the Punjab, most of the King's troops were paid their arrears and dismissed, and claims to rent-free lands and pensions investigated, though not with the sensitivity shown in the Punjab. 'The whole machinery of British Government started on the latest and most approved systems', as young George Lawrence, the son of the elder George, and therefore Henry's nephew, noted.

Henry Lawrence was only fifty when he came to Lucknow, but he had lived to the limit and was already an old man. Herbert Edwardes, who was his closest friend outside the family, wrote to John Nicholson after the news of his death had reached Peshawar: 'Grief had made him grey and worn, but it became him like the scars of battle . . . he had done with the world except working for it while his strength lasted.' Young Henry Daly was passing through Lucknow to take command of the Guides. His wife Susan has left a picture of Henry Lawrence in old age: 'He certainly, more than any one I ever knew, gives one the feeling of living for another world. He is perfectly cheerful, active and interested in this, yet every now and then some little observation falls from his lips which proves how fully he is imbued with the feeling of the transitory nature of our present existence, how perfect is his faith that the real life is to come.'

Lady Daly, as she became later, acted as his hostess during this time, and observed his total indifference to social circumstance and convention, his universal benevolence and friendliness, his munificence towards any project aiming at the service of others, and his perfect indifference about his own comfort. She gives a rare picture of his home life:

> Sir Henry Lawrence is a most charming person, his manners so kind, so cheerful, so affable, it sets everyone at his ease. He is full of life and animation, ready to talk on every subject, grave or gay, and so sympathising with all. He is worked hard from morning to night and often looks sadly weary, but he is hospitable and sociable in disposition and likes to collect people around him . . . We have . . . dinner parties every evening. It is my business to write the invi-

tations, Sir Henry sends up all the cards of all the people who call on him and desires that all may be invited to dinner. I have to arrange them as well as I can but, being a stranger, do not always bring the right people together, and in India we are prodigiously touchy about matters of Society, precedence and so on.

Once she invited an 'uncovenanted' clerk, who looked miserable all the evening, and at another time she nearly invited the son of an artilleryman whom Henry had known at an earlier stage of his career and about whom he had said, 'I should just as soon dine with his son as half the people I know, but we should have all the rest of the company up in arms.' One day George Lawrence 'came up to tell me his uncle had forgotten to mention that he had invited about twenty more in addition'.

> Henry is evidently a great favourite with Sir Henry and this is very gratifying to know. He sends his bearer to call him at daybreak, to go out riding . . . When they come in Sir Henry has his easy chair, books and a cup of tea in the verandah into which our rooms open. Little Bo has already grown quite familiar with his godfather. Always good natured and kind to children, Sir Henry takes a great deal of notice of him; the child runs up to him without hesitation, pulling his coat, touching his book. I rush out to fetch him in and apologise, but Sir Henry laughs and says 'I have little children of my own'. At breakfast we have strawberries which have just come in and are somewhat rare, he always remembers baby and takes some up to him. The breakfast is the agreeable party here, a meal that lasts from 10 till 12 or 1 o'clock, gentlemen constantly dropping in; the conversation animated and pleasant . . . Sir Henry himself so spirited, so agreeable in discourse. Colonel M., Mr Christian, Dr Ogilvie, my Henry – all clever men and quick in conversation.

She adds, 'He has saved about £20,000 and says this is enough for his three children. "The boys will be good for nothing, unless they have to work for themselves . . . " You know Sir Henry is my husband's beau ideal, so now Henry laments that our boys will be too rich. Poor little fellows, I don't think they will be ruined by the amount of their fortune!'

He gave his first impressions of Oudh in a letter to his brother-in-law, Dr James Bernard:

> I was never so well housed. My health is better rather than worse. I am calmer and quieter than I have been for years, and take intense

pleasure in my daily work, looking about this immense city in the morning, and dealing with authority all day in matters affecting many millions' welfare. All hands seem glad at my coming, the natives especially. For the first time since annexation have the doors of the Residency been open to the nobles and the traders, I have held large Durbars for both classes separately, and now the individual members of each class come to me daily. General Outram writes to me that he is glad I am come as he is sure I [he] could not have restored order. His wife, a nice gentle creature, writes to me that she too is very glad as, when she was here in January last, everyone was wretched, and all wanted a firm kind hand.

The Civil Officers, whether civilians or soldiers, may well be glad of the change, for in the whole course of my service, I never saw such letters as have issued from these offices. Evasion, misrepresentation etc. were common words flung about right and left. I tore up two drafts of letters that came to me that day and altered three others. Mr Jackson was not altogether to blame.

In a letter to Charlotte, Henry explains what he meant: 'Mr Jackson . . . is an able and energetic man but, like us Lawrences, has strong passions not under much control.'

The letter to Dr Bernard continues:

When thwarted he [Mr Jackson] could not restrain himself and lost his judgment. He stayed eight days with me, and was very amiable, though I told him he was very wrong in some of his acts, and in more of his expressions. He put into my hands the chief letters referring to despatches and they did astonish me. The government letters are nearly as bad as his own. All the impertinences of all Lord Dalhousie's letters during my stay in the Punjab, hardly amounted to what was poured out on Mr Jackson in a single letter. How he remained an hour in office any time this six months, is to me very wonderful. He ought to have resigned last July. The delay in letting me join after I had accepted the berth, seems to have been to enable Government to write half a dozen letters; each of many sheets, all dated March, and all pouring out with vituperations on Mr Jackson. He was on bad terms with five out of six principal officers (civil) and also with the Civil Secretary. The Judicial Commissioner, as also the Revenue one, were at bitter feud with him. The first is not a wise man, jealous of interference and yet fond of interfering. Mr Ommaney is his name . . . I took an early opportunity to let him know that he was not to lead me by the nose. The first occasion was regarding a *Thuggi* jail, in which I found all sorts of people mixed up with *Thugs*, and the sentries, all with muskets in their hands, at the mercy of the prisoners. On the spot I put the sentries into safe positions, Jackson was with me, and expressed surprise at my daring to interfere, in as much as in one of his despatches he had been told by Government that the Judicial Commissioner had plenary power in jail matters. As soon as I came in, I wrote an official letter to Mr Ommaney saying I did not wish to interfere in details but that the case was urgent as I was mobbed by life prisoners mixed up with those confined for misdemeanours and that all could escape when they liked . . . The Revenue Commissioner is a better and abler man, whom I like. He may be a more troublesome coadjutor. He has strong views about breaking up estates and destroying the aristocracy. To a certain extent I agree with him, where it can be done fairly. He also professes to advocate low assessments, but in some quarters he has enforced high ones. We have however sympathies in common, and he, Mr Gubbins, was so tremendously mauled by Mr Jackson, that he, even more than the others, has hailed my coming.

The military and political arrangements are perhaps worst, and mostly owing to General Outram. The position of the troops, magazine treasury etc. are all as bad as bad can be. All scattered over several miles, the infantry in one direction, the cavalry another, the artillery in a third, the magazines in a fourth and almost unprotected. The Governor-General seems in some alarm regarding the state of affairs, though I hope there is no serious reason. A few days ago he sent me more than a sheet of paper from an officer in Oudh, whose name he did not mention, giving a frightful picture of the state of irritation afloat in Oudh. I fear his picture of the revolutionary schemes of many (i.e. of the officials) is quite correct. A dead level seems to be the ideal of many civil officers, both military and civilians.

This letter from an anonymous officer reads in part:

The Civil Officers appeared intoxicated with the prospect of the work before them . . . that nine-tenths of the *taluqdars* had any legal title to their estates no one conversant with the past history of Oudh will be bold enough to avow, but it savoured more of frenzied zeal than statesmanlike discretion to overturn the entire proprietary body at one blow, in two months, without investigation . . . To force, suddenly, this alternative on a hundred thousand men accustomed to wear and use their swords was unwise. In the district of Fyzabad alone, so complete has been the summary ejectment of the *taluqdars* under the dictum of Mr Gubbins, that it is confidently believed that an armed rising must be the result, and if such be the result, not a civil functionary will live to relate how it all came to pass.

[This picture was overdrawn, but it shows the problems. The anonymous officer continues:] The fungus tribe that followed their masters from the old provinces have secured the petty offices about the courts from that of the *amlah* down to that of *chuprassy*. One and all of these harpies extort, grind and oppress to such an extent that they are also alienating the good will of even the peasantry, who first welcomed our advent . . . But what greater proof of their [the civil officers] unfitness to incorporate Oudh with British India than their own personal encounters with one another? Forgetting their duty to the state, they have first thought of their relative self-consequence and hence an amount of offensive correspondence has passed among them, which, dictated in becoming terms and devoted to legitimate ends, would have sufficed to secure the confidence and prosperity of the people of Oudh . . . Blessed by nature, man is its chief curse. And from all I hear, both from white and black lips, I solemnly believe that nothing but the spirit of Malcolm or Munro can secure it from a convulsion which must reflect disgrace on the good name of England.

The anonymous author then welcomes the prospect of Henry Lawrence's arrival, 'so thoroughly are the traditionary characteristics of officials understood and appreciated throughout India'.

Although many unwise things had been done in Oudh, these could all have been put right with a little more time. It was the disastrous, and largely accidental, outbreak at Meerut, and the still more disastrous failure to pursue the mutineers, which made the Indian Mutiny inevitable.

But why did the Indian Mutiny take place at all, and why did it happen when it did? In the first place, the fatal example of what had happened in Kabul fifteen years before had never been forgotten. Henry Lawrence had written about this in 1843 but, by a chapter of accidents, it had never been published. To some it has seemed almost uncannily prophetic of the situation which suddenly unfolded itself in 1857. It reads in part:

Asia has ever been fruitful in revolutions and can show many a dynasty overthrown by such small bands, as, on 2nd November 1841, rose against our force at Kabul, and British India can show how timely energy . . . has put down much more formidable insurrections . . . Dissensions among our enemies have raised us from the position of commercial factors to be lords over emperors. Without courage and discipline we could not thus have prevailed, but even these would have prevailed little had the country been united against us . . .

Perhaps our greatest danger arises from the facility with which these conquests have been made, a facility which . . . has betrayed us into the neglect of all rules for military occupation. Our sway is that of the sword, yet everywhere our military means are insufficient. There is always some essential lacking at the very moment when troops are wanted for immediate services. If stores are ready they may rot before carriage is forthcoming. If there are muskets, there is no ammunition. If there are infantry, there are no muskets for them. In one place we have guns without a man to serve them. In another we have artillery standing comparatively idle, because the guns have been left behind.

To come to examples, is Delhi . . . better prepared than Kabul was, should 3000 men arise tomorrow and seize the town?

It will be remembered that the mutineers from Meerut fled to Delhi, seizing the city and the titular emperor, and that the restoration of the Mogul dynasty became a potent symbol of the revolt.

Let all this happen in Hindustan on 2nd June [in fact it happened on 10th June 1857] . . . and does any sane man doubt that twenty-four hours would swell the hundreds of rebels into thousands and that if such conduct on our part lasted for a week, every plough-share in the Delhi States would be turned into a sword. [In fact, the peasants, throughout, just waited to see who would prevail.]

And when a sufficient force had been mustered by bringing European regiments from the hills and native troops from every quarter (which could not be effected within a month at the very least . . .) should we not then have a more difficult game to play than Clive had at Plassey or Wellington at Assaye? We should then be literally staking for our existence at the most inclement season of the year, with the prestige of our name vanished.

The reference to native troops was out of place. Henry was imagining a revolt of malcontents, not the disaffection of the whole Bengal army. And in sixteen years the overland route through Egypt had been developed and there were steamships, so that help from Europe could arrive much more quickly.

I have endeavoured to put the case fairly. Delhi is nearly as turbulent and unquiet a city as Kabul. It has, residing within its walls, a King less true to us than was Shah Shujah. The hot weather in India is more trying to us than the winter of Afghanistan . . . At Delhi the houses are fully as strong and the streets not less defensible. Here, if we act with prudence and intrepidity, we shall, under God's blessing, be safe, as we should with similar conduct there. Our chief danger in India is from within, not from without. The enemy who cannot reach us with his bayonets, can touch us more fatally if he lead us to distrust ourselves, and rouse our subjects to distrust us . . . At Kabul we lost an army . . . but I hold that by far our worst loss was in the confidence of our native soldiers. Better had it been for our fame if our harassed troops had rushed on the enemy and perished to a man, than that surviving *sepoys* should be able to tell the tales they can of what they saw at Kabul.

To what extent did Henry Lawrence foresee the Mutiny? This has become a disputed question. Kaye quotes Sir Robert Montgomery as saying:

With all his love for the people and their interests, he felt the rule of strangers was only tolerated because they could not help themselves. His conversation constantly turned to the subject of what measures should be adopted in case of any general disturbances . . . Passing along the parade ground one afternoon, where there were several hundred young Hindustani recruits at drill, he suddenly stopped and pointing to them, said to me, 'Do you see those fine young fellows? Mark my word, the Government is nourishing young vipers in their breasts and unless care is taken they will one day turn upon us.' This was five years before the Mutiny. With all this, he never showed any distrust of them, but ever studied their interests and feelings.

He did not foresee the occasion of the Mutiny. He did perceive its causes.

It seems incredible that the British arrangements should have had such fatal defects: perhaps the words of Baron Ochsenstjern to his son contain the ultimate wisdom: 'Consider, my son, with what little wisdom the world is governed.' Enough has already been said in quotations from Henry Lawrence about the entire absence of a 'career open to talent' for natives of ability in the Indian army. In the British part of the service promotion was by seniority, and there was no retiring age, with the result that senior officers were often in their dotage. No less an authority than Lord Roberts observed that those who were at the head of the army were no more heard of after the first stages of the revolt, which inevitably brought younger and more vigorous men to the fore. In a letter to Lord Canning written on 24th May, Henry had expressed himself vigorously: 'From top to bottom there are very few [officers] who both know and do their duty. The instances of gross ignorance and apathy that I daily encounter are most lamentable. I have been obliged to speak plainly and even roughly to many, and to record my opinion in orders. I have awakened some and probably incurred the hatred of others.'

The European element in the British forces, on whom alone we could rely, come what may, had been cut to the bone. In 1856 it was about one-seventh. The native forces had been wonderfully faithful over a hundred years of the British Raj, but there was a limit. It would be an anachronism to speak of a generalised Indian patriotism at this stage. Its place was taken by a strong feeling of belonging to a local community or to a caste. This is not to say that Indians did not have many things in common, things which distinguished them sharply from the British. These factors might have led them to combine for a specific purpose, but the combination would have been inherently unstable. None but Moslems, who were of course a minority, would want to restore Mogul rule. Hindus would have other ideas.

The military arrangements beggar description. Cantonments were often dispersed in the most haphazard way and magazines were left almost entirely unguarded. Henry Lawrence was prominent among those who had warned most urgently against all these defects, but nothing had been done. Moreover, the army was drained of its most talented officers, for every man with ambition aspired to a political post and the rest had lost interest in their duty, and sometimes in their men too. The days when the commanding officer had been the *ma-bap*, the mother and father of his troops, were far gone. Well-meaning regulations had deprived the senior officers of the power to dispense all but the smallest punishment and rewards. And there had been a steady decline in the discipline of the Bengal army since the beginning of the century. Officers were all too inclined to stand up for their men, whatever the merits of the case. The civilian population was ill protected against the exactions of soldiers. But when all is said and done it remains remarkable that the mutiny was confined to the Bengal army. It never spread either to the armies of Bombay or Madras. Both these armies had much better discipline, and ignored caste. A *brahmin* and a low-caste man stood together in its ranks.

It was indeed remarkable that there had not been trouble before, but there were particular reasons why it came to a head in 1857. Dalhousie had tried to do too much too quickly. He had been a leveller, one who was tempted to alter the relations of a complex and ancient society. It is true that, in the last generation, the Government of independent India has 'levelled' much more than entered into the dreams of Dalhousie, but that was an independent India, and it was a hundred years later, when all sorts of influences, some of them from

Europe, had had time to mature.

The celebrated case of the cartridges brought all this to a head. At any other time this would probably have passed off without much trouble. But it was believed that the cartridges had been greased with a mixture of cow's fat and pig's fat. The rule, at first, was that they had to be bitten. This would destroy a man's caste and was an abomination to Moslems. And there was an absurd story that ground bones had been surreptitiously smuggled on to the bazaars. Obviously this was a ruse of the Government to make everybody Christians. And no explanation of the Government was accepted. There was a total loss of confidence. There were, of course, in every regiment some men who were bent on mischief. It was easy for them to murder a British officer and then make out to their comrades that, having done that, they had no option but to join the Mutiny. Moreover, for many the *Foujki bheera*, the general will of the army, was almost irresistible.

There was moreover a 'general service order' which made every man in the Bengal army liable for service overseas. The Bengal army, in its origins, had been almost more of a militia than a regular army. The men depended on regular home visits. Their wives were not with them and home visits had been possible, when the Bengal army's sphere of activity reached from Bengal to the Sutlej and no further. But now it went from Peshawar to Burma, where the people had utterly different customs. The *sepoys* enlisted to serve in India, and in India only. They were originally compensated with special and generous allowances, if they were asked to serve further afield. But these had been abolished. There had formerly been special general service units who might be required to serve anywhere. Now every man in the Bengal army was conscripted, willy nilly, for general service. The food regulations of the Hindu were such that a high-caste Hindu could not cook on board ship. During a voyage he must subsist entirely on parched corn. Otherwise he would have to undergo a lengthy and costly purification from foreign contamination. Writing to Lord Canning, Henry quoted what had been said to him by an old *soubadar*: 'Anything in India is better than wealth beyond the sea.'

Though the Mutiny broke out at Meerut, Oudh was the flashpoint, in Oudh alone was there anything that approached a national rising. The *sepoys* could put two and two together. First the Punjab was annexed, then Satara, Nagpur and Jhansi. Dalhousie made no secret of his belief that British rule was preferable to Indian. And now Oudh, from where so many of the sepoys came. Oudh had always scrupulously performed its obligations to the British. Where would it end? Not until there was no more annexation to be done in the whole subcontinent and what would be the use of an army after that? As Britain's foreign enemies decreased, the importance of the *sepoy* became less. Brahmins from Oudh were the mainstay of the Company's recruitment. One cavalryman from Oudh told Henry: 'I used to be a great man. When I went home the best of the village rose as I approached, now the lowest puff their pipes in my face.' Such was the unintended consequence of annexation.

In a talk with an artillery *jemadar* who was about to be promoted, Henry learned from the man's sullen and stubborn honesty of the distrust which had now almost universally laid hold of the minds of the *sepoys* belonging to the Bengal Army.

He did not conceal that he and all others saw no absurdity in the ground bones *atta* belief, but that he considered we were quite up to such a dodge and that it was quite consistent with our whole career of fraud. 'You took Bharatpur by *dagha*. You got Lahore in the same way.' 'No. No,' I replied, 'all quite false,' to which he replied, 'Who broke the bridge at Sobraon?' – 'The Sikhs,' I replied, 'in their funk.' I was there. 'Yes,' he said, 'I know, you were there.' But he was not the more satisfied. 'I tell you they are like sheep. The leading one tumbles and down all the rest roll after him.'

In a letter to Lord Canning, Henry summed it all up in a quotation from a letter he had received from an 'old regimental officer'. This officer had said, 'If the *sepoy* is not speedily redressed, he will redress himself.' But Henry then continues:

I would rather say, unless some openings and rewards are offered to the military, as have been to the native civil servants and unless certain matters are righted, we shall be perpetually subject to our present condition of affairs. The *sepoy* feels we cannot do without him and yet the highest reward a *sepoy* can obtain at fifty, sixty, seventy years of age is about one hundred pounds a year, without the prospect of a brighter career for his son. Surely this is not the inducement to offer to a foreign soldier for special fidelity and long service? I earnestly entreated Lord Hardinge's and Dalhousie's attention to the fact, and more especially the point that *jemadars'* pay, though he is a commissioned officer, second in rank to the highest, is only twenty-four rupees a month or less than thirty pounds a year, while the average age of *jemadars* in the Bengal army is not less than fifty. The pension rules are perhaps the greatest of all the grievances. No soldier in the Bengal army can retire after any length of service, until he is incapacitated by ill health.

Recently the rules had been made more stringent. The previous rules had been that a man could retire on pension after fifteen years' service, provided he could make out that he was an invalid. Gubbins writes:

> It was a matter of surprise to see young and strong men, in the full enjoyment of health and vigour, relinquishing a service which offered them certain promotion and increased pay, in order to retire upon this scanty pittance. And yet it was so. Men starved themselves for months and became weak and emaciated, solely to pass for invalids. The Government granted an increase of pay for length of service . . . still the love of home proved too strong.

Henry Lawrence instances a man who had been for years a leper but was nonetheless sent back to his unit.

In another letter to Canning on 2nd May, Henry turned his attention to the press:

> Whatever may be the dangers of the native press, I look on it that the papers published in our own language are much the most dangerous. Disaffected native editors need only translate as they do, with or without words of admiration or exclamation, editorials from *The Friend of India* on the duty of annexing native states, on the imbecility, if not wickedness of allowing a single *jaghir* and of preaching the Gospel, even by commanding officers to raise alarm and hatred in the minds of all religionists and all connected with native principalities and *jaghirs*. And among the above will be found the large majority of the dangerous classes. We measure too much by English rule and expect [that Indians] . . . should like our own dead level and our arrogation to ourselves, even where we are notorious imbeciles, of all authority and all emolument . . . The politics of the editors are chiefly to be gathered from pithy exclamations . . . How good! wonderful! mutiny! More fires! with plentiful supply of the words mutiny, disobedience, disturbance. I would not trouble any of them, but with your Lordship's permission, I think we might squash half of the numbers by helping one or two of the cleverest with information, even with editorials and illustrations. Dr Ogilvie tells me that more than one of the English illustrated papers would, for a good purpose, sell cheap their half worn plates. An illustrated vernacular paper cleverly edited would sell well and do good politically and morally. I would be glad of your Lordship's sanction to a trial not involving above 5,000 rupees or £500. Of course, I would not appear and would use the present editors, at any rate, try to do so.

Henry's way with the press was original but it was effective, as a story told by Captain Wilson illustrates. One day the European editor of a

Lucknow paper wrote 'a very mischievous article against Government' which seemed likely to exasperate the native population.

Sir Henry sent for him and warned him that if he wrote again to excite the natives he would suppress the paper. Soon after this, Sir Henry was riding by the house where the paper was edited, and seeing the name up said to his staff, 'Let us go in and edit the paper for Mr K.' Going in, he said, 'Mr K., to show you I bear no ill will, I am come to write you a leading article.' He then made the staff sit down and give Mr K. all the military news of the day, while he himself dashed off a rapid review of all the resources at the command of Government for meeting and putting down the mutiny.

(ii) Before the Siege

Who is the happy Warrior? Who is he?
That every Man in arms should wish to be?
But who, if he be called upon to face
Some awful moment to which Heaven has joined
Great issues, good or bad for human kind,
Is happy as a Lover; and attired
With sudden brightness, like a Man inspired;
And, through the heat of conflict, keeps the law
In calmness made, and sees what he foresaw.

Wordsworth

By the end of May the situation had become tense, so Henry telegraphed to Lord Canning: 'Give me full military authority. I will not use it unnecessarily.' He was given full military authority with the rank of Brigadier General. The choice of a strongpoint for the defence of Lucknow was a matter of great difficulty. Unlike Delhi and Agra, Lucknow was not a fortified city but a huge collection of native streets and houses with a large population. There were neither walls around the town nor a citadel within it. The Kings of Oudh, secure in the protection of the British alliance, had taken no trouble to build themselves a fortified castle. They had spent their money on gaudy palaces.

The Chief Commissioner's house, known as 'the Residency', stood a little south of the river Gumti, which is a shallow stream some sixty yards wide and fordable in dry weather. The Residency, with its gardens and grounds, contained a church and houses for the other English officials. It was surrounded by a network of narrow streets which in many places abutted on the Residency grounds. Military opinion was that this unpromising site was the best available, but the defences had to be improvised from day to day, with no certainty when the blow might fall.

When the news of the Mutiny at Meerut came in, Henry Lawrence began to get in supplies from the country. People did not realise why he was doing it. These supplies were so ample that after Sir James Outram and Sir Henry Havelock had drawn on them, at the first relief of Lucknow, there was still a surplus when Sir Colin Campbell finally relieved Lucknow at the end of November 1857. As the revolt spread there was still hope that a close siege could be avoided. On 20th May Henry had been warned, through a native, that the Mutiny would come at evening gunfire. He was dining at his house in the cantonment, and he had said in grim jest, 'Your friends are not punctual.' Almost as he spoke, the rattle of muskets and the sound of running feet were heard.

Three officers were killed but a general massacre was prevented. Henry, with a hundred men and two guns, blocked the approaches from the cantonment to the city while Brigadier Inglis dealt firmly with the situation in the cantonment. The next day the mutineers were in full flight. They were pursued for ten miles with heavy losses. Henry was at the head of the pursuers. In a hasty postscript to the Governor-General Henry summed it up: 'We are now positively better off than we were, for we now know our friends and enemies. The latter have no stomach for a fight but are capital incendiaries.'

Disturbances spread through Oudh and completely obliterated the British Government. Some of the *taluqdars* did all they could to help those who were now refugees, while others did little or nothing. On 12th June, Henry wrote to J. R. Colvin at Agra that 'every outpost, I fear, has fallen, and we daily expect to be besieged by the confederated mutineers'.

The month of June was a prelude to the siege. In Lucknow everything that could be done was done. Already in the middle of May Sir Henry had sent for Simon Martin, the Deputy Commissioner of Lucknow, and told him to lay in supplies to last for three thousand persons for six months. 'That officer opened his eyes in astonishment. In common with the rest of the European community, he had never dreamt of the possibility of having to stand a siege, and he already had his hands full as magistrate and administrator of the great city, but Sir Henry continued, "Put everything else on one side, if need be; and mind I shall hold you equally responsible with the commissariat officer, if ever supplies run short before the end of six months.'"*

Meanwhile, the makeshift fortifications of the Residency were strengthened, while at Cawnpore mistakes were made. The position chosen was indefensible, everything was ready for a massacre, which duly took place owing to the treachery of the Nana Sahib, the representative of the once mighty Mahratta power.

Henry had been in weakened health when he came to Lucknow. The prospect of new work buoyed him up but the ordinary labours of his task tried his strength to the full. And the added responsibilities of the crisis, and then the Indian 'hot weather', would have worn down the strongest person. At first he rode about but latterly he went in a carriage. 'He lost appetite and sleep and his changed and careworn appearance were painfully visible to all', according to an eye witness cited by Kaye. But he worked on until he got in such an alarming state of exhaustion that the doctors advised him that further application to business would endanger his life. On 10th June he was ordered by Dr Fayrer, the Residency surgeon, to take a complete rest from responsibility for twenty-four hours. This was extended indefinitely the next day and he handed over his responsibilities to a council. Unfortunately Gubbins brought this period of rest to a sudden close by a flagrant disobedience of orders. Henry's object was to gather to the support of the English garrison all Indians who remained 'faithful to their salt'. This was well known. But Gubbins wanted to rid himself of all coloured troops, and persuaded a bare majority of his colleagues to agree. He therefore ordered the dismissal on leave of all remaining *sepoys* of the Lucknow regiments after the surrender of their arms. This was obeyed with reluctance. Henry, fortified by a doctor's report, thereupon reassumed his duties and countermanded the dismissal of the *sepoys*. McLeod Innes, who was there, said, 'The world has shown no nobler examples of military fidelity than that of the *sepoys* of the Lucknow garrison.'

Every observer speaks of Henry, even after this illness, as one whose body was now indeed weak but whose spirit mastered his physical weakness. Even after this illness 'he seemed never to rest. All hours of the night he was up and doing. That he derived great access of unexpected strength from prayer is not to be doubted. Often those who entered his room found him upon his knees praying for wisdom . . . and imploring mercy for the poor people committed to his charge.'[1] Brigadier Inglis, who afterwards succeeded him in military command of the garrison, testifies 'that his powers of mind were unabated, his orders clear and concise, his advice excellent and to the point'. Towards the end of June, McLeod Innes records a conver-

*Information supplied to my father from Mr Simon Martin.

[247]

sation with Henry while he was looking on at the construction of some batteries in the Machi Bhawan: 'I said to him, with a laugh of course, "These batteries will never be used." On this he turned round on me sharply. "What, you think we will not be besieged!" "Not so, sir," I said, "but when they come near enough to be under our fire, we shall have concentrated in the Residency." "Quite right, my boy! Their movements depend upon Cawnpore, a siege there will certainly be, and a long siege, and it will be months before aid can reach us."'

Martin Gubbins was an able man and very brave. He had earned Henry's high praise for his bravery but he had a bee in his bonnet about energetic measures without considering the resources to back them. In a letter to Colvin at Agra on 12th June, Henry wrote: 'Mr Gubbins would be continually sending fifty men on elephants, forty, fifty and more miles off. He is perfectly insane on what he considers energetic, manly measures. His language has been so extravagant that, were he not really useful, I should be obliged to take severe measures against him. He is the one malcontent in the garrison.' Merivale observed that of Gubbins' 'character, with its mixture of talent, courage, audacity and imperfect judgment, much might be said'.

There is no doubt that he was responsible for some of the mistakes of the Oudh administration. In a letter to Commissioner Tucker at Benares, Henry wrote: 'Gubbins is a fine fellow but he thinks ill of all who will not cut about the country. He looks too much to what he desires to do and forgets our means. His schemes would have destroyed this force ere this.' On the other hand Colonel Edgell wrote, in a private memorandum quoted by Merivale, that: 'Mr Gubbins did right good service with his rifle after we were besieged . . . His personal exertions and pluck throughout the siege were conspicuous, so was also his kindness and attention to the sick and wounded in his own house, which was always full. Mrs Gubbins aided him in this respect in every way, both have been I think very unjustly maligned.'

On the night of 29th June it was learnt that the advance of the mutineers on Lucknow had begun. They were at Nawabganj about twenty-five miles from Lucknow. Gubbins thought there were fifty foot and fifty horse but Henry doubted this. He wrote: 'Captain Forbes and Lieutenant Tullock were followed at 2 p.m. to the Kukrail Bridge [a tributary of the Gumti] seven miles on this side of Chinhut and only three miles from Lucknow. I write in the presence of Captain Forbes and Lieutenant Tullock (4.5 p.m.) and feel satisfied that now there are two or four thousand men at Chinhut, and in the morning there will be many more.' Nevertheless Gubbins demanded a decisive blow against the mutineers. Gubbins argued his case with all the force of his ardent and impetuous spirit and, in the end, Sir Henry yielded and ordered an advance. During the lull which preceded the battle,

Henry retired into a mango grove to be alone, presumably with God. The precedent was not encouraging to other generals, for the battle of Chinhut was a disaster.

After a march in the scorching heat, a halt was called for breakfast at the Kukrail where there was a bridge over the river, but the rations had been forgotten and the men were already exhausted and desperately hungry. Bad staff work was the plague of Victorian armies. Riding forward Lawrence examined the country ahead with a telescope but saw nothing, and had just sent a message ordering a withdrawal to Lucknow when he suddenly saw a large body of men moving forward in front of him. Countermanding his order, he instructed his troops to advance. It had been expected that the battle of Chinhut would be no more than an engagement between advanced detachments, not a battle with the whole force of the enemy. Moreover an extraordinary mistake had been made. The battlefield was well wooded. No pickets had been placed in the line of groves on the left of the British position. So the rebels' right wing was able to advance in force through or behind the grove without being seen. They brought an overwhelming fire to bear all round. This decided the contest at once. Henry Lawrence was to be seen everywhere at the points of greatest danger. The rebels were, on this occasion, well led. At the end of the day the defenders had lost at least 200 men with '8 wounded or overcome by the heat as well as some of the best officers and NCOs'. Five guns were lost because the *sepoys* who manned them deserted in the heat of battle. Only 1,720 able-bodied men were left for the defence of the Residency. The situation was saved by a bluff. Henry placed guns on the bridge with their port fires lighted. There was no ammunition left but the enemy did not know that and the survivors straggled back to Lucknow. They were given most welcome milk and water by the villagers on the way. Henry had sent out his carriage to Chinhut, intending to return in it, but after the disastrous action the horses were required for other purposes and he was conveyed to Lucknow on a gun carriage in a prostrate condition. Brigadier Inglis says that 'weak and prostrated by illness before he started, it was a miracle he returned alive. It needed no words to explain the result, the utterly exhausted state of our poor fellows as they came in told its own tale.' On returning to Lucknow Henry said, 'Well, Mr Gubbins has at last had his way and I hope he has had enough of it.' As he watched the last stages of the retreat he was heard to say, 'My God! My God! And I brought them to this.'

Reporting the disaster at Chinhut to Sir Henry Havelock, who was marching to an abortive relief of Lucknow, Henry wrote: 'The enemy have followed us up and we have now been besieged for four hours, and shall probably tonight be surrounded. The enemy are very bold and our Europeans are very low. I look on our position now as ten times as bad as it was yesterday . . . unless we are relieved quickly, say in ten or fifteen days, we shall hardly be able to maintain our position.' In fact the siege of Lucknow lasted nearly six months. The rebels were surprised at their victory and neglected to follow it up. A really determined attack would have captured the Residency in a day, but the mutineers were badly led. This was not surprising since no one in the native army was allowed to rise above a rank roughly equivalent to a sergeant major and the mutineers were riven by the old rivalry between Moslems and Hindus.

General McLeod Innes, one of the most thoughtful of those who lived through the siege of Lucknow, has this to say:

> Throughout the Mutiny, while some of the *sepoys* were embittered and fought with their whole heart, the bulk of them, who had simply followed, sheep-like, some truculent and self-appointed guide, felt that they were fighting in a bad cause, and against their habitual leaders of whom they naturally stood in awe. Under such circumstances, their conduct in the field could not draw out their military qualities in a true light, whereas those who remained true to their salt were the real representatives of the valour of their race.

Innes gives details which reinforce his view:

> The siege was marked through its whole duration by this want of organisation, of discipline, of military knowledge, of skill or leadership on the part of the investing force . . . They kept their guns in isolated and sheltered nooks and corners and fired them at random . . . The most effective and mischievous step which they took was to excavate shelter-trenches, from which they rained a ceaseless fire of bullets, their marksmen systematically making our loopholes and embrasures their special aim. It was to this feature of their attacks more than to any other cause that our continuous daily loss of life was due . . . When in actual contact with the enemy, as in sorties, I personally never found them show either determination or malignity. If brought to bay, they fought.

In the destruction of houses occupied by the enemy, the engineer (McLeod Innes) 'was necessarily the last man, having to fire the mine and overtake the party after they had withdrawn sufficiently far from the site of the explosion, yet I never found the enemy pressing too closely on me, either collectively or singly, or shooting very straight'. On one occasion when a large party of rebels ran past him two or three yards away none of them fired at him, until mistaking them for our men he called out to them to turn the other way.

What did the population of Lucknow think of the siege? The aristocracy of Oudh seem to have regarded it as an interesting peep show, rather than as something on which the future of their country depended.[2]

As for the people, they did not like being looted. Rajah Maun Singh, who played a notoriously double game but whose evidence on this point can be accepted, for the truth would have been known to his brother *taluqdars*, to whom he addressed a letter on 20th July 1857, writes of the mutineers: 'They have plundered thousands of houses, and they consider every person's property to be their own.' The villagers retaliated by pillaging small bodies of mutineers when they could.

Sharar, who was born only two years after the Mutiny and was in love with the traditional culture of Lucknow, thought that 'The besiegers consisted of the disreputable elements of the town and unprincipled and headstrong combatants. There was not a single man of valour among them, who knew anything of the principles of war or who could combine the disunited forces and make them into an organised fighting force.' Much later, when the revolt was virtually lost, good leaders came to the front.

(iii) Never Give In

There had been three strongpoints in the defences of Lucknow: the cantonments, the Residency and the Machi Bhawan or Fish Pavilion. This last was a fortification in the centre of the city which helped to overawe Lucknow. The cantonments had already been abandoned. Now it was time to concentrate all the resources of the tiny garrison on the Residency. Lieutenant Innes was the engineer in charge of the works at the Machi Bhawan. He writes:

Whilst the fight was going on at Chinhut, the works and operations were being carried on as usual at the Residency and the Machi Bhawan. Carts were still bringing in supplies and the defences swarmed with labourers. It was clear that the approach of the *sepoy* army was not exciting the ordinary city population. The Machi

Bhawan was, by this time, cleared out of nearly all its supplies and of all the spare guns, but not of the guns at the west end of the position, nor of a large store of powder and small arms ammunition, for which room had not yet been found or made in the entrenchments. All of a sudden the work people disappeared as if by magic both at the Residency and the Machi Bhawan, and in the next few minutes the first fugitives from the fight [of Chinhut] made their appearance with the announcement of the defeat of the British force.

At both positions, the main positions were immediately taken to make the gates and entrances secure and to man the outposts and batteries. By degrees the troops of the Chinhut forces rejoined, the city meanwhile keeping quiet.

Henry had arranged to hold one of the bridges across the Gumti and the one other bridge was commanded from the Machi Bhawan, so that the mutineers had to cross lower down. The mutineers were therefore not able to surround the Residency till later in the day, when they fired into the windows causing a few casualties. The Machi Bhawan in the meantime was hardly molested. On the night of 30 June little happened but the next day musketry fire poured in from all sides and a shell was fired from the north of the river but with little result. In the meantime the ground intervening between the Machi Bhawan and the Residency had been occupied by the mutineers, so that the only communication was by semaphore. Henry sent a message saying, 'Retire tonight at twelve. Blow up well.' The garrison marched out expecting to be attacked at any moment. Twenty minutes later, as the rearguard came within the gates of the Residency, 'there was a great quake of the earth and thunderous report and a brilliant glare which announced that the Machi Bhawan magazine had been successfully exploded' (McLeod Innes). This was accomplished without a single casualty. The mutineers had chosen this night to loot the city. McLeod Innes records that this success 'was a great consolation to Sir Henry after the disaster of 30 June . . . Thus the first hours of 2 July saw the whole of the Lucknow force concentrated in the Residency entrenchments and prepared to hold it to the death, with an ample store of food and of ammunition, with more guns than they could man, and with defences which the result showed to be adequate for their purpose against the enemies investing the position.' The defences were indeed adequate for their purpose, but only just, and the garrison was very thin on the ground. So every soldier slept in his uniform, with his weapons beside him, throughout the siege.

Meanwhile, in Rajputana George kept things steady and, in the Punjab, John was entering his finest hour. His judgment was almost unerring, his resolution unfailing and his courage of the highest. He was often racked by neuralgia yet he combined these qualities with the greatest consideration for subordinates, some of whom were more than prickly. When John Nicholson, for instance, on his famous march to Delhi, calmly annexed the gunners of senior officers, John Lawrence at first asked gently for an explanation that he could pass on when asked. But when no answer came and Nicholson did exactly the same again, he contented himself with saying, 'You are incorrigible,' and left him to his own superb devices. But, with all his reputation for sternness, John Lawrence always wanted to temper justice with mercy, knowing full well how sorely the *sepoys* had been tried. His influence on the siege of Delhi was such that many of the natives found it impossible to believe that he was not actually present in the body before that city. His word was accepted as law and he gave unsolicited advice to generals and to the Governor-General himself. He was called 'King John' in the Punjab.

Calcutta was cut off from all communication with the Punjab during a great part of the Mutiny. And the Home Government, believe it or not, had sent reinforcements by the long Cape route instead of the much shorter overland route through Egypt. So the Punjab was left to work out its own salvation. It was in the Punjab that there was the largest concentration of European troops in India, but there were also large numbers of *sepoys*, whose loyalty was doubtful. By a masterly stroke the garrison at Lahore was disarmed. At first the local population were doubtful, though they had little sense of kinship with the 'Hindustani' *sepoys*, for whom they had their own words *'poorbeahs'* or easterners. But when they saw the vigour of the administration they rapidly came round to the British side. John saw at once that Delhi was the key point. He took risks denuding the Punjab of troops, and some of his best men, to send every available man to the siege of Delhi where the 'besiegers' were few and the 'besieged' were many.

Henry had chosen a room at the top of the Residency so as to direct the defence. Already the main building had received special attention from the enemy's guns. And on 30th June an eight-inch shell burst in the room where Henry and his secretary were sitting. Evidently the enemy knew just where to aim. On being pressed to change his quarters, he said in jest 'he did not believe the enemy had any artillerymen good enough to put another shell into the small room'. However he promised to change his room on the next day, which was 2nd July. Captain Wilson describes what happened next:

Towards 8 a.m. he (Henry) returned greatly exhausted, the heat was dreadful, and he laid down on his bed with his clothes on and desired me to draw up a memorandum as to how the rations were to be distributed. I went to the next room to write it but, previous to doing so, I reminded Sir Henry of his promise to go below. He said he was very tired and would rest a couple of hours and that then he would have his things moved. In about half an hour I went back into the room with what I had written. His nephew, Mr George Lawrence, was then lying on a bed parallel with his uncle's, with a few feet between them. I went between the beds and stood on the right side of Sir Henry's, with one knee resting on the bed. A coolie was sitting on the floor pulling the *punkah*. I read what I had written . . . and he was in the act of explaining what he wished altered, when the fatal shot came. A sheet of flame, a terrific report, a shock and dense darkness is all I can describe. I fell down on the floor and for perhaps a few seconds was quite stunned. I then got up, but could see nothing for the smoke or dust. Neither Sir Henry or his nephew made any noise, and in great alarm I called out, 'Sir Henry, are you hurt?' Twice I thus called out without any answer, the third time he said in a low tone, 'I am killed'. The punkah had come down and the ceiling and a great deal of the plaster. And the dust and smoke were so great that it was some minutes before I could see anything but, as it gradually cleared, I saw that the white coverlet of the bed was crimson with his blood.

The coolie who was pulling the *punkah* lost a foot but Captain Wilson was only slightly wounded and George was unscathed. A small fragment of the shell had struck Henry right at the top of his thigh. Dr Fayrer was called and, in answer to a question from Henry – 'How long do I have to live?' – he answered, 'I hope some time.' To which Sir Henry replied, 'I want a distinct answer. How long shall I live? I have a deal to do.' Dr Fayrer said, 'I hope about forty-eight hours.' Henry was surprised that it was so long. He then sent for Brigadier Inglis and Major Banks to whom he gave his last order. Foremost among his last instructions was 'Never give in'.

Henry received the Holy Communion at the hands of the Reverend James Harris, whose wife has left a valuable record of his last hours. Many of the officers and men made their communion with their chief. This Communion took place amid 'the din of the fight going on all around and the heavy guns firing from the garden at our very ears'. Mrs Harris continues: 'The balls were flying thick among us but not one of us was touched. Yet scarcely had he been removed into an inner room . . . when the casualties occurred at the very spot where we had so lately stood and knelt.'

After receiving the Communion he lay for nearly an hour, talking connectedly during the intervals of severe pain, sending messages to all he had loved. He asked forgiveness of those to whom he had spoken harshly in the course of duty and begged them to kiss him. He summoned to the front all his old servants, who were 'sobbing out their grief in the background'. He rewarded each of them and told them of the contents of his Will and who he wished to look after his children.

His sufferings as he lay dying were terrible but intermittent. Mrs Harris, who nursed him in his last hours, added that he took 'an immense quantity of champagne and arrowroot' and further that 'his grateful words and looks for those administrations were affecting beyond measure', but 'his screams were so terrible that I think the sound will never leave my ears'.

He expressed the deepest humility and repentance of his sins and said that he had been very ambitious all his life, 'and look how it has ended'. He spoke 'most touchingly of his dear wife', and looked forward to rejoining her, but at the mention of her name 'he burst into an uncontrollable fit of weeping which lasted some minutes. He again completely broke down in speaking of his daughter . . . There was not a dry eye there and many, seemingly hard and rough men, were sobbing like children,' according to Kaye quoting an eye witness. George Lawrence adds: 'He said that I had been like a son to him, and that, though he used to think me selfish, he had not found me so, and lastly he gave me his blessing.' And finally he said, 'Let there be no fuss about me. Let me be buried with the men. No nonsense.' Then after a short silence he added with a touch of his old sensitivity, 'Don't let me be maligned'. Throughout he made it very clear that the garrison should die to the last man rather than surrender, but he emphasised that no force of less than two thousand Europeans should attempt a relief and that this must be emphasised by repeated messages to the relieving force.

After the first day he never spoke very connectedly, though he still repeated prayers after the chaplain, even when it seemed that he was insensible to all around him, and from time to time, alternately with his prayers for the women and children whom he had particularly at heart, he said, 'Remember the Asylum, do not let them forget the Asylum'. And so the half-intelligible mutterings went on until the morning of 4th July.

Mrs Harris, who was present, writes:

His end was very peaceful and without suffering . . . His expression was so happy, one could only rejoice his pain was over. Half an hour before he died his nephew, Mr George Lawrence, was shot through his shoulder. I have been nursing him today, poor fellow. It was so sad to see him lying there in the room with his uncle's body, looking so sad and suffering. About twelve, the smell became so offensive I was obliged to ask James to have the body carried outside, so he called some soldiers to help carry the bed into the verandah . . . A party came begrimed and heated from the fight and, when told the nature of the service and for whom required, they first knelt down, subdued and sorrowing beside the bedside, and lifting the covering sheet from his face, one by one, lovingly and reverently kissed it.

Major Banks was killed in the worst of the fighting but his diary in which Henry's last instructions are recorded was found by chance after the end of the siege. The instructions have been slightly re-arranged to make the order more logical.

(i) Reserve fire, check all wall firing.

(ii) Carefully register ammunition for guns and small arms in store. Carefully register daily expenditure as far as possible.

(iii) Spare the precious health of Europeans, in every possible way, from shot and sun.

(iv) Organise working parties for night labour.

(v) Entrench, entrench, entrench. Erect traverses, cut off enemy fire.

(vi) Turn every horse out of the entrenchments, except enough for four guns. Keep Sir Henry Lawrence's horse, Ladakhi, it is a gift to his nephew, George Lawrence.

(vii) Use the state prisoners as a means of getting in supplies, by gentle means if possible or by threats.

(viii) Enroll every servant as *bildar* or carrier of earth. Pay liberally – double, quadruple.

(ix) Take an immediate inventory of all natives, so as to know who can be used as *bildars*, etc.

(x) Turn out every native who will not work (save menials who have more than abundant labour).

(xi) Write daily to Allahabad or Agra.

(xii) Take an immediate inventory of all supplies and food etc. Take daily average expenditure.

(xiii) Sir Henry Lawrence's servants to receive one year's pay. They are to work for any other gentleman or they may leave if they prefer to do so.

(xiv) Put on my tomb only this: 'Here lies Henry Lawrence who tried to do his duty. May God have mercy on him.'

Epilogue

Throughout the siege the Union Jack was hoisted again and again as often as the enemy shot it down. After that the flag was never lowered, night or day, up to the independence of India.

It was sad that Henry Lawrence died at the hands of *sepoys* whom he loved with clear sight, whose grievances he understood and whose rights he advocated more effectively than any of the British in India. Of all the tributes paid to him after his death, the best was given by his friend, Sir John Kaye, when he said: 'it was not so much what he did as what he was'.

This was echoed by Lord Stanley, the future Earl of Derby and a distinguished statesman in his own right, who said at a memorial service:

> Sir Henry Lawrence rose to eminence step by step, not by favour of any man, certainly not by subserviency to ruling authorities or to popular ideas, but simply by the operation of that natural law which in troubled times brings the strongest mind, be it where it may, to the post of high command. I knew Sir Henry Lawrence six years ago. Travelling in the Punjab I passed a month in his camp, and it then seemed to me, as it does now, that his personal character was far above his career, eminent as that career has been.

It would have consoled Henry Lawrence to know that many of the reforms he had at heart were acted on after his death. The army was reorganised on much better principles, there were no annexations, the English-style law courts were also reorganised on principles that were much more acceptable to the natives and it was a little easier for Indians to rise in the hierarchy. But Indians could still not occupy the seats of power until it was nearly too late. Before the news of Henry Lawrence's death had reached London, the Directors of the East India Company paid him the highest compliment which they could offer to their servants. On 22nd July a resolution was unanimously passed by them proposing to appoint Sir Henry Lawrence 'provisionally to succeed to the office of Governor-General upon the death, resignation or coming away of Viscount Canning, pending the arrival of a successor from England'.

It only remains to say that Indians, who are the most faithful of all mankind to someone they have loved, and whose faithfulness continues from generation to generation, still put fresh flowers on the grave of Henry Lawrence.

APPENDIX

The Calcutta Review: Henry and Honoria Lawrence's contributions

YEAR	ISSUE	TITLE OF ARTICLE
1844	Vol.I May-Aug.	The English in India. Our Social Morality, pp.290-336
1844	Vol.I	Lord William Bentinck's Administration, pp.337-371
1844		Recent History of the Punjab, pp.449-507
		The Administration of Lord Ellenborough, pp.508-62
1844	May-Aug.	Review of book of Children's Verse, pp.563-70 (seems to be by Honoria). See E&M Vol.2, p.12
1844	Vol.II	Military Defence of our Indian Empire, pp.32-72
1844	Oct.-Dec.	The Sikhs and their Country, pp.153-208
1844	Oct.-Dec.	Romance and Reality of Indian Life, pp.377-443 (by H.M.L. and Honoria together)
1844	Oct.-Dec.	Kashmir and the Countries around the Indus, pp.469-535
1845	Vol.III Jan.Jun.	The Sickroom in India, pp.71-101 (Honoria)
1845		Review of *Field Carriage of Sick and Wounded* by Dr Login, pp.vii-xiv
1845	Jan.-Jun.	The Kingdom of Oudh, pp.375-427
1845	Vol.IV Jul.-Dec.	Englishwomen in Hindustan, pp.96-127 (Honoria)
1845	Vol.IV Jul.-Dec.	The Mahratta History and Empire, pp.178-239
1845		Married Life in India, pp.394-417 (Honoria almost certainly)
1846	Vol.V Jan.-Jun.	Review of *Adventures of an Officer*, pp.348-72 (Not by H.M.L.)
1846	Vol.V	The Irregular Cavalry, pp.181-201
	No.IX	Mr Thornton's Last Volume, pp.145-80
1846	Jan.-Jun. No.XI Vol.V	The Countries Betwixt the Sutlej and Jumna
	Jul.-Dec.	The Sikh Invasion of British India in 1845-6, pp.241-304. Written by Edwardes but drawing information from H.M.L.

YEAR	ISSUE	TITLE OF ARTICLE
1846	Jul.-Dec.	The Scinde Controversy – Napier and Outram, pp.569-614
		Remarks on the Scope of Military Literature and History, pp.1-xxvii. Seems to be by H.M.L.
1847	Vol.VII Jul.-Dec.	Lord Hardinge's Indian Administration, pp.451-547 (See also *London Quarterly Review* No.55, June 1846, Article IX)
1848	Vol.IX Jan.-Jun.	*The Reigning Family of Lahore*, pp.511-24 (Review of Carmichael Smith's book)
1849	No.XXII Vol.IX	Baggage of the Indian Army, pp.445-92
1851	No.XXXI Vol.XVI	Recent works on Scinde. Review of *Dry Leaves from Young Egypt. Scinde or the Unhappy Valley* by Lt. R. F. Burton and *General Sir Charles Napier's Administration of Scinde* by Lt.Gen. Sir William Napier, pp.383-411
1854	Jan.-Jun. Vol.XXII No.XLIII	Sir Charles Napier's Posthumous Work, pp.208-90. Signed by H.M.L.
1856	Jan.-Jun. Vol.XXVI	The Indian Army, pp.177-210
1856	Jan.-Jun.	The Bengal Cavalry, pp.549-91
1856	Jul.-Dec. Vol.XXVII	Army Reform, pp.94-149

SOURCE NOTES

CHAPTER 1
1 Unless otherwise noted all quotations in this and the next chapter can be found in the opening pages of *The Life of Sir Henry Lawrence* by Edwardes and Merivale
2 *Life of Lt.Col. Alexander Lawrence*, p.4
3 *Life of Lord Lawrence* by Bosworth Smith, Chap.XIII
4 BS Chap.XII

CHAPTER 2
1 Unless otherwise noted all quotations in this chapter are from Edwardes and Merivale

CHAPTER 3
1 *Calcutta Review*, Vol.I, 'Lord William Bentinck's Administration'
2 BS p.332

CHAPTER 4
1 All quotations in this chapter are from Chapter 2 of Edwardes and Merivale

CHAPTER 6
1 E&M 1. 97
2 Herbert Edwardes in E&M.122
3 E&M 11.118
4 E&M 119
5 Letter of 31.5.50 to H.M.L.
6 E&M 123-4
7 See Eur MSS 85 Vol.2 F.36-7, second series
8 E&M 1. 123

CHAPTER 8
1 Report of H.M.L. quoted in E&M p.206
2 *Lawrence of Lucknow* by J.L.Morison p.95
3 Becher apud E&M 1 p.295
4 Letter of 13.5.41 from H.M.L.
5 E&M 1. 294
6 Letter of 27.6.42, H.M.L. to Clerk Vol.25
7 Eur MSS 85 2 folio 35
8 E&M 1. 344
9 Eur MSS 85/85. Letter of 23.2.42.F51
10 E&M 1. 299
11 EUR F85/70. Letters 5.4.42
12 E&M 1. 305
13 Vol.25 letter of 17.6.42
14 See letter to Kaye of 24.6.52 MSS Eur E 85/35A 1852
15 E&M 1. 317
16 Eur MSS 85/F43. Letter of 20.2.42
17 E&M 1. 328
18 E&M 1. 339
19 E&M 1. 333 Letter of 29.2.42 to Honoria
20 E&M 1. 342-3
21 E&M 1. 346

22 ibid
23 Eur MSS F 85/85, F111. Letter of 5.4.41
24 Eur MSS F 85/85, F113. Letter of 15.4.42
25 ibid, F118. Letter of 19.4.42

CHAPTER 9
 1 *Lives of Indian Officers* by Sir John Kaye
 2 E&M 1. 438
 3 E&M 1. 484
 4 E&M 1. 485
 5 Kaye, p.405
 6 ibid
 7 ibid, p.408
 8 ibid
 9 ibid, p.409
10 H.M.L. in a letter to Lord Auckland, 25.5.45
11 ibid
12 Morison p.139

CHAPTER 10
 1 Morison
 2 H.M.L. in a letter to Elliot 2.7.47
 3 Morison
 4 Morison p.211
 5 *Adventures of an Officer*, Vol.2 p.75
 6 Lumsden in a letter to H.M.L. 25.2.47
 7 ibid
 8 Morison p.197
 9 Charles Raikes, *Notes on the Revolt in the North-Western Provinces of India*,
    pp.35-6

CHAPTER 11
 1 Kaye p.401
 2 John Lawrence in a letter to H.M.L. 19.6.48, Vol.31 p.49
 3 BS Chap X, of H.M.L. to Kaye.
 4 GL Vol.31 p.18, J.L. to H.M.L. 4.5.48
 5 Eur. F.85 Vol.32, J.L. to Currie 30.4.48
 6 John Lawrence in a letter to H.M.L. 14.11.48
 7 Morison p.213
 8 Colin Campbell in a letter to H.M.L. 23.7.49
 9 Vol.11 p.657
10 BACSA Chowkidar Vol.1 No.1
11 Hodson in a letter to H.M.L. 12.11.49
12 Rennell Taylor in a letter to H.M.L. 15.11.49
13 Confidential letter of Hardinge to H.M.L. 24.2.49
14 Dalhousie in a letter to Sir George Couper 5.3.49

CHAPTER 12
 1 Memoirs of Sir Henry Dermot Daly p.370
 2 Merivale Vol.2 p.88
 3 First Punjab Report p.77
 4 Temple in E&M 2. p.188

5 *The British Conquest and Dominion of India*, Sir Penderel Moon
6 BS p.284
7 E&M 2 p.1157
8 Morison

CHAPTER 13
1 E&M 2 p.230
2 Morison p.271

CHAPTER 14
1 Kaye
2 *Last Phase of an Oriental Culture* by Sharar, Elec 1985

SOURCES

The primary sources are: the Henry Lawrence papers in the India Office Library, Henry's novel *The Adventures of an Officer in the Service of Ranjit Singh* (Henry Colburn, 1845), and Henry and Honoria's journalism, particularly Henry's articles in the *Calcutta Review* (see Appendix).

The secondary sources are: *The Life of Sir Henry Lawrence* by Edwardes and Merivale (Smith Elder, 1872); *Sir Henry Lawrence*, in the Rulers of India series by Lt. Gen. McLeod Innes; *Lawrence of Lucknow* by J. L. Morison (G. Bell & Sons, 1934); *Lives of Indian Officers* by Sir John Kaye (W. H. Allen & Co., 1889); *Reminiscences of the Great and Good Sir Henry Lawrence* by 'Y'. This was given to me by George Young of Culdaff. 'Y' was Robert Young of Culdaff, known as 'Salvation Army Young' (printed in Dehra Dun, 1893); notes on the Revolt in the North-West Provinces of India by Charles Raikes, but mainly written by Herbert Edwardes; *The Life of Lieutenant Colonel Alexander Lawrence* by his great-grandson Lt. Col. George H. Lawrence C.M.G. (privately printed, 1932); *Honoria Lawrence* by Maud Diver (John Murray, 1936); *Forty Three Years Service in India* by Lt. Gen. Sir George Lawrence (John Murray, 1875) and three admirable biographies of John Lawrence, viz. *Life of Lord Lawrence* by Ronald Bosworth Smith (Smith Elder, 1885), *Lawrence* in the Rulers of India series by Sir Charles Aitchison (O.U.P., 1892) and *Lord Lawrence* by Sir Richard Temple (Macmillan English Men of Action series, 1889). It would be worth some enterprising publisher reissuing some of these, perhaps the shortened version of Bosworth Smith, to which should be added the series of *Reports on the Administration of the Punjab Territories* (Calcutta Gazette Office, 1853–6).

Every one of the books on India which I have read have added to the background. Many of the books by and about the contemporaries of the Lawrences have been very useful. I should mention:

The Causes of the Indian Revolt by Syed Akhmet Khan Bahadur (Benares Medical Hall Press, 1873); *A Guide to Seringapatam and its Vicinity* by P. Stephen Basappa (Town Press, Bangalore, 1897); *Rider on a Grey Horse*, A

Life of Major Hodson by Barry Joynson Cork (Cassell & Co. Ltd, 1958); *Lady Login's Recollections 1820–1904* by E. Dalhousie Login (Smith Elder & Co., 1916); *Memoirs of General Sir Henry Dermot Daly* by Major H. Daly (John Murray, 1905); *Hindu Manners, Customs and Ceremonies* by Dubois and Beauchamp (Clarendon Press, 1924); *Memorials of the Life and Letters of Major General Sir Herbert Edwardes* by His Wife (Kegan Paul, Trench & Co., 1886); *A Year on the Punjab Frontier 1848–9*, Vols. I & II, by Major Herbert B. Edwardes (Richard Bentley, 1851); *An Account of the Kingdom of Cabaul*, Vols. I & II, by Hon. Mountstuart Elphinstone (Richard Bentley, 1839); *Journal of an Afghanistan Prisoner* by Lt. Vincent Eyre (John Murray, 1843); *Sale's Brigade in Afghanistan* by Rev. G. R. Gleig M.A. (John Murray, 1846); *An Account of the Mutinies in Oudh* by Martin Richard Gubbins (Richard Bentley, 1858); *A Lady's Diary of the Siege of Lucknow* by Mrs G. Harris (John Murray, 1858); *Twelve Years of a Soldier's Life in India* by W. S. R. Hodson B.A. (John W. Parker & Son, 1859); *The Comparative Merits of British and Native Administration in India* by J. W. Kaye (26th February 1868); *Lumsden of the Guides* by Gen. Sir Peter S. Lumsden and George R. Elsmie (John Murray, 1899); *From Sepoy to Subedar* edited by James Lunt (Routledge & Kegan Paul Ltd, 1970); *Lucknow and Oude in the Mutiny* by Lt. Gen. McLeod Innes (A. D. Innes & Co., 1895); *Signal Catastrophe* by Patrick Macrory (Hodder & Stoughton, 1966); *A Matter of Honour* by Philip Mason (Jonathan Cape Ltd, 1974); *The Men Who Ruled India* (Jonathan Cape Ltd, 1954); *Monty's Grandfather* by Brian Montgomery (Blandford Press, 1984); *The British Conquest and the Dominion of India* by Sir Penderel Moon (Gerald Duckworth & Co., 1989); *Field Marshal Lord Napier of Magdala* by Lt. Col. H. D. Napier (Edward Arnold, 1927); *The Hero of Delhi*, The Life of John Nicholson by Hesketh Pearson (Collins, 1939); *The Life of Sir George Pollock* by Charles Rathbone Low (W. H. Allen & Co., 1873); *Journey of Disasters in Afghanistan 1841–2* by Lady Sale (John Murray, 1843); *A Journey Through the Kingdom of Oude in 1849–50* by Major General Sir W. H. Sleeman K.C.B. (Richard Bentley, 1858); *Men and Events of My Time in India* by Sir Richard Temple (John Murray, 1882); *Ecrits et Discours Politiques* by Alexis Tocqueville (Editions Gallimard, Paris, 1962); *The Life of John Nicholson* by L. J. Trotter (John Murray, 1898) and *The Story of the Guides* by Colonel G. J. Younghusband C.B. (Macmillan & Co., 1980).

GLOSSARY OF ANGLO–INDIAN
WORDS AND PHRASES

Anglo–Indian:	Originally a British person who made his career in India, now a person of mixed blood
Adulatees:	A court of justice
Atta/otta:	Flour
Baboo:	Originally a native clerk who wrote English
Banya:	A caste of traders and money-lenders
Batta:	An extra allowance made to soldiers in the field or on other special grounds
Bearer:	A native valet
Bheestie:	A water carrier
Bildar:	A carrier of earth
Bundobust:	Any system or mode of regulation
Burj:	A tower
Burkundazes:	An armed policeman
Burra Sahib:	A great or very great Sahib, or a leading member of the ICS
Choga:	An Afghan long-sleeved garment, like a dressing gown
Chugprassy:	An office messenger with a badge
Clashee:	A tent pitcher
Cossid:	A courier
Crore:	One hundred lakhs (q.v.), therefore 10,000,000 rupees or about one million pounds sterling
Dagha:	Deceit
Dakoiti:	The act of robbery
Dharma:	Under the caste system each caste had its own duty
Dhobie:	A washerman
Dhoolie:	A covered litter or cot suspended from a bamboo pole and carried by two or four men
Doab:	A mesopotamia, literally two waters
Fakir:	An Islamic religious mendicant; also applied to a Hindu of the same type
Feringhee:	A European, derived from a Frank
Ferishstahs:	Angels
Foujki bheera:	The general will of the army
Ghazi:	Generally a fanatical Muslim warrior
Ghee:	Clarified butter
Gram:	Chick pea
Gurreeb:	Literally poor, figuratively humble, self-abasing
Guru:	A Hindu spiritual teacher

[265]

Hammam:	A Turkish bath
Jaghir:	A hereditary assignment of land
Jaghirdar:	The holder of a Jaghir
Jemadar:	The second rank of officer in the Indian army, roughly equivalent to a serjeant
Jezail:	A long smooth-bore musket generally with a forked rest at the end to keep it steady
Kardar:	An all-purposes agent of the government of Ranjit Singh
Kutchery:	An office of administration, a court house
Kyzilbashes:	Literally a red head, namely a person so-called from their headdress
Lakh:	A hundred thousand
Ma-bap:	Mother and father
Mahout:	The driver and tender of an elephant
Malik:	Chief
Munshi:	A secretary, an interpreter, a writer
Nimmuk huram:	Faithful, reliable, literally true to one's self. One who carries out his obligations
Nujeeb:	Half-disciplined infantry soldiers of good family
Nullah:	A watercourse, often a dried watercourse, a ravine. Corresponds to a wadi in Arabic
Omlah, ambah:	A native clerk of a civil court or Kutchery
Palkee:	A covered vehicle containing a couch and carried on men's shoulders
Piffers:	The celebrated Punjab Irregular Frontier Force
Panchayat:	A council properly of five persons assembled as a court of arbiters or jury
Punkah:	A large swinging fan suspended from the ceiling, made of cloth stretched on a rectangular frame. Used to agitate the air in hot weather
Pyarkurro:	To make love
Ressaldar:	The native officer who commands a ressala, or company, in a regiment of irregular horse
Rijot:	A peasant
Sahib:	A European gentleman or any European
Salaam:	The Arabic for peace (or the Hebrew Shalom). An oral salutation used by both Muslims and Hindus. Compliments
Sefku:	Put to the sword
Sepoy:	A native soldier drilled and dressed in the European style

Shikaree:	A hunter
Sirdar:	In Anglo-Indian usage a leader, or person in command
Sowar:	A native cavalry soldier
Sudder Board of Dep:	Board of Revenue
Sunnud:	A deed or grant
Soubadar:	The chief native officer of a company of sepoys. Its actual captain
Syce:	A groom
Suttee, Sati:	The burning of the living widow along with the corpse of her husband. Practised by certain castes among the Hindus
Taluqdar:	In Oudh a feudal landowner with extensive possessions
Terai:	A belt of jungle and marshy land stretching along the foot of the Himalayas
Thugs/Thuggi:	A secret society dedicated to the worship of the goddess Kali 'who sallying forth in a gang . . . and in a character of wayfarers, either in business or pilgrimage, fall in with other travellers on the road, and having gained their confidence' get a rich traveller by himself and then take the opportunity 'of strangling them by throwing their handkerchiefs around their necks and then plundering them and burning their bodies.' (From *A Glossary of Anglo-Indian Colloquial Words and Phrases* by Henry Yule and A. C. Burnell). They appear to have existed for centuries but were eventually discovered by the British shortly after the capture of Seringapatam in 1799
Tulwar:	A sabre
Tuppeh:	One of the sub-divisions with which Bannu was divided
Uncovenanted Civil Service:	Members of the Indian Civil Service entered into a covenant with the East India Company. An uncovenanted civil servant held a subordinate post and did not have a covenant with the Company. They were not received in good company
Vizier, Wazir:	A minister, usually the principal minister
Zamindar:	A landowner. A tenant in chief paying revenue direct to the government
Zubberdast:	A very forceful character

INDEX

Court, General Claude Auguste, 102
Craufurd, Rev. George, 35–8, 41, 104
Culdaff (Northern Ireland), 14–15
Currie, Sir Frederick: recommends HL's
  appointment to Ferozepore, 73;
  summons HL to Punjab, 126; HL
  reports to, 129, 136–7, 149; appointed
  to Lahore, 158–9, 173; and Second
  Sikh War, 159–61; Nicholson
  criticises, 168

Dalhousie, James Andrew Broun
  Ramsay, 10th Earl and 1st Marquis of:
  as 'leveller', 57, 241; relations with
  HL, 127; and HL's assistants, 142;
  succeeds Hardinge, 149; and Second
  Sikh War, 160–1, 163, 173; and HL's
  return to Punjab, 173–5; character
  and manner, 173–5; sets up Punjab
  Board of Administration, 176–9;
  achievements in Punjab, 192; and
  John Lawrence, 194, 197; and
  Kohinoor, 202; Napier opposes, 204;
  as administrator, 205; on HL's
  absences and travels, 206; and HL's
  appointment to Rajputana, 209; and
  annexation of Oudh, 232–3, 242; and
  army discontent, 243
Daly, Sir Henry, 193, 195, 210, 234–5
Daly, Susan, Lady, 234
Davee Singh, 103
Delhi, 27, 164–6, 239, 253
Delhi Gazette, 84, 104–5, 130
Derby, 15th Earl of see Stanley, Edward
  Henry, Lord
Dhulip Singh, Maharajah of Punjab: and
  Punjab unrest, 126, 128, 136; and
  Treaty of Bhairowal, 139–40, 151; and
  Second Sikh War, 162
Dhyan Singh, 97
Dina Nath, Rajah, 132, 138, 140–1
doabs (Punjab), 180–2
Dost Mahommed, King of Afghanistan,
  69–70, 81, 84, 89, 99; in Second Sikh
  War, 162, 164
Dum Dum (Bengal), 25, 35–6

East India Company: history, 25, 27, 30;
  Board praises Punjab administration,
  192; Charter reviewed, 223; see also
  Addiscombe; Haileybury
Ebden, Dr, 221
Edgell, Colonel, 248
Edwardes College, Peshawar, 144
Edwardes, Emma, 219
Edwardes, Herbert: on Alexander
  Lawrence's face scar, 4–5; on Angel
  Knox, 11; on HL's generosity, 18; on

HL's religion, 34, 36, 153; on Revenue
  Survey, 55; on HL's character, 56–7;
  on HL in Ferozepore, 77: on HL's
  prophecy of Afghan trouble, 84; on
  HL's mission to Peshawar, 91; on
  HL's reprimand, 100; on Afghan
  campaign, 102; on HL in Nepal, 113,
  117; and HL's Defence of Macnaghten,
  114; as assistant to GL, 130, 142, 144,
  159; injured, 133; in Bannu, 144–8;
  character, 144; defers to McLeod, 152;
  on HL's methods with assistants, 152;
  religion, 153; on Cocks, 154; dislikes
  Hodson, 155; success in Second Sikh
  War, 161–3; Nicholson and, 165, 167;
  succeeds Abbott at Hazara, 171;
  Dalhousie criticises, 175; on HL's
  quarrel with John, 198; on HL's
  departure from Punjab, 211; on HL's
  ageing, 234; A Year on the Punjab
  Frontier, 144
Edwards, John, 34–5
Ellenborough, Edward Law, 1st Earl of,
  96, 103–6, 109–11
Elliot, (Sir) Henry Miers, 160, 176
Elphinstone, Mountstuart, 25, 148
Elphinstone, Major General William
  George Keith, 84, 86–9
Erskine, Thomas (of Linlathen), 105
Eyre, (Sir) Vincent, 84

Fane, General Sir Henry, 71–2
Fayrer, Dr (Sir) Joseph, 247, 254
Fenning, Colonel Sam, 34, 36
Ferozepore, 73–9
Ferozeshahar, Battle of (1845), 126
Forbes, Captain (Sir) John, 248
Forster, E. M., 25
Foujdar Khan Alizye, 162
Foyle College, Derry, 14–17, 197
Francis, Philip, 29
Friend of India, The (newspaper), 58,
  217, 244

Gardner, Colonel William Linnaeus, 57
Ghora Gali see Lawrence College
Gilbert, General Sir William, 172, 174
Gorakhpur, 62, 65
Gough, Field Marshal Hugh, 1st
  Viscount, 126, 128, 160, 163, 172, 203
Grant, Lieut., 54
Grant, Brigadier, 39
Griffin, Sir Lepel, 74
Gubbins, Martin, 233, 237, 244, 247–9
Guides, Corps of, 142–3, 163, 183–4
Gujerat, Battle of (1849), 172
Gulab Singh, Maharajah, 97–9, 133–6,
  151, 170, 206–7

arrival, 64; friendship with HL, 77–9; named as Alick's guardian, 100; and HL's complaints in Kaithal, 110; and HL's appointment to Nepal, 110, 113, 117, 119; introduces Hodson to HL, 155; as Lieut.-Governor of N.W. Provinces, 178; in Agra, 191; on HL's explosive nature, 215

Thomason, Rev. Thomas, 35, 57

Thucydides, 199

Thugs, 186–7, 236

Timoor Shah, 84

Tippoo Sultan, 3, 5

Todd, Lieut. D'Arcy, 36

Trevor, Captain R. S., 87

Trigonometrical Survey, Northern Ireland, 48

Tucker, Henry Carre, 248

Tullock, Lieut., 248

Victoria, Queen, 202

Wajid Ali Shah, King of Oudh, 231

Waldemar, Prince of Prussia, 120

Wellington, Arthur Wellesley, 1st Duke of, 7, 81, 173, 203

Wild, Brigadier, 90–2, 94–6

Wilson, Captain T. F., 244, 253–4

Wordsworth, William: *The Happy Warrior*, 216, 245

Wraxall Hall, Wiltshire (school), 17

Young, James (HL's cousin), 15, 220

Young, Robert, 14, 215, 220–3